Bill

last

Vaughan

Once A Villain

ONCE A VILLAIN

A memoir

PETER VAUGHAN

First published in 2016 by Fantom Films
fantomfilms.co.uk

Copyright © Peter Vaughan 2016

Peter Vaughan has asserted his moral right to be identified
as the author of this work in accordance with the
Copyright, Designs and Patents Act 1988.

A catalogue record for this book is available from the British Library.

Hardback edition ISBN: 978-1-78196-160-5

Typeset by Phil Reynolds Media Services, Leamington Spa
Printed and bound by CPI Group (UK) Ltd, Croydon, CR0 4YY

Jacket design by Will Brooks

CONTENTS

PREFACE

I AM NOT A WRITER, so why am I writing this book? *Can* I write this book? As an actor, I am used to words; I've tinkered with scripts and written bits of additional dialogue from time to time – but that's all. At least I don't have to worry about a plot: *I am the plot!* Just my memories over the last four-score-and-ten-plus years.

I have never kept diaries or anything of that kind so I will have to rely on my brain dredging up remembrances, one thing with any luck leading to another. In the process I hope to learn a bit about myself – my real self, not the complacent, optimistic version I carry around with me. At the same time, anyone reading this book should find a few amusing incidents and anecdotes along the way to keep him or her entertained – let's hope so!

Here we go then.

1

A Shropshire Lad

THE TROUBLE WITH BEING A CHARACTER ACTOR, and therefore having assumed so many differing characters over so many years, is that it isn't easy to know who one really is. Reactions to real situations are subconsciously monitored, observed and stored away for use in some future, fictional situation. Eventually, through this constant process, the two become slightly blurred and it's difficult to know who or what you really are. As this process has been going on in my case for over seventy years, I think it's about time to try and sort it out by writing down what I remember of my life.

I was born Peter Ewart Ohm in a flat above Barclays Bank in Wem, near Shrewsbury, in April 1923. My father, Oscar Max Ohm, was a clerk in the bank and had married Eva Marion Wright a couple of years earlier. Max was also born in Wem where his father, Joseph, was headmaster of the grammar school. Like many immigrants from Europe, Joseph had done well for himself. The Ohm family came to England to work in the then thriving cotton industry in Bolton and Manchester. There was even an Ohm shop in Deansgate, Manchester, until the 1960s selling shirts and so on: an insurance company office block now stands on the site! Joseph Ohm married a Miss Cus of French and most probably Jewish descent. I say probably as this was never confirmed or denied in our household, I suspect because a hint of Jewish ancestry would not have gone down well in a small town, never mind at the time of the rise of Nazism in Europe. Assimilation was the order of the day.

Max, my father, was the eldest child; then there was Rene, then Cecil and finally Muriel. Rene became the art teacher at the local grammar school and was the doyenne of the local dramatic and operatic society. The well-known actor Peter Jones, the son of an antique dealer in the town, was greatly encouraged by her before he became a professional. Cecil was spoken of in slightly hushed tones: he became a stand-up comic in Birmingham clubs and was also a great sprinter, winning races for money and bets. Tragically he died of TB at twenty-nine; I am very sad not to have known him as he must have been a great character.

Muriel married and lived in Stratford, East London and later in Woodford Green in Essex. I liked her very much and had some good holidays with her when I was older. I remember going with Uncle Billy (her husband) to the Arsenal and seeing Alex James and Cliff Bastin in the team that won everything in the 1930s. We went once or twice to the music hall and saw Fats Waller at the Holborn Empire – my first taste of jazz! I was about twelve when I saw the great Max Miller there and was enthralled by his brilliance. My aunt and uncle were great speedway fans of West Ham and a couple of their Australian riders, Tiger Stevenson and Bluey Wilkinson – famous names in their day – were good friends. This was all very exotic to me in contrast to my small-town home life.

*

As I have written my father married Eva. She was a Manchester girl through and through. Her father was Jack Wright, the son of domestic servants in Yorkshire. He was obviously bright as he became a veterinary surgeon, passing out at vet college in Edinburgh. He married a Miss Hunter who had been born in the USA where her family worked building the railways. I suspect she had a bit of money and helped Jack through his studies. Anyway, he became a very successful vet in Manchester. Later when I stayed with them he sometimes took me on his rounds and there were great teams of shire horses to be visited belonging to the breweries. I also vividly remember going with him to Belle-Vue Circus to tend an elephant with a bad foot. The mahout made the elephant raise his foot so that Grandad could tend and dress it: this impressed me greatly at five years of age!

My mother had a sister, Meg, and two stillborn brothers. Meg was a sickly child, something which Mother resented greatly as she felt Meg got preferential treatment – perhaps true as Meg lived to be eighty-five and Mother died of lung cancer at seventy-four.

Meg married an engineer called Wilmot and I had some memorable holidays with them too. They lived in Coventry first and then moved to Leeds where Wilmot worked in a piston-ring factory. They loved music hall too and I remember seeing Nellie Wallace and many other comedians there but none could match Max Miller, oh, and most importantly, they took me to the silent movies in Manchester. I don't remember much of the film but I vividly remember the piano at the bottom left-hand corner of the stalls. Again I was about five!

Grandad's city-centre veterinary practice took a great hammering thanks to the combined effects of the decline in horse-drawn transport and the economic collapse of 1929, so he had to sell up and moved just outside Manchester to Heald Green, near Ringway airport, where he opened a smaller practice dealing with mostly cats and dogs. Ringway at that time was just a small airfield, and I was always thrilled whenever I saw a plane which in those days of course would be one-engined and double-winged. Grandad (or 'The Major' as he was known) was a great character. He had been in charge of hundreds of horses in France in the First World War, hence the Major! He was also well known in the dog world as both competitor and judge worldwide.

I spent a lot of my early childhood away from home with these various relatives, for reasons I'll explain a little later.

*

My father was a handsome man, very easy-going until roused, with a highly developed sense of humour. He was a great sportsman: a good soccer player and a fine all-round cricketer – much better than I ever became! I think he went into the bank because his father died aged forty-nine and he had to get a steady job in order to support his mother and his younger sisters. Then the First World War broke out and eventually he was allowed to join the army, on condition that he remained a private. Due to his background he couldn't even rise to a lance corporal, never mind an officer. I suppose the powers that be were fearful he might go over to the other side. Anyway he had an interesting time, first going to Ireland, then France. He was an artillery signaller, laying lines and telephones from one battery to another. Four of them set out one day doing just that near the front line when a shell landed on them, killing the other three and blowing my father into the air, filling his back and legs with shrapnel. He recovered in hospital and was able to play cricket again, though he suffered terribly from arthritis in later life and ended up very crippled. I think you can say he did his bit for his country – namely England!

My mother, Eva, was a lovely-looking girl seven years younger than father. They made a handsome couple. She was a proud person and could be autocratic, though also very loving. She was highly ambitious, could be very funny and wanted to be an actress but this was frowned upon in those days. She had been nursing badly wounded soldiers in a military hospital in Manchester during the war as had her sister, Meg. This gave her a somewhat hard and stern outlook on life and made her afraid to show too much emotion.

So there they were, these two disparate people; they met, they fell in love and married. I was born after a very difficult birth for my mother who was left unable to have any more children. This I think made her very possessive of me and she loved me dearly and I her. However, by the time I was three years old it became clear all was not well between my parents.

Father was moved to a different branch of the bank, at Wellington (now known as Telford). I remember we had a bungalow next to the abattoir and the shrieks and cries of the animals being slaughtered are strong in my mind; just like the smell of hops from the brewery adjoining the back yard of our Wem flat, pleasantly filling my nostrils as I lay in my pram! When I told Clement Freud of this and of a very early memory of a large bird alighting on my pram, it was published in an article in the *Radio Times* and a hilarious cartoon of this event accompanied it; the original is now hanging on my study wall.

We soon left the sounds of the abattoir for a new house on the outskirts of the town. The road wasn't finished and houses were still being built and I used to play on the building site with a boy next door. He didn't live long, like many of my generation: he was killed in a bomber over Germany aged nineteen. I called on his mother once or twice when I was on leave from the army. She was amazing and seemed pleased to see me; I suppose she saw me as a link with her son.

However, my stay in the new house was short-lived: there were angry scenes and a great deal of rowing, though this didn't worry me as it was the norm to me and I would run between them and hold on to Mother to protect her from blows. I am not too clear of the chronology of these events but at some point I found myself back in Wem, being looked after by my Aunty Rene whom I did not like at all. I must have been an inconvenience to her and I stayed some of the time at an infant school in the town and lived with the staff. I remember reciting a poem at a school concert which was rapturously received. That registered in my mind as being something I could do and which might be useful for the future.

There must have been some toing and froing between Wem and Wellington because once, when I was home, Father was very ill with pneumonia. Mother took me for a walk and, as we neared the house on returning, she looked up at the bedroom window and said: 'Your father is an evil, wicked man. I wish he was dead.'

Being five I believed her wholeheartedly.

The next vivid event in my mind was a terrible row going on between Father and Mother and a strange man I hadn't seen before. I was told to go and play outside; there was a car at the gate with its engine running and the front door open. Then Mother came out with the strange man, suitcases were loaded, I was hugged and that was the last I saw of Mother for what must have been some months.

So it was back to Wem and Aunt Rene and sometimes Granny Ohm who had married again and was now Granny Beattie. She was a marvellous cook and I can still taste her apple strudel in memory. Then one day I was walking up the High Street with Rene when Mother jumped out of a car and tried to drag me away. A tug of war ensued and my arms were nearly pulled out of their sockets. Mother won and I was bundled into the little car and taken to a bungalow at Kinmel Bay near Rhyl in North Wales. Again it was a new development with new roads and sand dunes. It was very windy and cold most of the time but I was happy to be there with Mother, visited from time to time by the strange man. Then I learned that she and Father had patched things up and he had been moved to the Uttoxeter branch in North Staffordshire near the Potteries. So, off we went to a flat there and I went to junior school. The strange man was never seen again.

*

I was now aged seven and the toings and froings were over, apart from holidays of course. Uttoxeter was, at that time, a pretty dull town. Apart from the races and a yearly fair – both of which excited me – nothing much happened. On race days some of us used to hide in the bushes far away from the stands and hear the jockeys work out who was going to win! This little bit of corruption has never tempered my love of horse racing, especially over jumps, and my enjoyment of a little punt; you'd think I would know better after listening to the jockeys at Uttoxeter! The fair, or Wakes as it was called, came for a week once a year and I was fascinated by it, thinking it must be the greatest life: packing up and moving on, excited crowds everywhere. I used to follow them on my bike for a mile or two as the steam traction engines pulling the packed-up dodgems, ghost train, hurdy-gurdies and all, streamed slowly out of town followed by the old lorries, brightly painted and towing caravans. Then all would be quiet and dull again.

By the time I was nine I had graduated to grammar school, and there I remained until I was sixteen. I was a poor student, not bad at English, French and History but useless at Science and Maths. The trouble was I was scared of the masters. My mind froze with a mixture of fear and boredom and I wandered off into my own world a great deal of the time. I dreamt of keeping goal for Stoke City and playing cricket for Lancashire or Derbyshire. I remember the first football match I saw: Stoke versus Bristol Rovers, in Division Two at the time. I was eight, the goalkeeper's surname was John, and I loved the idea of standing between the posts on my own, in a green jersey, different from the others: the last heroic line of defence! I was not much cop as a goalie, though I did make the school team later. The High School girls used to stand behind the goal to watch and you could chat them up when we were on the attack. Sadly this often led to lack of concentration, with disastrous results. Eventually I was dropped and was made to play at right back, but by then I knew all the girls anyway! I was better at cricket; and, largely due to my father's patient coaching on our small lawn, I developed into a fairly useful batsman. Strangely this ability stood me in good stead later on when I was an actor.

Mother didn't like Uttoxeter at all and was unhappy and restless and went back home to Manchester as often as she could. There was always tension at home: hardly a day went by without it boiling over. Some of the rows were humdingers, but usually Father refused to join in and remained tight-lipped causing Mother to hit the roof. However, sometimes she was very funny and her spontaneous variety acts would have me in hysterics. Her great hobby was breeding dogs and, like her father before her, she was a successful exhibitor and later a very good judge.

And so, in this way, life carried on. I was very much a loner with my own dream world to fall back on. I was constantly admonished by Mother: 'Don't do that, you're just like your father!'

I had one great friend, though: Denis Stewart. He was in the same form at school and we grew up together. Denis was the son of the local butcher and I was fond of his mother, a lovely lady. I spent a lot of time at their house and garden kicking footballs or bowling and batting and staying for tea afterwards with lovely home-made cakes. Denis was better academically than me at school and was a fine cricketer and soccer player. Unlike me, he was very even-tempered and steady as a rock. We were great friends and are still in touch to this day. He had a very successful career as a bank manager in London, including a branch in Shaftesbury Avenue. Perhaps knowing me helped him understand some of his clients!

As I said I was a very unremarkable student at school, not having any real idea of what I was going to do with my life, until suddenly I was in a school play. I played a French professor in a one-act play – and I *knew* exactly what I could do. That feeling of holding an audience in one's control was spellbinding. The play, and (dare I say) I, were rapturously received. I was fifteen and I was secure in my mind about my future at last. I remembered reciting that poem when I was five and I thought: this *is* what I can do.

Things moved pretty quickly after that. I appeared in other school plays, and I even sang Sir Joseph Porter in *HMS Pinafore* – that shows how confident I had become. The county of Staffordshire had a schools' drama teacher, Miss Joy Belford: I think she must have seen something in me because she took me under her wing and gave me scenes to study whenever she visited our school. This I did avidly and life was pretty good, especially as the High School girls from behind the goal were sometimes in the plays as well. Our headmaster found me, in the dark after a rehearsal, in a somewhat compromising position with my girlfriend of the time. I was terrified when the lights were suddenly switched on and there he was. I thought my time was up but all he said was, 'Ah, Ohm, caught you there,' and wandered off! Perhaps he liked my acting too!

*

The 1930s was a strange decade to grow up in. Unemployment was rife and there was real poverty. The economic collapse in 1929 had hit industry badly; even in Uttoxeter the main employers, Bamfords Engineering, had to lay many men off, and the rest were often on a three-day week. Remember, this was before the Welfare State and there was real hardship. Manchester was in a terrible state with the decline of the cotton industry. The working classes were really suffering. We were all right as Father had a steady and reasonably paid job, but many of my father's peers did not.

It all seemed so unfair; something had to be done. Fascism was rife in Europe. In my dreams I joined the International Brigade in Spain to fight Franco, and I formed very solid left-wing political views. The Soviet Union was the panacea. We didn't know that Stalin had destroyed *their* dream. And so I formed my views which I hold to this day.

Hitler marched into Austria and Chamberlain came back from Munich waving a piece of paper and saying, 'Peace in our time.' Hitler promptly occupied Sudeten Germany and Czechoslovakia; then in September he invaded Poland and that meant war. Our headmaster gave us a very solemn and gloomy lecture telling us what war would mean: 'Many of you sitting here today will die in it,' he said. He certainly wasn't far wrong: more than one of my form were dead at twenty.

Mother didn't like what I was growing into, especially my politics. Father was much more tolerant and, I think, secretly agreed with my passionate outbursts; he let me develop in my own way, and I grew to admire him greatly. We shared a rather weird sense of humour and he certainly didn't seem an 'evil, vile man' to me. *Don't do that, you're just like your father* – what's so bad about that I thought?

The war, or phoney war as it was known, was a bit of an anticlimax to begin with. We were all given gas masks and helped dig ditches to hinder German airborne troops landing, but none came. Food, clothes and petrol were severely rationed, and Father became an air-raid warden and Mother a part-time nurse – but not before we were investigated to determine whether we should be shipped over the Irish Sea and interned on the Isle of Man: the place where aliens and those of dubious backgrounds were sent. Nothing came of this but it was a little reminder to me that I wasn't totally bred of good old British yeoman stock.

I truly thought the war had to be fought and won: I believed it was a war to destroy the evil of Fascism. There was no TV of course, but I saw enough on the Pathé News on my weekly trip to the cinema and heard enough on the BBC radio to be certain in my young mind that the war had to be won and Fascism defeated once and for all. I must say, though, we had no idea what was going to unfold.

Then, war or no war, it happened: Joy Belford, the drama organiser, heard one of my scenes and said, 'Would you like to become a professional actor? I think you should be!' I jumped at the idea.

There was only one repertory theatre in the county, the Grand Theatre in Wolverhampton, and she arranged for me to meet the producer. By an enormous stroke of luck they needed a young lad to play 'Smith the Pie Boy' in a production of *Sweeney Todd*. I went into the producer's office and he looked me up and down and, after a preliminary chat, handed me the part and said, 'Read this.' I read it to him; he said nothing, left the room and came back with the manager, Basil Thomas, and said, 'Read it again.' I did. They looked at each other; Mr Thomas nodded and the producer, Hilary Fisher White, pulled out a large volume from his bookshelf and said, 'You start in two weeks; in the meantime go home and study this book. You are playing Smith the Pie Boy and probably another part or two, and you can help with the stage management.' The book was *My Life in Art* by Konstantin Stanislavsky, the great Russian acting teacher. I was on my way!

2
AN ACTOR'S LIFE FOR ME

I HAD NO IDEA HOW LUCKY I WAS. My salary, I was informed, was to be two pounds and ten shillings per week. I was then taken from the producer's office to the back of the dress circle to watch a matinee that was in progress. I was spellbound: the stillness, the control and power of these actors was riveting. I can do that, I thought; I know I can do it. I thought of the poem and the French play at school.

Indeed I was very lucky. Standing in that dress circle was only the second time I had been in a straight professional theatre. Music hall, yes. The year before I had been on holiday with Father to Blackpool and we went to a variety show at the Winter Garden. The first half of the programme ended with a short whodunnit and all was not revealed until the end of the show. In the meantime chorus girls tapped, magicians juggled and comics cracked jokes but I didn't care; I just wanted to be there and watch. Then I persuaded Father to take me to see Franklin Dyall (father of Valentine) in an Edgar Wallace thriller at the Opera House: real live straight theatre for the first time in my life. It was wonderful and Franklin Dyall became my idol, as George Arliss was in the cinema: two extraordinary character actors who were truly my inspiration.

As a boy before the war, I went to the cinema a lot, drinking it all in. Saturdays were the best: football at Stoke followed by a picture at the Majestic Hanley one week, and then the next week football at Derby and the pictures at the ABC. Derby was posher than Stoke: it was cleaner, being the home of Rolls Royce! Stoke was usually damp and foggy as the pottery kilns were all brick-fired at that time and filled the air with hazy smoke.

But to see Stanley Matthews float down the wing, leaving everyone in his wake – ah, that was magic, and real drama too.

So that was the extent of my theatrical background, reinforced by a desperate study of *My Life in Art*. I don't suppose I took much of it in during that fortnight, but it led me to *An Actor Prepares* later; and, although I am not a slave to the system, I use Stanislavsky to help me out when I need it.

Before I left Wolverhampton that day Basil Thomas, the manager, told me that I would have to change my name for acting purposes: 'Ohm is a central European name and it wouldn't go down well with an audience now we are at war, so think up a good British name and let me know what you come up with.' After much wracking of brains, the family conference decided on Peter Wright, using my mother's maiden name, but unfortunately it was no good as there was already an actor of that name so we had to think again. We were getting a bit desperate when Mother remembered an obscure relative called Vaughan; and so, Vaughan it was! Fortunately it was approved all round and ready in the nick of time for the *Sweeney Todd* programme. I never changed my name by deed poll, using Ohm in all private and legal matters. In fact it has come in handy at times to have two names and it separates one's professional self from the private one. This can be quite therapeutic at times and helps to keep one's sanity!

The Wolverhampton Grand and its sister company, the Alexandra Theatre in Birmingham, were run by the cousins Derek Salberg and Basil Thomas. In those early days the repertory season ran from March to November; large, spectacular pantomimes with big variety names were also staged over the Christmas season. I had stumbled into one of the highest standard companies of its kind in the country – me with no experience and no drama school behind me. Mind you, the war helped in that respect as young actors were becoming scarce due to call-up or volunteering to join the forces. Kenneth More had just left Wolverhampton to join the merchant navy. But for the war there would have been more competition for the part of Smith the Pie Boy.

The repertory movement became very popular in Britain through the 1930s and survived the war to have a boom in the forties and fifties until the coming of the age of television. Most commercial repertory companies put on a play each week; there were even a few who were doing fortnightly rep, but weekly was the bedrock and Wolverhampton was one of the very best. In the nine-month season some thirty-eight plays were staged ranging from comedy to thrillers to farce, from Shaw to Ibsen, an odd American play and even the occasional Shakespeare. A permanent company would be engaged for the season, and some of the actors would return year after year and become much loved by the audience. The company usually consisted of a producer, leading man and leading lady, leading character male and female, juvenile leads, second juvenile and second character. In addition there was a stage manager and two young assistants, all of whom acted when required. Sometimes the local amateur or semi-professional actors were called in. The most renowned in Wolverhampton was Gwen Berryman who gave many fine performances over the years and later became a household name playing Doris in *The Archers*. There was also a set designer and painter; and between us, assisted by the theatre staff, we put on a play a week!

The weekly routine worked as follows:

Monday: Dress rehearsal, followed by opening night.

Tuesday: Read-through of next play and set all the moves. After lunch learn the lines of Act One. Perform existing play in the evening.

Wednesday: Work on Act One knowing lines; matinee of existing play followed by evening performance. Burn the midnight oil learning Act Two for the next day.

Thursday: Work on Act Two knowing lines. Afternoon: learn lines for Act Three. Performance in the evening – again burn midnight oil.

Friday: Work on Act Three knowing lines followed by a run-through of the whole play. Afternoon, realise you don't know lines for next week so work feverishly on them! Evening performance.

Saturday: Run-through of next week's play with more detailed direction from the producer, followed by the matinee and evening perform-ance of existing play! As soon as this was over the scenery would be struck and all the props and set furniture would be stored away.

Sunday: The new play's sets would be erected by the designer and the stage management. New furniture and props set in readiness for the dress rehearsal on Monday morning.

The producer would do the lighting first thing on Monday and the dress rehearsal would begin about midday and probably continue until curtain up. Clothes were tried on for the first time; quick changes were worked out; lighting cues were practised (never take your hand off an electric light switch before the lights actually come on!). It was the first time the cast had walked onto the set as weekly rehearsals took place elsewhere (in a room in a pub!) so when you got on the set it would all be very different and had to be coped with very quickly. Adrenalin flowed and sometimes tempers frayed.

First-night nerves could reduce you to a shaking wreck but, once on stage and over the first few lines, the play took over and the communion between the audience and the cast began. If it didn't it was a pretty horrible experience I can tell you. Also it was not good for the week's takings, as many of Monday's audience were given complimentary seats. The town's shopkeepers who had lent furniture and props got a credit in the programme; if they didn't like the play or the performance, word would spread round the town like wildfire and business would be affected. This is to say nothing of the local newspaper critic sitting in the front row, pencil poised, with his opinion aired for all to see in the next day's paper! So Monday was a pretty stressful day in repertory, usually followed by a noisy post-mortem and wind-down in the local hostelry with a certain amount of imbibing going on!

When I first arrived in Wolverhampton I went into digs at Waterloo Road. The stage manager, Axel Moller, was in the same digs and he quickly set me to work as his 'gofer'. I was in my element, returning and collecting props and set dressing to and from the various shops in the town who had lent them in return for a credit in the programme. As I said, we rehearsed in a nearby pub; the shape of the set was taped onto the floor, with pub chairs and tables as make-do set furniture. Smith the Pie Boy was not a large part: the Demon Barber saw to that, knocking me out, putting me in the barber's chair and dispatching me to the cellar below. I had to quickly learn how to fall on stage, realistically, without hurting myself and also how to go down the trap in the middle of the stage and land on a mattress twelve feet beneath, also without hurting myself! I hadn't spotted any reference to this in *My Life in Art*, but I had a good teacher in the Demon Barber: the company's leading man, Gerald Cuff. In the years to come I realised what a tremendous actor Gerry was; I learned so much from him.

Sweeney Todd came and went without too many bruises; other small parts followed, and I rushed around at Axel's beck and call doing all the backstage chores: checking prop lists; helping with set changes; going round the dressing rooms knocking on doors – 'Half-hour please,' 'Fifteen minutes please,' 'Five minutes please,' 'Overture and beginners please,' 'Act One beginners please,' etc. at the appropriate time. There was a staff bar under the stage at the Grand and some of the company liked to have a pint or a Guinness on their dressing places in the intervals, while others wanted the inevitable brew-up. Acting is always thirsty work, but acting in weekly rep – half-exhausted, relying on the adrenalin of the performance – was even more thirst-making!

At this stage I was not allowed in the prompt corner to run the play (that is, give all the lighting cues, bring the curtain up and down, give any acting prompts and so on). However, at rehearsals I often had to be 'on the book' – in other words prompting, a tricky job in rep with some of the actors struggling with their lines. The best and most efficient actors would say 'please' or snap their fingers when they needed a prompt; others would be all over the shop and blame you if you prompted in the wrong place. This could sometimes lead to tantrums and much humiliation for the wretched prompter. I vowed later in my career always to be nice to prompters in rehearsals and I do my best, but there are two things I really find irritating: firstly, when the prompter is not following the lines properly and *you* remember the line before *they* can find it in the book; and secondly, the over-enthusiastic one who prompts by reading several lines when you only needed one word. Enraging!

Then I was brought down to earth with a thud: I was told that there were no more parts for me that season and, as I was only helping out with stage management, I would have to go. This bitter pill was sweetened somewhat in two ways. First, I was told there would probably be a regular place for me for the whole of the next season as an assistant stage manager and small-part player. Secondly, I was cast as Octavius Moulton Barrett in *The Barretts of Wimpole Street* at the Salbergs' third company in Hereford. Occy was the youngest of eight sons of the tyrannical father, Edward Moulton Barrett, and he stood out because he had a really bad stammer. It was my best part so far, and I think it went well; but that was it, no more work, just a promise for next season some four months away.

Back home I went and Father said I must go back to school and take my Higher School Certificate, the equivalent of A-levels today. The atmosphere at school was unbearable and my fellow pupils resented me, or I thought they did. I was disconsolate. I left after a couple of weeks after a serious punch-up over some tiny incident. My opponent was no great friend of mine and I think he was jealous of my situation; sadly he was killed when in the RAF.

So I was out of work and out of school. Father was very firm and told me, 'You can be an actor but I haven't any money to support you. You must pay your own way, and you can't live at home except for holidays.' This was quite a brilliant way of dealing with my future: if I wasn't going to make the grade as an actor obviously I would have to find another sort of job, so it made me determined to succeed! It turned me into even more of a *What Makes Sammy Run?* character; I would have to work just that bit harder and be just that bit more single-minded, and I don't think I have changed in all my long career.

*

I was already reading *The Stage* every week and scouring the 'Wanted Artists' column, and then I had a bit of luck.

Frank Kenyan of the Macclesfield Repertory Players wanted a stage manager/juvenile actor to start at once. I wrote immediately, embellishing my limited experience so that I sounded like an old hand – well, old for seventeen that is! I got the job and off I went to Macclesfield, a silk town on two levels not far from Manchester.

The company was ensconced in the town hall; after the wonderful Grand Theatre Wolverhampton with its plush seating, orchestra pit, bars, stage door and comfortable dressing rooms, it was going from the sublime to the ridiculous. The area under the stage served as one large dressing room divided in the middle by a hessian curtain – men on one side and women on the other. There was no running water, just water in a bucket to wash in.

My wages were twenty-seven shillings and sixpence a week and my digs were twenty-five shillings all in. Even in those days with beer at eleven old pennies a pint and fags about the same, I obviously couldn't make ends meet. In addition actors had to provide all their own clothes for the plays; this meant a suit, sports jacket and flannels, various shirts and ties and the inevitable dinner jacket. By now my post office savings book was pretty low in credit – not that it was ever high despite my being a careful saver (which

I still am). Something had to be done, so I went straight to Mr Kenyan and told him I needed a rise in order to live. He saw the point and gave me an extra five shillings a week. Big deal!

As it happened I didn't have time to spend money anyway, as I usually had a big part to play as well as running the stage management. I did everything except paint the scenery, and I was in my element – Sammy was really running! I became pretty nifty at the stage management side of things: doing lighting cues and effects, prompting, and raising and lowering the curtain at the beginning and end of each act. Of course, sometimes I was on stage myself at crucial stage-managerial moments, and some fairly strange exits into the wings took place to deal with the situation. The trickiest of all was if I had the last line of a scene, in which case someone else had to ring the curtain down (or across, as it was at the town hall). If the whole company was on stage at the time then a way had to be invented to get someone off stage to do it without the audience noticing anything unusual!

Although it was a small and pretty basic company, it wasn't a bad one by any means. There was a good leading man called Harry Shacklock who was a brilliant light comedian. Alec McCowen had been in the company before I arrived whilst on vacation from RADA, and was spoken of in slightly respectful tones: a real live RADA student. The leading lady was the lovely, vibrant Margery Mason, who continued to be brilliant until she passed away in 2014 a few months after her hundredth birthday. We talked affectionately of our time in Macclesfield when we met again in 1997, some fifty years later, preparing for the film *Les Misérables*. In the film, although we hadn't a scene together, she played a nun and I a bishop: sanctity at last for both of us!

Business wasn't too good at the theatre/town hall, principally because the Luftwaffe bombing campaign had started in earnest and Liverpool and Manchester were being targeted. We regularly heard the planes droning overhead during performances, and not many people wanted to venture out in the blackout. At one matinee we played to fewer people than were in the cast! I remember that audience exactly: two in the stalls on the left, one RAF bloke in uniform on the middle right, three kids and their mother on the front row; seven in total, and there were eight of us in the cast. Mr Kenyan asked them if they wanted to have their money back or stay and see the show: they opted for the latter. It was a slick light comedy, normally with lots of laughs. Harry and I were the two leads and we played it with good pace and with no interruptions for laughter. We reckoned it was the best and truest performance we had given. Another lesson learnt.

At Christmas we did a play; I can't remember the name, but there was a tableau of Britain through the ages to follow it. This was the spectacular special attraction for Christmas. The whole company had to dash into a quick change, a tatty old table draped in a Union Jack was rushed centre stage and we took up our positions round it. Margery was Brittania and I was Saint George; Harry was King Charles in a terrible wig that made him look more like the dog of the same name. It was truly awful and we found it hysterically funny to do; the things people paid money for in those days!

In the New Year I signed up as promised for the 1941 season at Wolverhampton, starting in February. My salary had gone up to £3 a week; better than Macclesfield, to be sure, but I had had a great time there and also learned so much. I left at the end of January, having paid my way and feeling entitled to a week's holiday at home!

*

Walking from Wolverhampton station to the Grand Theatre on a bitterly cold day, dragging two suitcases through a couple of inches of melting snow which soaked my suede shoes despite my galoshes, I felt an aching in the pit of my stomach. I was nervous, I was apprehensive. I was now an integral part of the company and I had to justify the Salberg faith in me. Could I do it? Would I be good enough? No longer *this is something I can do*, remembering school plays or a poem I'd recited as a five-year-old. There was much much more to it than that – and don't forget I had to pay my way.

I was experiencing the anxiety of the professional: that dual innate self-belief on the one hand and the fear of failing on the other. This feeling never leaves you or gets any easier: in fact, just the reverse. You get a role sometimes against great and distinguished opposition, totally sure you are best for the part... then you have to actually do it. Doubts and fears set in until you find how to do it – or think you have found how to do it. And so the process goes on; sureness and doubt, certainty and fear. Then there's the audience: *will I hold them? If I don't believe it, they won't believe it* and so on. And I got real pangs of this that first morning in Wolverhampton.

Axel Moller had gone home to neutral South Africa and Donald Master was the new stage manager. I got on with him like a house on fire from the start. He was exempt from military service on medical grounds, knew his job thoroughly and was great to work with.

The company was still headed by Gerald Cuff although it was accepted that he would be called up at some time during the season. Kenneth More pays tribute to Gerry in his book, and he was without doubt a superb actor. He had a large family and a house in the town and so had settled to stay in repertory. This was Wolverhampton's gain and London's loss and locally he was much idolised. He could play any style equally well, be it Coward, farce, Shakespeare, Ibsen or Shaw. He had toured and played with Esmé Percy, the great Shavian, for some years. What a gift it was for me to work with him and watch him work. He was also a master of make-up and able to assume any character he chose. He never minded me sitting and watching him make up, especially if I had brought his pint up from the bar! I learned about wigs and character make-ups, how to wear period costumes and how to move on stage, how to time laughs and how to hold audiences, how long to pause and many other things from Gerry. It was all about different rhythms really, and he had them all.

Gerald Lennan was another character actor much adored in the town and very good in comedy in particular. He loved his Guinness and would always be found in the stage bar in his waits and would time his entrances from there to perfection. Well, perhaps not quite always... Sometimes there would be panicked shouts of 'Gerry, you're on!' There was the odd occasion when I had to listen for his cue, open the door of the set and push him on. He would then proceed to play the scene perfectly! He was a great character and terrific company to be with.

Lee Fox was the juvenile lead, a very charming man and, like Donald, exempt from military service. When Gielgud came to Singapore in 1946 and gave the troops his superb Hamlet, Lee Fox was Horatio. After years in the army, to see that production was inspiring; I have never forgotten it.

The ladies in the company included the wonderful character actress, Aletha Orr, as well as the beautiful leading lady, Joan Haythorne, who later played in the West End and in several films.

Alongside my ASM work, I was playing more and better roles. In April, I was cast in the dual roles of Simon and Harry in *Mary Rose* by J. M. Barrie, a huge undertaking to do in a week; and other large roles were in the offing too, such as Tobias in *Tobias and the Angel*. I was now just eighteen but was tall and looked older, and I asked Basil Thomas if I could stop stage managing and concentrate on my acting. He agreed and put my salary up to £4 a week – and I didn't even ask for a rise!

Around this time Gerry Cuff was called up into the RAF and posted to some base nearby where he worked in the stores. What a waste: surely he could have done more for the war effort if he had stayed in rep? But of course acting was never a reserved occupation, I'm afraid! I believe he did save up his leave and give the odd performance or two later in the war, and his appearances were cheered to the rooftops.

It was a real step up for me to become solely an acting member of the company, although my stage management experience remained invaluable especially as there was more of that to come later in both London and America. Good parts continued, and I started to be asked to various parties after the show. These I accepted with alacrity because food was rationed; I never knew where all these goodies came from – the Black Market possibly!

Once a tall, well-built rugger-playing type asked me to his house; a rather severe lady let me in with a very quizzical look and disappeared. 'Ere long I was being chased around the room and pinned against the wall, held in a bear hug as he tried to kiss me. I kneed him in the groin and fled. Not for me that scene: I was far too interested in having as many embraces as possible with the odd usherette, shop assistant and one or two nubile fans who were turning up! I have been hetero all my life but I have many friends and acquaintances who are homosexual by inclination, and a great deal of fun, laughter, brilliance of mind and wonderful acting experiences I would have missed without them. What a strange word 'gay' is to describe their sexuality. I suppose it's better than 'queer', 'iron hoof' (poof), 'woofter' and so on; but 'gay' seems to trivialise the serious, lasting and sometimes painful relationships equal in every way to those that so-called normal people have. What on earth is normal anyway?

Speaking of 'gays', I started to do the odd play with the main company at the Alexandra Theatre in Birmingham and there were several there who were real fun to be around with an outrageous sense of humour. One, however, who was not gay was a cheeky, pugnacious bloke by the name of James Viccars: slightly older than me, with a huge personality, both on and off stage. We were in a play, *Young Woodley*, set in a public school. I played the po-faced head boy and Jimmy the school bad boy. He was brilliant.

Physically he reminded me of a young James Cagney. We did the play in both companies and the girls adored him.

Birmingham was frequently bombed at this time and Jimmy saved the Alexandra Theatre from being burned down when an incendiary bomb got lodged in the 'flies', high at the top of the stage. Jimmy crawled along the flies, forty feet up, and put it out: no problem!

Because of the bombing the shows started at 6 P.M., in the hope that the final curtain would be down before the air-raid sirens went off and the night bombing began. When I played there I would catch a blacked-out train back to Wolverhampton every night. Once I took a girl over to see me in something, I can't remember what. I had given my all in the show and, on the way back, I was more interested in what she thought of my perform-ance, rather than in her. What an idiot I was! She wasn't in the least impressed and I didn't see her again. Typical actor egocentricity which erupts like a volcano from time to time all through one's life.

The audiences at that time were superb; people needed to gather together and be transported from the fears and worries of their lives. Plays, films and concerts were always enthusiastically received. What with the air raids, blackouts, long working hours, food rationing and clothes rationing, there was a hunger for the arts.

In June, Hitler's armies marched into the Soviet Union and all we left-wingers pledged our support for our comrades in the Red Army, though what good that did them coming from a weekly rep actor I'm not sure!

During the summer I realised that Derek Salberg and Basil Thomas were both nuts about cricket and we managed a game or two on Sundays. Derek was a good player, but Basil was best described as keen. Derek was already in the army so must have been on leave at the time. They were only scratch games but at the time very precious.

Meanwhile, the rep season continued, not without its lighter moments. There was one classic spoonerism which I've never forgotten. I was on stage in a very tense scene in an exciting 'whodunnit'; the audience was hushed in silence, held in the palm of her hand by the superb Joan Haythorne. In the thick of interrogation, the detective asked, 'What happened next?' Joan paused dramatically and said, 'Mr Toft crapped at the window!' The cast struggled against bursting into fits of laughter; but so good was Joan, and so immersed were the audience in the scene, nothing was noticed and the play went on as if nothing untoward had happened!

As the season approached its end in November I registered for military service, which I was required to do on reaching the ripe old age of eighteen and a half. When the call-up papers might arrive was in the hands of the gods, or rather the War Office, so until the big day came I carried on as usual. I finished the season with an offer for the following one (beginning in February 1942) at £5 a week. There was a good chance of being able to do a few weeks before call-up and in the meantime I was taken on at Macclesfield again, where the set-up was much better than before. The management was now in the hands of Amy Viner; she was a Blackpool store-owner's daughter with a great love of the theatre and she looked after her actors well. I was happy there over Christmas and New Year, looking forward to the new season in Wolverhampton once more in February.

That 1941 season had been an amazing one for me. Peter (earns as he learns) Vaughan had a wonderful time, growing up as an actor and perhaps as a person too, though the latter not a great deal. Actors always remain children at heart whatever befalls them... well, this one has anyway!

3
SOLDIERING ON

Instead of my theatre season in Wolverhampton starting in February, I found myself on a train bound for Ossett, near Wakefield, Yorkshire, to report to the Royal Corps of Signals depot there. The weather was foul, with more and more snow the further north we travelled, and the train was hopelessly late arriving. A corporal met and escorted me and a few others from the station. My suede shoes were soaked from the snow and I was glad of my camel-hair overcoat which I had bought, having saved up my clothing coupons, not long before. It cost £6 from Montague Burton's and still my Post Office savings book was quite healthy.

Just like the previous February on Wolverhampton station, as I trudged through the snow there was an ache in the pit of my stomach. What was this very different kind of season going to be like, and how long was it going to run? It was not a promising start: by the time we arrived at the depot it was pitch black and the blackout was in full force. As it was so late our details were quickly taken down, we were given a couple of blankets and something to eat and sent to our billets. It was bitterly cold, but I was in a hut that at least had a wood-burning stove in it. The other occupants had already been there a couple of days and were firmly ensconced around the stove, but they were a friendly lot and shoved over to let me have a warm. I noticed some of them had their rifle bayonets in their hands; I thought this rather odd but asked no questions. I went to sleep on an upper bunk bed with no mattress, fully dressed, wrapped in my two blankets.

At 6 A.M. it was, 'Wakey wakey, rise and shine, get out of these pits.' It was freezing cold; our ablutions were rows of wash basins and latrines outside in a field. There was no hot water, only what was boiled in a large kettle and shared out for shaving and thawing out the cold water. From there on my feet didn't touch the ground. I was issued with uniform, equipment and rifle, and also a kitbag, mess tin, knife, fork and spoon. My flowing actor's locks were shorn and I was given the pudding-basin look, very short back and sides and just about ready for six weeks' rigorous basic training.

'Wakey wakey, rise and shine' turned out to be our drill sergeant who was a sadist, albeit one with a sort of grim sense of humour. He immediately called me 'Shakespeare': 'Shakespeare, wipe that smile off your face;' 'Shakespeare, get in step, you're not acting the bloody lead now!' We did marching drill, rifle drill and gymnasium work all day long. My feet, more used to gentle suede shoes, found breaking-in army boots hard to bear and I was soon covered in blisters. The medical officer gave me an 'excused boots chit', so for a few days I wore gym pumps until the feet healed up. This meant I had to do what the army calls 'fatigues' instead of drilling: keeping billets spotless for daily inspection, likewise the latrines and ablutions. These were pretty grotty jobs and I was pleased when the surgical spirit had done its job and I was back in boots again!

I quite enjoyed drilling: it had a rhythm to it, though our sergeant really put us through it and his language was pretty fruity. One thing we recruits learned early on was that, no matter how we were sworn at, we must not be called a bastard. An NCO could be put on a charge for calling any of his recruits 'bastard', so we listened very attentively in the hope of hearing that magic word. 'Wakey Wakey' was too old a sweat and too smart for that to happen, but it did add a bit of interest to the proceedings.

One bit of sadism he enjoyed was to drill us for a couple of hours and then march us to the local pub where he would drill us some more until we were on our knees – watched and jeered by the locals with foaming pints in their hands! However, he was good at his job and we were beginning to look like soldiers. 'Come on, hit those rifle butts, I want to see your hands bleed.' We had to be smart in our appearance too: uniforms pressed, equipment blancoed and all the brass polished. Rifles had to be oiled, with not a speck of dirt in the barrels. We had officers' roll-call inspection each morning parade and we would get spot-check inspections of the billets. 'Stand by your beds,' the NCO would yell, so it was quickly to attention to have all your stuff inspected. All this for fourteen shillings a week!

We looked forward to pay parade every Friday. The officer sat at a desk with his clerk and we all lined up in front of him. One by one we marched up, snapped to attention, saluted and called out our name, rank and number; the clerk would then check this and say, 'Fourteen shillings, sir.' One's cap was doffed and the princely sum would be placed in it by the officer. The money was then transferred to one's pocket, hat put back on again, another salute, smartly about turn and back into line. MONEY! Straight to the NAAFI canteen for a couple of pints and a packet of fags and perhaps a game of 'housey housey', now known for some reason as bingo. Then perhaps we went to the local YMCA where the ladies doled out free soup and sandwiches and where there were table-tennis tournaments and snooker tables. Some of the women were quite attractive so I naturally tried my usual chat-up line which had gone so well in the rep days. I needn't have bothered. I was just a squaddie with a pudding-basin haircut, without even a stripe, and my efforts were greeted with at best a polite smile and at worst a 'get lost' expression. Another lesson learnt: it wasn't me who was special, it was the glamour of the theatre and maybe the parts I played.

Back at the billet after lights out, we would sit with our rifle bayonets in our hands not making a sound, waiting for the rats. That was what they were doing the night I arrived; I don't think we ever killed any but it was good sport! No matter how much that billet was cleaned and polished it was still rat-infested and it was always a good idea to sleep with a blanket over your head.

The six weeks of square-bashing finally over, it was goodbye to 'Wakey Wakey' and on to the next stage of training which was to learn one's particular signals trade. I was to be an Operator Wireless and Line, which really meant learning to receive and send Morse code. In preparation for leaving Ossett I got into the full kit consisting of webbing harness to which was attached a large pack, a small pack, water bottle, gas mask, two ammunition pouches and a tin hat. Carrying a rifle in my right hand and the kitbag slung over my left shoulder (all my possessions in fact), I climbed into the back of a three-ton truck and was transported along with about twenty others to a commandeered woollen mill in Huddersfield. There was a completely different atmosphere here and, although we still did a lot of PE and drill, most of our time was spent in the classroom with earphones on and a Morse key in our hand tapping out and listening to the Morse code.

I liked Huddersfield and was happier doing the course although the weather was atrocious with heavy snowfalls. We were put to work with shovels and wheelbarrows, clearing the main streets in the town, and the shop and office workers would bring us hot drinks. Unlike Ossett, where the ratio of men to available women was about two hundred to one, here there were lots of lovely warm-hearted Yorkshire girls and it wasn't too difficult to get a date or two.

There was also a local repertory theatre and I went along one evening to see the play. I had very mixed feelings: I stood outside the stage door after the show waiting for the cast to come out, but I didn't have the heart to make myself known to them. I didn't belong, and I didn't go to the theatre again. This feeling of not belonging has remained with me. To this day I am nervous and shy of going onto a film set that I'm not involved in, even though I am appearing in other parts of the film. I feel I am intruding and I should not be there. I am not too good at going backstage after plays either, no matter whom I know in the cast.

*

I was pretty good at Morse: I found the rhythm easy to pick up and by the end of the course I could read and send about twenty words a minute. My next posting after a home leave was to Catterick camp in North Yorkshire. I was promoted to lance corporal (acting unpaid) and given a squad of about twenty to march about and teach Morse code to. Catterick was a huge peacetime army base, one of the biggest. As well as the signals garrison, there were the Royal Artillery Tank Corps and infantry head-quarters: many thousands of troops gathered together. The signals garrison was divided into lines of billets named after First War battles; I was in Le Cateau lines.

The garrison was a world of its own, with NAAFIs, football and cricket grounds and, lo and behold, a theatre! The 'Gaiety' was fully equipped to professional standards; concerts and plays were regularly performed, and very soon I found myself rehearsing a leading role in Priestley's *Dangerous Corner*. It was a pretty good company with an excellent director. I wangled with the powers that be to be allowed to grow my hair, saying that the pudding-basin style was definitely not right for the part! As the first night approached my hair was looking quite respectable and one day on parade, being inspected by a very senior officer, I heard: 'Get that lance corporal's hair cut!'

I quaked: had my wangle been in vain? Then I heard the sergeant major reply: 'Lance Corporal Ohm, sir: excused haircuts as he is in the play.'

'Oh yes,' said the colonel. 'How's it going?'

'Fine, sir,' I answered.

'Good – carry on!'

I glowed!

Another huge perk was being allowed to visit the officers' married quarters to borrow props and furniture for the plays. To sit in a properly furnished room, sipping tea and saying to some major's wife, 'That lamp standard would be just right for Act Two,' and getting it, was a coup indeed! In fact I remember these moments of escape from regimentation more than the actual performances of the play itself, although the army audiences were unforgettable.

Spring had now given way to early summer which was as hot and sunny as the winter had been cold and icy. I played cricket, opening the batting for the battalion, and even had a couple of games for the garrison side which had several Yorkshire professionals in it. I was getting pretty fit. At a PE compulsory boxing match I realised I had a good right hand, putting my opponent into hospital with a broken nose and a mangled face! In consequence I was asked to join the garrison boxing squad and, although the training was extremely hard, the great advantage was being excused guard duty and fire pickets. Guard duty was two hours on and two hours off, saying, 'Halt, who goes there?' with fixed bayonet and being terrified out of your wits if an owl suddenly hooted! Fire picket was four hours on and four hours off and involved touring the camp and making sure that the blackout was strictly observed. One night I saw one billet with all its lights blazing and went in to read the riot act. There was a stillness: something very new, something very different. Cards were being quietly played, letters being written, cigarettes smoked on bunks. These were men resting, recovering. They were commandos who had been on raids in Europe and had come to do a signalling course. I asked politely if they would attend to the blackout: there was a long pause, a nod to someone from the sergeant and the job was done in a leisurely way. They had made their point: to them, a strict blackout on a Yorkshire moor, miles away from anywhere, was bullshit. They had my respect; they had been through it – they were real soldiers.

By now I was in the boxing squad and training every night at the double with my arms never lower than my shoulders, an hour at a time. I met one or two better opponents and didn't much like the punishment, injured my hand and dropped out of boxing forever. A great southpaw lost to the world!

Nevertheless things weren't going too badly. I enjoyed the Morse teaching and my extracurricular activities such as cricket and drama. Most Saturdays there would be a liberty truck to either Richmond (the North Yorks version) or Darlington, and I saw some active service by the river-side at Richmond and at the dance hall at Darlington! The locals were really warm towards us, and we had some good booze-ups too. We used to bet who could drink a pint the fastest and, being young, we usually won. My fastest was three and a half seconds; it was a good way to augment one's pay! We then caught the 23.59 liberty truck back, sat on our bunks and discussed the vagaries of the evening.

Around this time a huge army exercise involving the whole of Northern Command was planned. It was to last a week and involved infantry, tanks, signals et al. I got the job as wireless operator at the general's HQ. This was a really good number as my wireless was in a mobile truck and I had a tent to sleep in and very good food. The general was very friendly and, apart from the cook and one or two others (a few infantry to guard us), we were on our own. I had tuned in all the correct frequencies to the various HQs and everything was hunky-dory; messages were going through loud and clear, the weather was glorious and on the second day, a Saturday, I was sitting alongside the general having something to eat in a lovely wooded clearing somewhere in Bedale, beautifully camouflaged and with not a care in the world. Suddenly a fresh-faced second lieutenant from the Green Jackets burst into the clearing. He was sweating and panting and had obviously pulled off a brilliant forced march which no one else had thought of.

'Sir,' he panted, 'I have orders to arrest you and take you prisoner.'

Members of his platoon frog-marched me, hands in the air, to my wireless truck and made me de-net all my frequencies. We were totally without communication and completely taken prisoner. I was delighted: it was Saturday and I had visions of Darlington that evening and a few cushy days off until the rest of the exercise was over. Then a staff car drew up and a major wearing a red armband got out, apologised profusely to the general and bollocked the poor second lieutenant for breaking the rules of the exercise. I had to laboriously send out my call sign and tune in all my HQs again! I often wonder whether that second lieutenant survived the war: I hope he did but he seemed a bit too keen to me.

Our Royal Signals Colonel-in-Chief (an honorary title usually given to someone really eminent) was the Princess Royal of that time, and a real tartar she was too! We knew she was coming to inspect the camp and troops at least a month in advance and immediately everything had to be cleaned, polished and given a lick of paint. Even the coal bunkers were distempered white. All our uniforms and equipment were pressed and blancoed and brasses polished. On a previous inspection she had had someone put on a charge because the backs of the buttons on his greatcoat were not polished: everyone was terrified of her!

On the day of her visit not all of my Morse equipment was working, much to the alarm of the officer in charge. When she came round on her inspection some of the people with earphones on were pretending to read Morse although no sound was coming through; we held our breath and got away with it! That day I really learned the truth of the phrase 'bullshit baffles brains', which has stood me in good stead all my life – sometimes as a practitioner but more often than not when practised on me.

At about the same time as this nonsense the Battle of Alamein was raging in the desert and, although it was a great victory, there were many casualties. This meant many overseas postings as replacements and there was a great clear-out from the camp, irrespective of persons; footballers, cricketers and a young actor/Morse instructor were all on their way. Then the Entertainments Officer, an older man who had lost an arm in World War One, stepped in and decreed that I would be wasted as a wireless operator and should become an officer. He was totally wrong about this as by now I was really good and quick at Morse and would have been much more use at that than telling a lot of men what to do. However, I was selected for the six-month course and remained at Catterick. Perhaps he thought I would be available a bit longer for plays at the Gaiety Theatre, but there was no time for that sort of thing!

Our feet didn't touch the ground. There were ten-mile forced marches carrying the PIAT anti-tank rifle (weighing thirty-six pounds); twenty-mile route marches at night in gas respirators; battle camp in the Lake District. Highlights of battle camp included climbing the three-thousand-foot mountain Hellvellyn in full equipment and carrying rifle (fortunately it was a misty day because I hate heights), doing the assault course and then the mock battle. This entailed crawling up a stream with live bullets just above us, tossing grenades and firing mortars. All perfectly safe of course, until we heard about the lads who had set up their mortar gun too high and too near the tree branches, fired it and that was the end of them.

We then moved down to Kent and there was more physical training to do including running up and down the famous steep Wrotham escarpment in full kit until exhausted. I later explained this to Sidney Lumet when I went to talk to him about his film *The Hill* but he was not impressed and I didn't get the part. We also learned to drive trucks and ride motorbikes; that was great fun as we had scrambling courses and learned how to lay the bike down at speed and roll away. All that side of the training, the physical side, I was reasonably good at; but we also had a month's technical training and I was truly awful. Stick a diagram of a super-heterodyne receiver in front of me and I freeze! My brain just couldn't take in the technical stuff. How I passed out as a Signals Officer, supposedly versed in radio sets and telephone exchanges, I will never know, but I did! Apparently my report said I was a natural leader of men, whatever that means.

In the spring of 1943, just after my twentieth birthday, I found myself at Western Command Signals, stationed in Chester Castle, in charge of a line section. This meant I was responsible for sixty men, six large trucks and trailers, nine fifteen-hundredweight trucks, six Lease-Lend Harley Davidson 750cc motorbikes and a van, later to be replaced by a jeep. Our job was to lay overhead and underground telephone lines. The area we covered was huge and included Liverpool docks, Lancashire, Cheshire and the whole of Wales as far south as Barry Docks. Fortunately I had some wonderful NCOs, well versed in the job, and a great section sergeant called Nebby Ward, a regular soldier who knew every trick in the book. Nebby taught me what to do in the early days and steered me through many snares and obstacles.

Western Command was very stuffy and correct so it was good to work away. We were a completely self-contained outfit with our own cook and we could move off at any time, without notice. In between working away there was nothing to do but train on the famous Roodee race course, drill, keep fit and generally engage in bullshit in the time-honoured army way!

Because of my civilian background, I was made unit entertainment officer. This really meant looking after the unit dance band which was very popular in the district. I had to deal with booking the band for gigs, paying the boys and keeping the accounts. This was a very good number for a twenty-year-old lad in an officer's uniform, and it continued for about a year. I remember thinking, it won't go on forever, so let's enjoy it while it lasts!

*

By the spring of 1944 there were lots of rumours about the second front in Western Europe, the first being of course the Russian Front. We found ourselves posted as a unit to a holding battalion in Kirkburton near Huddersfield to await developments, but nothing happened; we hung around for a month or two and I played a bit of cricket in the Huddersfield league. Eventually we moved down in convoy to Chislehurst in Kent, dodged a few doodlebugs and hung around a bit longer.

The doodlebugs were interesting. You were quite safe if you heard them above you as they would crash further on; the ones that shut off before reaching you were tricky as in a few seconds they could land very near you indeed. One day we were doing some training in a field when one came lurching towards us and there was some very fast sprinting from the lads! Fortunately, it landed a couple of streets away and no damage was done.

Everything was shrouded in secrecy at that time. D-Day had come and gone, but eventually we were ordered in convoy to Tilbury docks where we embarked onto a merchant ship with all our transport and gear and set off, presumably for Normandy. It certainly wasn't a direct route as we were on board for over twenty-four hours, eventually transferring all our stuff onto a landing area at Arromanche. Ours was an uneventful journey, though another ship in the convoy had a hairier time of it when a bomb landed amidships; fortunately for them, it did not explode.

While on the journey I gave one or two lessons in basic French, and also in how to behave towards the local population. Nebby was more pragmatic: 'When you move into a town always go for the ugly girls. They are most likely to be clean and will be very grateful!'

We were, almost to a man, the same unit from Western Command; and we did the same sort of work, laying and repairing telephone lines and cables and getting exchanges working again, using most of the lines for military purposes.

Initially we were attached to the First Canadian Army who suffered dreadful casualties, many of them Canadian Français. The French people heartily disliked them, rather in the same way that Americans weren't too popular in Britain. I got on well with the Canadians, but I could have done without the trick of testing the Limey's bottle (i.e. mine) by driving unnecessarily through shelling areas. You nipped in between shells – that was the theory anyway! But in general we were well at the back, out of harm's way; we just had to look out for snipers, check for booby traps in any room we entered and be very careful when riding motorbikes in case there were wires stretched across the road at neck height.

Not everyone was thrilled to be liberated by the Allies; after all, the Wehrmacht had been there for four years and many of the populace did well out of supplying their needs. Some of the local girls had married or had fiancés. The POW camp in Bayeux had every nationality among them: Germans, Italians, Poles, Belgians, Dutch, French girls – the lot. There were even some Russians who did pioneer work for the Germans: anything for something to eat and a warm uniform. Nine hundred were repatriated to Murmansk at the end of the hostilities and Stalin promptly had them shot on the dockside.

In the main, though, we were rapturously received. Flowers were thrown on the trucks, Calvados was brought out, even champagne that had been hidden from the Germans, but mostly it was wine that was offered whenever we stopped the convoy. It was an incredible atmosphere of joy and relief to be rid of the German occupation. The resistance had dealt summary justice on collaborators and many girls wore turbans to hide their shaven heads. I wondered how many personal scores and jealousies were settled in this way, '*cheveux coupé*'.

Everything was 'every man for himself' and 'catch as catch can'; we never knew what was around the corner. For instance, we were sent over without bedding or tentage and were sleeping rough when we came across a store being guarded by the FFI (French Forces of the Interior). These were resistance fighters, now issued with uniforms and working with the Allies. They were under strict instructions to guard this store; I managed in my best French to persuade them otherwise and we loaded up tentage and comfortable bedding for the entire unit! A question of 'bullshit baffling brains' French style, but the lads didn't get wet any more!

After a spell just outside Dieppe, we moved to Boulogne and Calais and there we parted company with the Canadians and were given the job of doing the line communication for Pas de Calais and the Lille area. I set up our unit HQ in a German blockhouse in the centre of Calais and split the lads up into groups: some were in Lille Roubaix and Tourcoing and some in Boulogne, but most of us were in Calais. Just up the road were twenty thousand crack German troops who had been bypassed in the advance and were being held by a Czech anti-tank brigade. I liaised with the latter and did their communications layout for them.

The Czechs were an interesting lot, especially in view of the future. Because they were already a Communist brigade they either saluted in the army style or with a clenched fist; I often replied with the latter. We were all very red in those days: we were fighting the war to end Fascism once and for all. We would join up with our comrades in the Soviet army and the left would triumph throughout Europe. That was our fervent hope and expectation; we did not yet know of the Jewish persecution, but we knew enough to know that they had to be saved from Nazism. Of course we had seen the newsreels of Kristallnacht and heard stories from refugees who had escaped to Britain, but the full horror of the final solution came later.

We settled in for the winter, and a bitterly cold one it was too. Calais was a dismal place at that time and the local people were nearly starving. We had a queue of children at our cookhouse every day and the lads would give a bit of their rations to them: little grey faces standing in the cold, patiently waiting for a scrap or two of food.

Even so, some of us managed to get our 'toes under the table', an army phrase meaning being invited into a civilian's home. I often used to visit the family Danglot. I would take tins of food and cans of beer to share with the family, and Madame Danglot would work miracles in the kitchen. They were very kind people and so, spending time with them and working with the local PTT (*Postes, Téléphones, Télégraphes*), my French came on well.

Meanwhile my work meant that I travelled a great deal up and down from Bayeux to Brussels. A detachment of my troops was based at the main telephone exchange in Lille so I had to visit them frequently. There was a lovely telephonist there of whom I was very fond and who made my visits very worthwhile indeed. She was charming and very attentive! She once sent me a message urging me to come and see her; it ended: *Je t'embrasse ardemment, passionnément, tendrement – ton amour, Elaine.* I later found out that one of my lads, who was stationed there, was also being ardently embraced by her, only more regularly as he was on the spot! It must have been quite a coup for him to nick his officer's girlfriend.

Things were pretty peaceful during that winter. There seemed to be a sort of unofficial truce between the crack German troops at Dunkerque and the Czechs. It was well known that the odd German would slip through the lines into the nearby town of Gravelines at night but nothing was ever done about it – a blind eye was turned! Christmas came and went, and apart from a very thorough bombing raid which killed several hundred civilians and von Rundstedt's Ardennes offensive, which threatened to cut us off in a great pincer movement and so concentrated our minds for a little while, things were cold but fairly quiet.

Eventually, in early May, the war was won. My second-in-command, Harry Webster, a thirty-five-year-old schoolteacher, went to accept the German surrender at Dunkerque. The proud Nazi CO refused to surrender until three days after the official surrender in Germany, thereby claiming his troops were never defeated. You can't keep a good Nazi down!

I was just twenty-two and therefore young enough to be posted to the war against Japan which was still not over. So, after a short leave to Paris, I was sent to a holding battalion in Bruges ready to be posted out to the Far East; and thus my association with my line section came to an end. Nebby and I said farewell and that was that. We had been together for two years. At least I could say that no one got killed or hurt, but I think that was more down to good luck and not being exposed to much nastiness. It was, however, a profound experience for me. I still don't automatically expect a light to come on just because I press a switch, or water to be in taps, or telephones to work; I can't stand wasted food and I look over my shoulder a lot!

*

From Bruges I went to Aldershot and, after a short leave at home where I slept non-stop for seventeen hours, I went on to Southampton to board a troopship, having been rigged out with my tropical kit.

I can't say that I was overly thrilled at the prospect of what might lie ahead: I would much rather have seen my time out in Germany, or gone to Prague with my Czech friends. I couldn't understand why we didn't march into Spain and liberate the Spanish from Franco; after all, it was meant to be the end of Fascism. Instead we set off through the Bay of Biscay, through the straits of Gibraltar, along the deserted Spanish coast (that was the nearest I got to taking on Franco!) and on past Malta before arriving at Port Taufiq at the entrance to the Suez Canal.

There was a troopship going in the opposite direction full of Fourteenth Army Burma veterans being repatriated home. There were many jeers and catcalls from them as our white bodies sailed by: 'Get your number dry! Get your knees brown!' They had mostly been out East without leave for four years and their skin was a mixture of dark tan and jaundiced yellow from taking malaria tablets. We took on water and supplies while Egyptian youths swarmed round the boat begging, trying to sell things and diving for coins that were thrown into the water; the Orient was beginning and the West was being left behind.

The Suez Canal was amazing as it twisted and turned; to look across the desert and see a boat ploughing its way through the sand was extraordinary. By day it was almost unbearably hot, and the boat was crowded; but it was lovely to be on board at night when it was cooler and the moon shone brightly, quite beautiful after the grey, cold winter in Europe.

We stopped in Aden where it was so hot in the middle of the day the sun's rays could be seen bouncing off the deck. Then on we went through the Indian Ocean, in glorious sunshine, accompanied by shimmering flying fish, to Bombay, gateway to India. What a culture shock this great city was to me. Teeming with people, brilliant colours, strange smells, the Taj Mahal, coffee shops, bazaars, beggars everywhere, buses with people hanging all over them, crowds, crowds and more crowds! I thought it was mind-blowing.

I was soon sent by train up to Indore to a big signals depot there. The train journey was amazing. The railway stations were not like those of British rail! Many people would be lying down on the cool platform with their luggage around them; others were eating and feeding their families. I saw sad beggars, women with babies, the blind, men with elephantiasis, amputees, slashes of red that looked like blood on the ground where the betel nuts had been chewed and spat out, all accompanied by a cacophony of sounds. As the train left Bombay, people selling cigarettes and matches and various other goods, or just begging, clung on to the side of the train and only jumped off at the last second as the train gathered speed.

The big city was soon left behind and was replaced by the worst slums and shanties imaginable. Everything, good or bad, seemed larger and more extreme than anything I had ever known. I was only in Indore for a short time, but it was long enough to learn that a sweeper with his broom was an untouchable and the bearer bullying and ordering him about was of higher caste. I had time to marvel at the skill of these bearers and how silent they were. Billets were cleaned and *dhobi* (laundry) taken away whilst you slept. There were some who could shave you without waking you, but I never had that done to me!

After a couple of weeks there I was posted to Mountbatten's head-quarters in Kandy in Sri Lanka (then Ceylon). This was quite a journey, being over three days by train down to Madras, then on the ferry from Danashkodi to Talamanaar, and then by road into Colombo and eventually up-country to Kandy. There was one memorable night as we chugged along on that train. In the middle of the jungle we crossed a viaduct which was followed by a steep incline. Half way up, the engine slowly ground to a halt and rolled backwards down the incline onto the viaduct. The driver tried again and the same thing happened again; the incline was too steep for the engine, and more steam was needed. So the driver and guard set off up the track to a village station a few miles away to telegraph for an extra engine! Things never moved too swiftly in India, but this was a major problem and our engine didn't arrive until morning. There we were all night on this viaduct surrounded by the jungle; it was so still, yet stealthily alive, and the silence was only broken from time to time with roars and shrieks. I didn't sleep at all, and spent a wonderful moonlit night in that impenetrable jungle, watching and listening. It was quite unforgettable.

The ferry was interesting too. All forms of transport in the East seemed to be loaded and full to the gunnels and the ferry was no exception. We landed in Ceylon accompanied by chickens, sheep, goats and their owners, the old ferry having groaned its way across the water.

Kandy was a beautiful place and the air was lovely and fresh after the humidity of the coast. I wasn't there long enough, but had time to visit the Temple of the Tooth and watch the elephants at work: gentle, intelligent creatures moving huge logs with great precision.

I was put in charge of a line section responsible for maintaining the telephone lines and cables between Kandy and Colombo, a distance of ninety-six miles. A compound had been put up exactly forty-eight miles from each town. There was nothing there, apart from a few billets, some barbed wire, the odd snake and several salamanders. I was there for six weeks and the lines constantly went down, largely due to having been laid through paddy fields and becoming inundated.

Those six weeks were the loneliest and most boring of my army life to date. I didn't know the troops, and couldn't mix with them anyway for disciplinary reasons, unlike my old section in Europe who knew each other for two years. My only friend was my 350cc Matchless motorbike. Sometimes on off-duty days I would ride to Kandy, and sometimes to Colombo where there was an officers' club, just to fill the time.

I also had an army radio set in my room and used to tune into American Forces Radio on which I heard some music that really made me sit up and take notice: Lionel Hampton, Count Basie and Duke Ellington for example. I was enthralled, and my love of jazz was reinforced. In general, though, it was not a happy time, although I loved Ceylon and its people with permanent smiles on their faces.

My next job was to help prepare and load equipment and stores on to ships, ready for the recapture of Singapore (the so-called 'Exercise Zipper'). There weren't so many smiles among the stevedores as they were having a dispute and were unwilling to work. I'm afraid my left-wing trade-union ideals went out the window as I shouted, pushed and bullied to get them to work: our stuff just had to be loaded – they could go on strike later if they liked! My mode of transport to Singapore was to be on an aircraft carrier for about four days, transferring onto a landing craft for the last bit of the journey. Tension was greatly relieved because by now atomic bombs had been dropped on Nagasaki and Hiroshima, so the war was over. This was very fortunate for us as the Japanese were well dug-in in Singapore and Malaya and would have given us a tough reception; not so fortunate for the tens of thousands of Japanese civilians who perished.

Billeted in the notorious Changi jail, we set to work on our customary line-laying tasks. To assist us we had two hundred Japanese POWs digging trenches for new underground cables, supervised by us. Needless to say they were hardly popular with us as we had already seen the state of our own POWs returning from the 'Death Railways' and other camps. They had been treated like animals and were in an appalling state of mal-nutrition and illness; the ones we saw were survivors on their way to gradual rehabilitation and rest before returning home. We were outraged at what we saw and heard, but still treated our prisoners within the rules of the Geneva Convention. As they dug the cable trenches in the extreme heat, watched by their medical orderly, patrolling up and down, it was not uncommon for a Japanese to faint in the trench. The orderly would stroll towards him, pull him out, give him a swig of water from his water bottle and slap his face until he came round. Recovered, the POW would then bow, pick up his shovel and start working again. No one else stopped working while this was going on or displayed any interest in the proceedings; one must not lose face under any circumstances.

Once or twice I had to supervise roll-call in front of their own officer. Their way of meting out punishment for misdemeanours was interesting: the miscreant would be paraded in front of the officer, his offence barked out by his NCO and his officer would knock him down with a swipe across his face. He would then get up and bow; the process would be repeated a number of times dependent upon the misdemeanour.

Their whole culture was completely alien to ours. As prisoners they were grovellingly obsequious and tried to ingratiate themselves into our good books and so disarm us, but we had nothing but contempt for them.

One of my corporals went too far, though. He had lost a brother on the Death Railway and was not above laying about him; he made them run up hills behind trucks until exhausted. I had to stop this and warn him about the Geneva Convention, but I felt for him and recognised his anger.

*

Demobilisation was now under way, albeit slowly. We were given numbers based on our age and length of service: my number was 44 and, as they had only reached 14, I knew I was in for a long wait! About two numbers a month were getting away and I reckoned my number would come up in about fifteen months, in other words the end of 1946. The only thing to do was to enjoy things there and at the same time prepare for the civilian life that lay ahead.

I got in touch with the local radio station, Radio Malaya, and started to work for them in my spare time. The chief producer was a very efficient lady called Adza Vincent, who later became an agent in the UK and worked very closely with Christopher Fry as his assistant. Adza gave me various things to do; I read the news and documentaries as well as acting in many plays.

Quite the most shocking and moving thing I had to do was read Richard Dimbleby's account of what he found in Belsen. The horror of the Holocaust was brought sickeningly home to me, and I wept. It was so strange to be so far away, when I had been so near only a few months before. I remembered so clearly those grey, drawn faces of the forced labour workers who managed to get home to France and Belgium as their factories were liberated, and here I was in lush, verdant Singapore. Yet here I also saw and heard of the torture and starvation of our POWs by the Japanese; and I was horrified, too, to learn the details of Nagasaki and Hiroshima – and yet those bombs ended the war. How many of us would have survived Exercise Zipper if the war had continued? Not many from what I saw. It was all profoundly disquieting. How could a supposedly civilised country like Germany carry out genocide, murdering six million Jews? I couldn't come to terms with it then and I can't come to terms with it now; having some Jewish blood myself made it all the more disturbing and distressing.

My radio work took up a lot of my spare time, doing a couple of evenings a week. I love radio drama: the bounds are limitless and I got a great grounding while in Singapore. Cricket, too came back into my life and I played a great deal, including playing for an army side who took on the local teams as a sort of goodwill and friendship exercise. We played mostly on matting wickets and mostly against Indian sides. They had some wonderfully graceful players with exquisite wrist timing when batting and full of spinning wiles when bowling. We were practising fielding one day when the colonel's very beautiful daughter rode by onto the ground. This distracted me and a ball hit me above the left eye, temporarily knocking me out. I carry the scar to this day as a permanent reminder of the dangers of the opposite sex!

Work continued in the usual way, though we did have a good time at the naval base, HMS *Terror*, over the causeway into Malaya at Johor Bahru. They were not called the Senior Service for nothing: they ate, drank and slept in more comfort than the PBA (Poor Bloody Army). Christmas came and went and it was strange to have a swimming gala to celebrate it. The monsoons came and the crickets and bullfrogs celebrated with even more noise at night. Rain was glorious after the heat and I remember standing out in it getting drenched – wonderful!

I loved Singapore in those days: Raffles Hotel, only one skyscraper which housed Radio Malaya, rickshaws everywhere, wonderful street markets cooking superb food. The population was of course Malay but there were even more Chinese. The popular idea that the Chinese are inscrutable and humourless couldn't be further from the truth. That is a front: they are emotional, gregarious and have a huge sense of humour. Many Chinese worked in the army camps and they would work and slave diligently for months until they had enough money to get home to their families. They would set off with good intentions only to get no further than the gambling dens and whorehouses in town where they would do in all their money! A month later they would return to work and start all over again. There were large centres of Chinese-run entertainments called the New World and the Happy World and these housed the Chinese Theatre, dance halls, wrestling and boxing matches, bars and restaurants, teeming with people of all colours and creeds. A great town to be in, and it was recovering quickly from the occupation.

*

I then heard that the CSE (Combined Services Entertainment) had a headquarters on the island; and, in my quest for practice for civilian life, I applied to join them. I was interviewed by the head of the administration, Major Bob Wilson, and he made me second in command as his assistant. The posting came through: I was made an acting captain, and this is what I did for the last six months of my army life. No more Signals songs:

Don't turn away The Royal Corps of Pigs
They may be needed by and by,
For every man in the Royal Corps of Pigs
Is willing to do or die – I don't think!

No more of that. Bob was a civil servant in civilian life – a land valuer for the ministry – but with a great love of the arts, especially drama and literature. He became a great friend. Together with a marvellous Malay assistant, he ran the office of the unit which Peter Nichols immortalised in his play *Privates on Parade*.

When I arrived the unit was in its infancy and being set up. Some very clever people were there, including Stanley Baxter who did a very funny Frank Sinatra parody. Reg Varney had a show, and I had to look after the

39

great Tommy Trinder when he came out to entertain the troops.

One day a pale waif-like creature turned up in the office, weighed down with full kit and rifle. It was a stifling hot day and I was not in the best of moods. 'What do you do?' I asked.

'I'm an actor,' he replied.

To my everlasting shame and remorse I said, 'My God, they'll be sending us bloody performing seals next.'

This eighteen-year-old, Kenneth Williams, was quite brilliant, with talent pouring out of him, and he became an immediate star in the unit. Later, in the fifties, my then wife was in a play with him in the West End and we visited him in his flat in the St Pancras area once or twice as we lived nearby. It was as well to go to the loo before visiting him as his bathroom and lavatory were strictly out of bounds! Otherwise he was the perfect host. We would sit on cushions in his sparsely furnished sitting room, whilst he held forth on some obscure subject with brilliant erudition. I travelled on a bus with him once and anarchy reigned: he was obscenely, outrageously funny and the bus was in an uproar.

Many years later, in the 1980s, he offered me a part in a play he was producing. I wrote back explaining why I couldn't do it and mentioned our days in Nee Soon Transit Camp, Singapore, saying nostalgically, 'Ah well, I suppose it's all high-rise flats now.' He wrote back a charming letter and the idea of high-rise flats covering our unit amused him greatly. He told me the production wasn't much good anyway and that I wouldn't have enjoyed it and wittily described why this was so. Shortly afterwards he was dead. Until I read his diaries I knew nothing of his dark, tragic side. To me he was one of the funniest people I ever knew, with the sharpest and most brilliant of minds, and I was saddened by his far too early death.

*

I had nothing to do with the artistic side of the privates on parade, only administrative matters including pay parade. It amuses me to think that the world-renowned film-director-to-be, John Schlesinger, must have picked up his Malay dollars a time or two from me. I was still very busy at Radio Malaya, though; and I did one CSE play, *The Two Mrs Carrolls*. The cast were mostly civilian actors and actresses from London, including my old friend, Jimmy Viccars, now demobbed from the navy.

We did the play in the famous Victoria Theatre, a lovely old theatre but overwhelmed by starlings who chattered loudly in the roof all through the performance. I had a lovely criticism from the Artistic Director of CSE who told me to stick to radio and never go on stage again. Very encouraging. Mind you, I was playing the young juvenile lead and my weight had gone down from twelve stone to nine due to skin disease. I had suppurating sores all over my body which spread like wildfire when they broke open. When I went to the MO for treatment he took off his shirt and showed me his skin disease. There was nothing to do but knock off a bottle of scotch together and call it a day. I also had malaria bouts despite mosquito nets and tablets. So for a juvenile lead I must have looked a bit odd.

Then, lo and behold, in October 1946, number 44 came up and I was on my way. I stepped onto the boat leaving my wonderful Indian bearer, Nagasar, prostrate and weeping on the dockside. After a week we got to Bombay where we waited for other troops to fill our ship. We were there for five days and there was tension in the air. '*Jai Hind!*' was the cry and there was a complete alcohol ban. Even the officers' club was dry, so another cricket lover and I went to the Brabourne Stadium to watch a fine match – West v East Zone, I think it was – and with glorious Oriental *sang-froid* the bars were open and we were able to drink lovely ice-cold beer all day.

And so eventually to the long voyage home. There were sing-songs at night with the popular number one on the Singapore hit parade, 'Rose, Rose, I Love You', sung rather wistfully for past memories and certain mixed feelings for what lay ahead. Eventually we reached Liverpool, the weather getting colder and colder; then on to Aldershot to hand in equipment and be issued with a demob suit, shirt, tie, shoes and trilby hat.

It was all over, Captain Ohm. The 'run' had lasted four years and ten months (a bit longer if you counted the demob leave). A pretty ordinary and unexciting time compared to some people's exploits.

In 1942 when I was a cadet in West Malling, a fellow trainee called Tubby Galbraith whom I hardly knew came and sat on my bunk and asked if I would be interested in training for special operations: being dropped into Europe, that sort of thing. I turned him down – didn't have the nerve, didn't have the bottle. Pity: the Morse code would have been really useful then.

4
CIVVY STREET

S ITTING HUNCHED OVER A SMALL COAL FIRE in the sitting room at home in Uttoxeter in early December 1946, I felt gloomily depressed. Coal, food, clothes and petrol were strictly rationed, and after Malaya I felt cold, very cold. Worse still though, I didn't feel as though I belonged or fitted in. I walked into the odd pub, looked around, froze and walked out again. I was a bit like a racehorse refusing to go into the stalls. I just didn't feel a part of the life I saw around me. I was moody and morose, and Mother found this terribly annoying. I really had to pull myself together and do something.

I had an unsigned three-year contract with Radio Malaya (six hundred and twenty-five Malayan dollars a month, a free bungalow and an *ayah*) in my pocket. This was very tempting to take up: a lovely way of life, a girlfriend waiting there, and very interesting and creative work. I thought I might spend a year or two there and then go on to do radio in Australia, a big industry there at that time.

However, my heart was really set on going back into the theatre and so, my skin trouble having cleared up and back to normal weight, I went to see Basil Thomas in Wolverhampton. The wonderful Salberg family welcomed me back without a qualm. 'You'll be a bit rusty,' said Basil, 'so we'll put you into our Hereford company until the new Wolverhampton season starts in February.' Off I went, just like that. The die was cast. I often wonder what my life would have become had I taken the other path back to Malaya. The loyalty and generosity shown to me by the Salbergs was wonderful and formed the basis of my future development as an actor.

Despite all this, I carried with me a huge chip on my shoulder. I was a creature of moods, very arrogant and with a violent streak. I really did think the world owed me a living. I don't know why I felt like this. I suppose my army experience, training and attitude had something to do with it, but others seemed to cope perfectly well with adjusting back to normal civilian life. I didn't, and sought refuge in my work, more determined than ever to succeed, or at least survive. Not a very nice person I'm afraid, but at least I could act and I got on well with my fellow players.

Despite heavy snow, followed by serious flooding, the company did well in Hereford. Gerald Cuff was also de-rusting and waiting for the Wolverhampton season; Arthur Lowe was there as a character actor and his wife, Joan Cooper, was stage manager. A young Irish doctor, recently turned actor, named Richard Leech was the leading man.

Most entertaining of all was the scenic designer, Michael Ellis, who went on to become the head of C & W May, the theatrical costumiers who were based in Garrick Street. I often dropped in on him over the years for hilarious liquid lunches. He was a rare generous spirit and very funny. Gays and straights mixed easily in those days and seemed much less segregated than perhaps they are today. There were no gay pubs, just pubs.

My major from CSE in Singapore, Bob Wilson, was back in London living in Redcliffe Square, Earls Court, and married to Toni, a truly beautiful, red-haired lady who had appeared on the cover of *Vogue* during leave from the WAAF. Bob and Toni were so supportive of me in those early days. There was always a bed when I needed it and we remained friends until his sad death some years ago.

The 1947 Wolverhampton company had six resident men: Gerry, Colin Laurence, Hugh Falkus, Leslie Yeo, Tony Sagar and me. There was also a lovely married actress in the company and we became close – perhaps too close sometimes for the good of my work. The management had a word, and so too did Gerry. He told me to concentrate on my work because I had it in me to become a 'proper actor'. What a wonderful phrase, and what an accolade coming from him. *A proper actor*: that is what I vowed to try to become, and still hope to be.

Colin Laurence was a lovely man with a great sense of humour and a love of life, only to be killed in a car crash two or three years later. Hugh Falkus gave up acting later and became a wildlife expert, appearing on TV and writing books on the subject. Leslie Yeo was great company, a brilliant light comedian and leading man and immensely popular with audiences. After doing a couple of seasons in Newfoundland, he eventually settled in Canada where he was very successful.

Tony Sagar and I were the two youngest, although he was senior to me. Tony was a fine cricketer who had been on the Lancashire ground staff and was a top club player. I've already mentioned the Salbergs' love of cricket and we played every Sunday under Derek's captaincy. The summer of '47 was sublime, the weather perfect and it was glorious to be playing regularly again in England. The rep season closed for two weeks in mid-summer and we went on a cricket tour, playing every day. The team was called The Reptiles and most of our games took place in Buckinghamshire: that was where I first played at Datchet, a club I was to join in later years. I also found time to get to Lords one day and saw Denis Compton in full flight during that vintage Edrich-Compton season. Denis hit six fours for twenty-four in one over all round the wicket off the great Somerset all-rounder, Arthur Wellard. At the end of the over, Wellard turned to the Tavern and threw up his arms as if to say, *What can I do?*

The crowds were enormous for both sport and theatre in those days, with everyone celebrating the end of the war, although life was still pretty austere with food and fuel severely rationed. I saw *Annie Get Your Gun* at Drury Lane and stood and cheered at the end. I'd never seen such energy on stage before. In the cinema I saw *Les Enfants du Paradis* and this has remained my number one film to take to the proverbial desert island: Marcel Herrand, Pierre Brasseur, Arletty and all. The film was shot in Nice during the occupation, and any actor not working became an extra to avoid being sent to forced labour by the Germans. The writer was a Jew hiding out in the mountains above Nice and clandestine visits to him had to be made to get more pages. A truly great film made in extraordinary circumstances.

*

The Wolverhampton season had been a great success, playing to packed houses. I was asked to remain with the company but decided it was time to move on. Tony Sagar was staying: he was getting a lot of parts I wanted to play and I was getting a bit frustrated about this, so I made the break.

I got a part in a new play at the Central Library Theatre in Manchester.

We rehearsed in London and the dress rehearsal was in Manchester at 3 P.M. on a Sunday. I missed the train from Euston for amorous reasons, arriving just in time to see the train move out. I was mortified and got on the Liverpool train, changed at Crewe and arrived in Manchester hours late. It was time I started thinking through my brain rather than from between my legs!

The play opened the following night, and in it I had a very long duologue scene with a not-very-confident actor. The scene started all right but then he went completely blank. He couldn't take a prompt. I tried to help him with a line or two but was met only with glazed eyes. He left the theatre (well, his brain did) while his body remained serenely on stage. I did my best to get the gist of the scene over by saying my own lines and tailoring some of his; but from him there was nothing. He looked so relaxed, while I in total contrast was in a state of some tension. It was a nightmare, and I don't think he ever acted again after this play.

The pay-off was the notice in the *Manchester Guardian* which said the play would be better once Peter Vaughan had learnt his lines! Ah well, whoever said the theatre was fair?

I stayed out at Heald Green where my grandmother was very ill in a coma and about to die. Auntie Meg was living there and looking after her. She had long become a widow. Wilmot had died of pneumonia after the piston-ring factory in Leeds lost its roof in a fire and they worked on regardless. My chief memory of him was driving his bull-nosed Morris around the leafy lanes of Yorkshire taking bends on the wrong side of the road like a racing car. 'Easier to steer,' he said. So he probably wouldn't have lived long anyway.

Meg never married again but devotedly looked after her mother until her death, and then her father until his death. Gran had a small amount of money to leave which all went to Meg. Mother had a real bee in her bonnet about this, believing Meg had made Gran alter her will and had guided her hand as she signed. She also believed Meg told her that I had been killed in the war in case she left anything to me. Mother nursed this grudge until her own death.

One day I was sitting with Grandad and he said to me of his wife: 'She's mad, you know. Doesn't know what's going on, but I'm all right.' He then pulled out a notebook and went through all his engagements for that year. I sat awestruck. I never saw either of my grandparents again.

I returned to London and got my first agent. Not exclusive, you understand: just me and practically everyone else who was out of work at that
time. The routine was to climb the steps to her office in Cambridge Circus
each morning and greet the lugubrious Smithy in the outer office. If there
was nothing, that was as far as you got; but once in a while you were
summoned into the inner sanctum where sat the great Miriam Warner,
doyenne of the special weeks.

The repertory system was booming with companies springing up
everywhere. These companies often needed augmenting, and Miriam had
cornered the market. She liked me because of my Salberg experience,
thinking I was a bit classy. I went in one day: 'They're doing *Charley's Aunt*
at Louth in Lincolnshire for Christmas and want someone for Jack,' she
said. 'Twice nightly and three shows on Saturday, twelve quid a week; take
it or leave it, dear.'

I took it, and shared digs with a student about to go to Yugoslavia
volunteering to dig roads for Marshall Tito. Left-wing idealists abounded
but there was not much sign of change in Britain despite the huge Labour
majority: Ernest Bevin saw to that. Still, we did get a National Health
Service, nationalised mines, iron and steel, railways, gas, electricity and so
on, so on the home front much was achieved.

On the days when Miriam had nothing for me, it was on to the
Salisbury and various other pubs in the area. There was bound to be someone around to have a beer and a natter with. No arrangements to meet
were ever made, it just happened; and that set the social pattern for years to
come – a loosely knit crowd of friends and acquaintances all regaling each
other with amazing stories and with ears flapping for any hint of work.

There were one or two other agents slightly upmarket of Miriam. I got
as far as the door of one once, froze and left. I hadn't shaken off this feeling
of being an outsider, and to a degree I have it still. I hate parties and social
occasions, getting very nervous and throwing drink down my throat at
every opportunity.

*

Philip ('Putz') Stainton, an ex-Salbergian, had by now definitely made it,
appearing in leading parts in several films such as the Ealing comedy,
Passport to Pimlico. A large jovial character actor, he retained his interest

in repertory by running a company in Warrington. When not otherwise engaged he directed the plays and made occasional appearances. He engaged me as juvenile character lead, and I knew I would get better parts than by returning to Wolverhampton. So, one Sunday morning in Euston station, I met up with one or two others who were obviously joining the company too. We were easy to spot by our theatrical baskets being loaded into the guard's van. These were quite large affairs carrying all our modern stage wardrobe, make-up etc. We travelled up together to Warrington with the inevitable change at Crewe.

Although we were wary of one another at first, the atmosphere soon became very convivial with lots of jokes and anecdotes. One of the girls asked me where I was staying; I told her my digs' address. Could she come too, she asked, as she had not fixed her digs? I was bagged before we even got as far as Crewe!

However, I was determined to be more disciplined in this regard. No more missing trains or being hauled up for not giving my all. Work was definitely going to come first. I wanted to become a proper actor above all else. We quickly agreed that there would be no love-making until we both knew our lines for the next day. We would hear each other's lines and then leap into action. It certainly added piquancy to the situation!

There were no matinees at Warrington for the simple reason it was twice-nightly weekly rep: two performances a day at six and 8.30. Putz was a fine actor and good director but he could be blunt and autocratic. On our first dress rehearsal I made an entrance and shut the door but it flew open behind me. A voice boomed out from the auditorium: 'Didn't they teach you to close a door when you come on stage at Wolverhampton?' This in front of the whole company.

I went stone cold and advanced to the footlights. 'When your scene department makes doors that shut properly I will bloody well shut them!'

There was a tense pause: was I on the next train back? Then he laughed, and I laughed; and we became great mates after that.

The audiences in Warrington were tremendous and the locals were so good to us. The local butcher often gave us a steak or two on top of our food coupons to take back to our grateful landladies. The lovely old Victorian Theatre Royal was packed to the rafters most weeks, and boy how those audiences responded, especially to comedy where there were always gales of laughter. As I said, the houses were at six and 8.30, and by the end of the week we often had to 'top and tail'. This meant speeding up and cutting our big speeches as we went along. You would precis the speech, making sure you gave the cue line. This called for some dexterity of mind. I am sure it didn't always make sense, but no one seemed to notice. It had to be done so that the second houses ended in time for people to catch the last buses and trains: there weren't too many cars about. It also meant the intervals could be stretched to increase the bar trade. All good for business, but there was no mention of this in Stanislavsky.

It was the company custom to have a Guinness or two in the local after rehearsals on Saturdays in celebration of the end of another week. Like everything in Warrington at that time, the pub was teeming and full of life and characters.

One week a rather severe middle-aged lady came up to me and said, 'I am director of the Warrington Amateur Drama and Operatic Society and I come to see you every week. I could tell you what I think of you if you like.'

'Oh yes,' I said, 'please do.'

'Are you sure?' she said.

'Yes, it's so important we get opinions and criticism otherwise we won't improve.'

'Well,' she said, 'you're stiff for a start, and that girl you're with is always the same.'

The trouble is she was quite right on both counts. In fact the 'girl I was with' was becoming a bit tricky. She was talking of setting up together at the end of the season in a flat and wanted me to go and meet her parents. This made me extremely uneasy, and I am afraid the relationship had to be terminated. We had a week's break in the middle of the season and that was the time to do it. There was much wailing and gnashing of teeth (she even pretended she was pregnant) but she finally accepted the situation and moved on to other digs. This left me free to explore the local scene which I did with enthusiasm. I am not pleased and proud of my ruthless behaviour; I am merely reporting it and, as I look back, I am appalled at some of the ways I treated people, especially the opposite sex. Anyway, the amateur critic was right: she was always the same!

There were some great people in the company in Warrington. One such was a vivacious and stunning character actress called Phyllis Montefiore. She was tremendous fun with a great personality. She was a bit deaf but you would not have guessed this was due to ill-treatment by the Japanese for three years in an internment camp in Manila.

We also had a very good leading man, Maurice Durant. He had been an officer all through the Italian campaign, during which he managed to purloin a German staff car which he filled with home comforts, including an Italian girlfriend who went through the campaign with him in the back of the car. My own anecdotes failed in comparison.

I really enjoyed my season at Warrington. I had some really good parts and my work came on a great deal, especially in comedy roles where my timing gained in sureness. Well, it would have been hard to fail with those audiences.

When the season ended the company arranged to do a play at the huge RAF depot at Pudgate. There was no part for me in it, but at the last minute the juvenile lead had to drop out so I was roped in, never having seen or read the play, with only the dress rehearsal to go. Fortunately it wasn't a huge part, but it was a bit hit-and-miss. However, a company of 'top 'n' tailers' pulled me through, and there was rapturous applause from the airmen and a few extra quid to go back to London with.

*

I found myself in a nice bedsitter in Baron's Court which a fellow thespian recommended to me. In the next room to me there was a young actor with whom I soon became very friendly. He was tremendous company: very funny with his own unique sense of humour. Although he did some acting at Oxford Playhouse and elsewhere, it was obvious he was destined to be a comedian. He had a stand-up act in which he told terrible jokes, died a death deliberately with the audience and then was hilarious in his discomfiture. He tried this out in the South and was a riot but when he went up North the audience started to love the bad jokes. The further north he went the more they loved them. Such jokes as: *Why did the chicken cross the road? To go to the movies to see Gregory Peck* went down a storm in Sunderland, so the whole point of the act was lost.

As he regaled us all in the pub with these disasters and others he was even funnier and had us all on the floor with laughter. There was no doubt that even at that early stage Tony Hancock was a comic genius, though he was skint and stuffed his shoes with newspaper to save having them repaired. He was also a fine actor as he later proved when he did Gogol's

The Government Inspector. In fact all his work was brilliant acting, as I witnessed myself in 1963 when I made a guest appearance in an episode of his TV series.

The same year I also had a small part in his film *The Punch and Judy Man.* One morning on the film I had a tricky scene to do involving a lot of business and opening and shutting of doors in conjunction with dialogue. Hank wasn't in it but came and watched. When it was finished by about 10 P.M., he said, 'That was a hard scene. You need a drink.' He took me to his dressing room and cracked open a bottle of champagne. He was a lovely man and I admired him greatly. His problems and tragic early death are well documented and so sad: such a loss.

However, he would have loved Willie Rushton's story. Willie was in Sydney at the time of Tony's death there and, as he was about to return to England, was entrusted with the task of taking Tony's ashes back with him. Willie's tale of bringing the urn through Customs was a classic.

'What have you got there?'

'Tony Hancock's ashes… honestly!'

The subsequent story of the urn being taken away to be checked that it did not contain illegal substances was pure Hancock and Tony would have howled with laughter.

The last time I saw him was one early evening in the pub next to the Thames Television studios in Teddington. He was sitting alone in the corner of the bar, waiting to do a show. He looked a tired, forlorn figure. 'Life's a bugger, Peter,' he said. We left him to his thoughts, and that sad image of him remains with me always.

However, back to the end of 1948 and the bedsit in Edith Road, Baron's Court. Through Hank I met quite a circle of comedians-to-be, and great fun they were too. Repertory was thriving and there were several good companies in the London area such as the Intimate Theatre Palmers Green, Sidcup and the Penge Empire. Special weeks were not too hard to come by, especially if Miriam liked you. However, I was in negotiation with Harold G. Robert for the 1949 season at the Gaiety Theatre in Douglas, Isle of Man, having answered an advertisement in *The Stage.*

There were some classic adverts in *The Stage* at that time. I remember one for a fit-up company: that is, a company doing three or sometimes four different plays in a week in small towns and village halls. The advertisement went as follows: *Wanted for first-class Fit-up company, juvenile lead, must be willing to help with stage management and assist in box office. Quick study essential. Able to drive lorry a help. Lazy bones out 10 mins.*

Negotiations for the Isle of Man were complete except for signing the contract when I got a letter from Basil Thomas. They were starting up a rep at the Theatre Royal Leicester, a really lovely old theatre; would I join the company? It was to be fortnightly repertory. I jumped at it. A play a fortnight meant much more detailed rehearsal time and was a real step up for me. Harold G. Robert was miffed, but this was too good a chance to miss. I've never been to the Isle of Man and I have a sort of yearning for it. I don't know whether it's because the family weren't sent there in 1939, or because I didn't play the Gaiety, or go to the TT; or could it be Income Tax at 6p in the pound?

Actually the Leicester season was a bit of a disappointment. Leicester was a hotbed of amateur theatre at that time and I don't think they were too keen on professionals in their midst. Business was not too good and it was clear it was going to be a struggle to sustain fortnightly rep there. In addition, I thought the director was poor.

When Basil told me what the takings were, I smelled a rat. We had a front-of-house manager of the old school and I couldn't believe the returns he was putting in were so poor. Business was not that good, but not that bad either. I told Basil of my fears.

'Oh, I know he's fiddling,' he said. 'All front-of-house managers fiddle a bit. It's the ones you don't know who are fiddling you have to watch out for.'

This philosophy annoyed me. I would have had him out on his ear. I am not sure this *laissez-faire* attitude served the Salbergs well in later years, but that is not my business to speculate.

In the company there was a brilliant character actor called Peter Collingwood. A very clever man, we shared the same political views and became good friends. One night after the show we went to a ball where Richard Attenborough, by now a huge young film star, was guest of honour. He was also on the council of Equity, our trade union. Peter and I waylaid him after many drinks and gave him some heavy left-wing stick about him not being militant enough. I am afraid it was more a harangue than a debate. I never met Dickie after that, and he never employed me in anything or even interviewed me for anything. I wonder...? Oh no, that's paranoia. He just didn't like my work. Anyway, belated apologies my Lord for being boorish, but not for the views I expressed. Peter later emigrated to Sydney where he has done some great work. I have bumped into him once or twice on his visits to England. He was as delightful as ever.

Marguerite Stone, a charming and beautiful actress whom I first met at Hereford, was in the company and we became good friends. When the season ended in the summer she went on to the Sheffield Playhouse and I used to go up and see her when I could, or she would come down to Birmingham where I had moved on to the Alexandra Theatre. A young actor called Patrick McGoohan was in the Sheffield company. He was to become involved in my life more than somewhat in the future.

It was good to be back with the Salbergs; the Alexandra was by now fortnightly too and doing extremely well. (Ironically, after the Salbergs abandoned Leicester, the theatre was then taken over by none other than Harold G. Robert who made a great success of it with commercial plays doing twice-nightly weekly.) Of course I was playing cricket for the Salbergs again on Sundays and we had another Reptiles tour.

My digs in Edgbaston were with Mrs Airey, a lovely lady with a large rambling house and garden. Michael Langham and his wife were there too. He was director of Sir Barry Jackson's Birmingham Repertory Theatre, probably the most prestigious theatre outside London. Michael (a left-winger too) and I were kindred spirits and we would talk far into the night. I was one of the very few actors ever to move directly from the more commercial Alexandra Theatre to the Birmingham Rep: when Michael asked me to play in a *commedia dell'arte* version of Molière's *Le Malade Imaginaire* called *Doctor's Delight*, I had made it to the top of the repertory tree: from twice-nightly weekly in Warrington to four-weekly at the Birmingham Rep in less than a year. The only trouble was, Michael saw me as a romantic lead and I found myself playing a lovesick young man with a lute serenading the beautiful Daphne Slater from under her balcony, *à la* Romeo and Juliet. I had to sing, too, and I felt extremely uncomfortable.

I must have got away with it, though, because I was next cast as Algernon in *The Importance of Being Earnest*. This production had a quite brilliant cast. John Neville was John Worthing, his wife Caroline Hooper was Cecily, Lally Bowers was Lady Bracknell, Jacqueline Squires was Gwendolen, Michael's wife, Helen Burns, was Miss Prism and last but not least Donald Pleasence was the Reverend Chasuble, DD. I loved Michael's detailed meticulous direction and I think I was good in the part; I felt good, anyway, and I was certainly in good company. The acting was uniformly brilliant, but I shall never forget Donald as Dr Chasuble and his delivery of the line: 'Patience, my dear Miss Prism, patience. None of us is perfect. I myself am peculiarly susceptible to draughts.'

The Birmingham Rep had a theatre school attached and, earlier that summer at a party, I met one of the students there. Not quite nineteen, Lillias Walker was gorgeous. Quite tall with a perfect young figure, full of life, intelligence and energy, with bone structure that would last her forever, lovely pale skin, a generous mouth and the largest, deepest eyes I had ever looked into. There was a sort of casual inevitability about our meeting. One night in my dressing room at the Alex I told her my real name. I don't know why, and I don't think it surprised her. I just wanted her to know who I really was. Perhaps I subconsciously realised that here was my destiny, even if not then. There were long journeys for both of us before that was to be fulfilled.

*

At the end of the run in Birmingham a tour of Holland was arranged for *The Importance*. Donald Pleasence and I had by now become tremendous friends and were to remain so for the rest of his life. Never in each other's pockets, we would go for long periods without being in touch but would always pick up again with the same easy friendship.

Don, four years older than me, was like the brother I never had. Already married to Miriam and with two young children, Angela and Jean, his philosophy on life amazed me. He always spent slightly more than he earned to spur him on to get a better-paid job. This served him well over his hugely successful career. He was a true friend, always available if you were in trouble. He never criticised, just accepted what the situation was and tried to help. In my tribute to him at his funeral I said all he asked for was that he be accepted too, whatever situation he was in. Unstintingly generous, he was one of the funniest men I knew with a marvellous laconic view on life.

In the war he was a tail-gunner in a Lancaster and was shot down over Northern France, parachuting from a burning plane. He was first put in Saint-Omer prison where the young Nazi in charge would come to his cell and tell him he would be shot at dawn. This was given credence by the fact that the Nazi in question was regularly shooting civilian prisoners. It was 1944 and, to avoid the Allied advance, Don was transferred to a Stalag in Poland. This journey and his final release by some Russian guerrillas would have made an exciting film, but he didn't wish to do it. After these experiences it was small wonder he had a rather amused, detached view on life.

The Holland tour was a huge success. We played every sizeable town, staying with local families wherever we went. I was amazed by the Dutch grasp of languages: English, French and German seemed obligatory, and Italian and Spanish were often thrown in for good measure. Their English was so good they would often pick up the nuances of Wilde quicker than Birmingham audiences had. We did a matinee for children in Amsterdam and the auditorium looked completely white from the stage, as each child had a copy of the play open to follow the text and there was a loud swish at the end of each page as about two thousand were turned over at once.

The Dutch people were so warm and hospitable to us and the audiences were wonderful. I had one or two tricky moments, though, with my passport which had to be surrendered in each town we played. Of course it was (and still is) in the name of Ohm. This was not always popular, it being a German name. Once I tried to mollify the official by saying I had been in the war for five years.

'But on which side?' came the reply.

Despite these inconveniences the tour was a great experience for me and some of the theatres, especially in The Hague and Amsterdam, were quite beautiful. One of the towns we played was Hilversum and we did an excerpt from the play on the famous Radio Hilversum, reminding me of my days with dear old Radio Malaya.

5

FROM THE WEST END TO BROADWAY

Back in London, I learned that the Birmingham Rep adaptation of *Le Malade Imaginaire* was to be done in London after a national tour. Still called *Doctor's Delight*, it was to be a lavish production with choreography by Walter Gore and starring the great veteran actor A. E. Matthews as the invalid and the huge German star of film and theatre, Elisabeth Bergner, as the maid. Daphne Slater and myself were the only two in the cast who had been in the Birmingham production, though very fortunately I was no longer her ardent lover: that role went to Peter Cushing, thank goodness. I was cast as the scheming, conniving Potion the chemist, doing down the poor invalid at every turn. Much better casting!

My partner-in-crime in the play was none other than the great Tod Slaughter, famous for his *Sweeney Todd, the Demon Barber of Fleet Street* and other great melodramas performed with his own touring company. Tod was by now pretty elderly but still on great form. I had great affection for him, perhaps partly because of my own beginning as Smith the Pie Boy. Rumour had it that he once had a correct £75,000 winning pools coupon but forgot to post it and so had to carry on acting, but I never dared ask him if this was true.

Stuart Latham was in the company too. Stuart later gave up acting to become a theatre director and eventually the head director at Granada TV. He always encouraged me, giving me a lot of work and telling me I would never really make it until I was forty and to keep on going. Strangely my understudy was Julian Amyes, a former Birmingham Rep actor who had left to take a BBC TV director's course which he had now completed. He took the understudy job whilst waiting for a position at the BBC. I don't think he was too thrilled to be understudying and rushing about as a townsperson. Two years later, firmly ensconced at the BBC, he gave me my first part in TV. It was a walk-on! It was good experience and I got eight guineas. Many years later when he was head of drama at Granada, Julian gave me a script to read, then rang me up and seemed extremely doubtful about whether I should do it. It was a part I thought I could do standing on my head but I agreed with him and said I wasn't right for it. I don't think he ever really got over that understudy job.

Stuart Latham, though, gave me one of my best parts ever on TV: Tarleton in Shaw's *Misalliance.* It was a live production and if someone dried the sound was clicked off while the prompt was given. There are a lot of words in *Misalliance* but William Mervyn and I sailed through it, driven I'm sure by fear and the experience of years in repertory.

Rehearsals for *Doctor's Delight* began in January 1950 for a month and then we were on the road. It was my first big English tour. My old friend Jimmy Viccars was stage manager, and I was soon into the routine of finding digs in each town, staying a week and then the train call on Sunday and on to the next town. I loved it, and A. E. Matthews was a joy. By now eighty-two, 'Matty' was a legend and the originator of the famous quote: 'I look in the obituary column of *The Times* at breakfast and, if my name's not in it, I go off to work.' A giant of a man with boundless energy and zest for life even at his age, he was a master of comic timing and once said he could get a laugh on any word in any sentence he chose. He asked us to nominate a word in a sentence and proceeded to get a laugh on it, though the word had absolutely no connotation whatsoever. I watched him en-tranced every night. He once told me he had earned a million pounds in his long and distinguished career in films and theatre but women had taken it all. What about the long nights of poker and a few drinks, I thought.

Elisabeth Bergner, our leading lady, was an international star of stage and screen and she certainly behaved like international stars were supposed to behave in those days. She was a *prima donna* hiding behind a dazzling smile and waif-like appearance. The whole point of the production from her point of view was to shovel this huge personality out into the audience with a smile like a laser beam. Although Michael was directing, she had her own director in the background: her husband, the German film director, Dr Paul Czinner.

He made sure she was always in the best positions and perfectly lit.

It has to be said that audiences adored this sweet, dazzling actress. Backstage, however, she was not so sweet and Jimmy Viccars had quite a time with her. His ASM, whose job it was to look after her and her props during the performance, was a perfectly efficient and personable young man. However, Elisabeth took against him for no apparent reason and said he must be fired because she didn't like his face and it was affecting her performance. Jimmy refused to fire him, so she said the boy could stay as long as she never saw him again during the production. One of the girl dancers who was very beautiful and whose face she apparently liked had to do the job instead.

She would also do rather alarming things in performance. There was a drinking scene and, as the maid, she served foaming drinks during it. One night she came out with no drinks and just stood with her lovely smile. She had suddenly decided that, as a star leading lady, she should not be serving drinks to other actors, even though she was playing the maid. It took a great deal of persuasion to get her to play the scene properly thenceforth.

One of our dates on tour was the Devonshire Park Theatre Eastbourne and I came alone out of the stage door one evening after the show. It was still daylight, and there on the steps leading up to the street lay a crumpled heap in floods of tears and groaning in apparent agony, with a sprained ankle. It was Elisabeth Bergner. I remember thinking quickly, if you want to keep this job you had better give a good performance and play this very carefully. I knew she was staying at a hotel only two or three hundred yards away, so I picked her up and carried her there, saying what I hoped were all the right things. In the foyer I sent for her husband Paul who rushed up and took her from me. I had done my stuff. The following day was a matinee day and so there was a full rehearsal for the understudy right up to curtain up. As the curtains parted, there, in one of the boxes only a few feet from the stage, was Elisabeth accompanied by her husband Paul. It is a huge advantage for any actor actually to witness a performance of a play they are in from the front. Copious notes were made by Paul so that changes could be made to her advantage. That evening – yes, you've guessed it – the ankle was miraculously cured and she was back on stage again.

But in general it was a happy time with lots of laughs. Tod seriously warned the young Daphne Slater to get plenty of drink in England as we were going up to Scotland which at that time was completely dry on

Sunday. The idea of anyone not having alcohol for a day really worried Tod.

We had quite a complicated curtain call and one night it went hopelessly wrong. The idea was that the dancers and townspeople would prance across the stage, half from one side and half from the other, crossing in the middle, followed by pairs of principals. Tod and I went on together crossing Stuart Latham and Hugh Pryse coming from the opposite side. One night the leading townsman – my erstwhile understudy, Julian Amyes – completely missed the cue so by the time he came on with his team of townspeople, principals were coming in from the other side in complete confusion. Tod saw this and, with his trembling hand, grabbed mine saying, 'On laddie, on, it's a heterogeneous bloody mess, but on laddie, on.'

Our tour over, we opened at the Garrick Theatre in Charing Cross Road. I had made the West End. We ran for nine weeks so it was not a huge success, but I had made the West End.

Many years later (twenty-six to be exact) whilst I was touring in a play in Europe there was a reception after a performance in Zurich. A frail old lady in a wheelchair was wheeled in. I tried to remind her of *Doctor's Delight* all those years before but was met only with cold eyes and a dazzling smile. Did she really not remember, or was it because I wasn't playing the lead?

*

Out of work, I went up to Didsbury, Manchester and did a few plays in the rep at the ABC cinema there, temporarily given over to a repertory season. My chief memory was of the cinema organist, who played at all intervals and before and after the show, coming up from the bowels of the earth with his signature tune 'I Want to be Happy' which he played at the beginning and end of all his selections. This tune was all right for comedies and farces, but was a bit unsuitable for thrillers and tragedies. A rasping rendition of 'I Want to be Happy' at the start and finish of a tense act didn't really help. However, he was very popular, perhaps more so than the thespians.

I stayed with Aunt Meg at that time and one cold, damp, foggy night standing at the bus stop after the show, I heard a couple of ladies also waiting in the drizzle:

'How's Henry getting on?'

'Oh, didn't you hear? He had all his teeth out and bled to death. Of course, he always was a bleeder you know.'

Coming to that job from the West End was somewhat from the sublime to the ridiculous, but then that is how I have always operated. Better to be working than not has always been my philosophy.

Back in London I heard that Christopher Fry's new play *A Sleep of Prisoners* was about to be put on as part of the 1951 Festival of Britain. It was about four prisoners of war imprisoned in a church at the time of the English Civil War circa 1642, and would be performed in an actual church, St Thomas's in Regent Street. It was a beautiful piece and an unqualified hit when the reviews came out. The cast of four were Denholm Elliott, Stanley Baker, Leonard White and Hugh Pryse; I managed to get myself hired as stage manager and understudy to Leonard and Stanley. Although in a way this was a bit of a step back into stage management, in another way it was a very valuable time. Michael MacOwan was the director and I had never worked with anyone of his experience before, so it was a huge learning opportunity for me, especially during the month's rehearsal period. As far as the stage-management side was concerned it was just a question of calling on my old repertory experience and so was no problem.

During the run in London I played Leonard White's part for a few performances and thoroughly enjoyed myself. It was wonderful to be playing a leading role in London in a seriously beautiful play, if only for a short time. Stanley Baker said he didn't want to work with me again because I was too good. I thought he was joking at the time, but when he later became a film star and producer he certainly kept his word! Not a day's work did he give me.

The Korean war was in progress at the time and I was opposed to it. To me it was an imperialist war against socialism. Britain was involved and, just in case more troops were to be needed, I got my army reserve papers. It was called the Z Reserve and was to be a two-week army-camp refresher course to get us all in readiness. I refused to go, thereby becoming a conscientious objector. This was a tricky situation as being an ex-officer I had sworn allegiance to the crown. Police called on me but I was adamant. I wrote an impassioned letter to the exemption board saying I was prepared to fight Fascism but not Communism. Christopher Fry interceded on my behalf, and to have such a famous pacifist on my side must have worked because the War Office quietly let the matter drop. Christopher was wonderfully helpful to me over the whole matter and it was a privilege to know this great man.

Romantically my life was continuing without much incident. Marguerite and I were unofficially engaged but we didn't see each other much, both of us pursuing our own careers. When the run ended a short tour was arranged and this was quite tough on the stage management as we had to strike the show on Saturday nights, travel to the next town with everything loaded into a Pickfords truck and have it all set up by Monday. Lancaster to Eastbourne was quite a busy weekend! However, I was really excited that one of our touring dates was a church in Birmingham. A chance, perhaps, to see Lillias Walker again. Lillias had now left the theatre school and had become a member of the Birmingham Rep company with an excellent reputation. I remember Eric Porter telling me she was brilliant. She had been often in my thoughts, and I was thrilled when she agreed to meet me at the Market Hotel bar next to the theatre on the Monday lunchtime.

I walked in and there she was looking absolutely radiant. We embraced warmly. It was so good to see her again. Then an extremely good-looking young man joined us.

'Oh,' she said. 'This is Peter Burton, my fiancé.'

I was shattered. That's the end of that, I thought.

Although I was really miffed at the time, later on we agreed that it was a good thing that this happened. Two such volatile and, in my case, arrogant people would have been disastrous for each other at that time. Peter and Lillias were married the following year and, although the marriage didn't last too long, they produced, in 1955, two gorgeous twin girls named Alexandra and Victoria.

*

A New York season followed by an American tour was arranged for *A Sleep of Prisoners* and in July 1951 off we went. We turned up at Heathrow and boarded a Pan Am four-engined turboprop (no jets in those days) called a Stratocruiser. We set off for Shannon where we had to refuel before crossing the Atlantic. On the way Leonard invited me to look out of his window and there was a propeller not going round at all, standing quite still. We told the crew and we returned to Heathrow, landing gingerly on three engines.

We were put up at a hotel whilst the engine was repaired, and next day we set off once more. Over Shannon we heard the American captain's voice on the intercom: 'Ladies and gentlemen, I always want my passengers to know what the situation is. I can't get the undercarriage down. There should be a green light come on but it's red. I'm sending my engineer down to see if he can operate it manually; meanwhile I'm circling the airport jettisoning my fuel.' The voice moved from reassuring calm to some anxiety during this speech.

Macho Stanley Baker went very white indeed and fiercely held hands with his wife Ellen; but Leonard and I had to deal with a recently married air hostess who became completely hysterical, crying, 'I want my husband, please God let me get down, please let me get down, I want my husband.' It's the only time I've ever had to calm down an air hostess. The plane landed all right in the end, but people's various reactions to the situation were revealing.

I think even the pilot must have decided this particular aircraft wasn't much cop, so we waited eight hours for a replacement. This plane was fine but we were buffeted around the sky in a first-class hurricane before landing at Gander in Canada where we refuelled before going on to New York La Guardia. The whole trip took almost three days instead of the scheduled twelve hours, I think it was!

New York, New York, it's a wonderful town goes the song, and it certainly was. To walk among those skyscrapers for the first time and feel the rhythm of the place; energy seemed to crackle from those rocks and the place was throbbing with life. Shops were open until 1 A.M. and many restaurants and clubs until four. Evidently no more than three or four hours' sleep was necessary. And everyone seemed so rude. They weren't really; it was just the terminology. Politely asking for two well-done fried eggs, please, on toast, thank you so much, would be greeted with scorn and derision. Gimme two eggs on rye all fried both sides, OK? was the way to do it.

I soon got the hang of it and loved the place, especially the ethnic mix. Jewish humour was everywhere. We set up in a church, around 74th Street and Park Avenue I think it was. I remember when our stuff was brought into the church one stage-hand said to his mate: 'Take your cap off. Show respect to the choich.'

The other guy replied, 'Aw Hell, I never know whether to take my hat off in choich and leave it on in the synagogue or voici voica.'

The play was greeted with great acclaim and had rave reviews. Because of this, and because we were British, we were asked to lots of parties and social occasions with even me, the stage manager, being invited along. The Korean war was at its peak and I don't really know how with my political track record I managed to slip into America at all, as the place was virulently anti left-wing. Politically, people were very scared to speak their minds as Senator McCarthy was just beginning his witch-hunt. Undeterred I held forth my views without inhibition. At one smart party I remember someone who shared my views whispering to me to shut up unless I wanted to be deported. America was paranoid about Communism at that time and even practised the evacuation of office blocks and skyscrapers in case of air raids. Who they thought was going to be able to drop a nuclear bomb on New York I am not sure, but it was an amazing sight to see hundreds of people pouring out into the street in practice alerts.

My salary was a hundred dollars a week, not bad in those days despite tax deductions of about forty per cent. Most of this was withholding tax to be recovered and I got myself an accountant to help achieve this. His office was pretty shambolic behind an imposing entrance, and I found that life was just as much of a struggle as anywhere else behind the façade and all the hype of New York.

I got the cheapest hotel room I could find, just off Times Square at ten bucks a week. My view was out on to Times Square about thirty storeys up and neon lights advertising movies flashed into my room most of the night. It didn't worry me as I was out most of the time and only slept now and then.

'Hullo, and how are you today?' our scrupulously polite elevator operator asked us every day without fail.

'Just fine,' we replied; and we were.

Donald Pleasence was in New York too, playing Enobarbus in *Anthony and Cleopatra* with Laurence Olivier and Vivien Leigh. We saw quite a bit of each other, and one Sunday we climbed the Statue of Liberty together ending up in the arm that holds the torch. Quite a view of Manhattan, but not as high as the Empire State. Another Sunday another supporter of our play, Louise Lortell, who had a lovely house in the country, invited our company to a party there. A lady friend of hers offered to drive me out there, about a couple of hours into gorgeous Conneticut in the fall. It was a great spot; Louise even had her own theatre there. We all had a great time but unfortunately my charming driver turned out to be a bit of a lush and got completely, paralytically drunk. Around midnight she handed me her car keys murmuring, 'Take me home darling, I can't drive.' This was my baptism of fire driving in the States: not knowing the route, with bright lights of oncoming traffic blinding me, multiple lanes and slip roads and my charming companion fast asleep in the passenger seat. More by luck than judgement I got back, parked and hastily retreated to the safety of my hotel.

There was so much to do and see: skaters at the Rockefeller Centre, movies with a live show combined, Radio City Music Hall, Tony Bennett at the Paramount and Rosemary Clooney too – 'Come on to my house, baby.' The great, one and only Judy Garland opened for a season on Broadway to ecstatic acclaim. I managed to get in one matinee. The young Max Bygraves opened the show and was very funny, and Judy was spellbinding. What a great artist. I felt the audience was walking a tightrope of emotion with her through the show, and there was a sort of relief mixed with acclaim at the end. Little did I know that years later she would be a fan of a play in which I was appearing in London and that I would get to know her a little.

On Broadway, about ten minutes from my hotel, was a club called Birdland. This was the great age of modern jazz and Birdland, named after Charlie 'Bird' Parker, was the hub of it. I had always hankered after jazz since I first heard it seriously on the Voice of America radio station when I was in Ceylon. I became an *habitué*, paying my dollar entrance fee, buying a beer for a quarter and watching and listening entranced. Almost every night after the play I would slip down there. I never saw Charlie Parker; I had to make do with Miles Davis, Dizzy Gillespie, Lester Young, J. J. Johnson, Lee Konitz, Milt Jackson, Wes Montgomery, Charlie Mingus, Philly Joe Jones, Art Blakey, Thelonious Monk, Bud Powell, Bill Evans, Zoot Sims, Stan Getz... I could go on and on but only aficionados would not be bored. The bill there for Christmas 1951 and New Year '52 consisted of Dizzy with his all-star seventeen-piece band supporting none other than Ella Fitzgerald, and the Dave Brubeck Quartet with Paul Desmond making their New York debut having just come over from the West Coast. That was a magical month. Ella was superb, and some nights other singers like Ruth Brown and Dinah Washington came in and jammed with her: '*I put my left leg on your shoulder and left my right leg on the floor, and if that ain't going to get ya then don't come round here no more.*'

I had some wonderful nights there and, although in no way a musician, I felt a great affinity with the music, which has had a strong effect on me. To have such command over one's instrument to be able to extemporise on a theme in a group setting and to be driven along by a tasteful and brilliant rhythm section is truly wonderful. Why couldn't we do it as actors, I wondered? After all, it's all rhythm: a collective heartbeat. Comedians could do it: Lenny Bruce, the Goon Show, even Lex McClean in Glasgow – they all blew their solos within a rhythmic form. Radio, relying solely on voices, gives the best chance in drama. I was lucky enough to work once or twice with Nigel Anthony, my favourite radio actor, and I think we blew well together! Nigel, a great jazz enthusiast, gave me a rare tape recorded in Birdland at the time I was there. It even has the voice of 'Pee Wee' Marquette in it. Pee Wee, standing about four feet high in a stiff dickie shirt and tuxedo, was the manager. When things got quiet sometimes late on and not many people were there he would exhort the musicians, 'Come on, blow; what do I pay you for, blow!'

Alas, Birdland did not survive the onslaught of rock and roll and is long since closed. But the music lives on as strong as ever all over the world. It is a true art form; and it gives me deep pleasure that my son, Dave Ohm, is a successful professional modern jazz drummer.

The season in the Manhattan choich over, we took the play on tour, mostly along the eastern seaboard: towns like Baltimore, Washington, Pittsburgh and so on. It was a good tour, enhanced by my close friendship with the lady in charge of publicity for the play. It was her job to meet us in each town, attend the opening night, give a drinks party for the local critics and dignitaries and then move on to the next town to make the arrangements there. This was really good for me as I had a very warm welcome everywhere we went, but only for a short time which left me free for the rest of the week to engage in the social life which was quite abundant.

The tour over and back in New York, I got myself taken on by an agent at MCA, probably about the best in town. British actors were at a premium and could do no wrong in the States at that time. My background in repertory and having appeared in the West End was enough to get me an audition for the juvenile lead in a Somerset Maugham play, starring and being directed by Cyril Ritchard, destined for Broadway after an out-of-town tour. I got the part, salary four hundred dollars a week. Unquestionably my biggest break ever.

However, there was one potential snag. At that time American Equity decreed that there must be a six-month gap between engagements for non-resident foreigners. As I had not acted in the US, only stage-managed, MCA argued that this rule did not apply in my case. Equity did not agree and so I was not allowed to take the job. I went back to the hotel and I must have looked a bit downcast; my friend the elevator man asked me what was up and I told him my sad tale.

'Ah, Broadway,' he said. 'For every light bulb there's a broken heart.'

My heart wasn't broken but I was pretty disappointed. As a matter of fact I probably had a lucky escape as I would have been playing opposite Adrienne Corri, an experience I found not the happiest many years later.

I toyed with the idea of sticking around doing any old odd job until I was free to work in the theatre again. At least I could go to Birdland. However, this idea was short-lived and I decided the only thing to do was to go home. I flogged my return air ticket with some difficulty and bought a single on the Queen Mary instead, saving quite a lot of dollars. It was unforgettable to sail out of harbour standing on the deck of the great liner, watching that Manhattan skyline get smaller and smaller and finally disappear from view.

The journey back was not without incident as we encountered a really heavy Atlantic storm which lasted most of the voyage. The ship rolled slowly from one side to the other and pitched and tossed violently at the same time. This double movement was too much for most passengers and they retired to their cabins. Hugh Goldie, the assistant director of *A Sleep of Prisoners* and therefore my boss, was on board too and we more or less had the boat to ourselves. There was plenty to eat as long as you could hold on to your food and cutlery. The games room was always free but we had to abandon table tennis most of the time.

There was an old Yorkshire farmer who, like us, never missed a meal. He had been somewhere in the Deep South visiting his brother, whom he had not seen for many years. I asked if he had enjoyed the visit.

'Not much,' he replied. 'Too many blackies.'

6

THE SMALL SCREEN

S AFELY BACK IN SOUTHAMPTON I was disembarking to who knew what. The near miss of a leading role on Broadway, a New York agent: they were just memories. I was out of work and starting all over again. I couldn't go home for a holiday: Mother was outraged at my objection to the Korean war and told me I had a yellow streak right down my back and virtually not to darken her door again. I didn't mind much as it took the weight of trying to conform off my shoulders. Anyway, she was probably right about the yellow streak.

I took a room in Hyde Park Gate. It was huge with a view over the park and it was very cheap. It was amusing to think of Churchill living just up the road, which he was. I wonder what that room would cost today; but this was February 1952.

I did a bit of rep, and then I heard about a new play called *Lion's Corner* going out on a pre-West End tour. The play was put on by John Forbes Sempill, an extremely pleasant and gregarious fellow who also cast himself in a leading role. I don't think he had done much acting before; he had a disconcerting habit of backing upstage on almost every one of his lines so that scenes that started near the footlights would end up near the back-cloth. I am sure there was no attempt to upstage anyone in this process; I think he was just a bit nervous. He was, however, great company and he sometimes invited me to travel between dates in his smart sports car, stopping for convivial lunches en route.

It wasn't a very good play, but it just got by thanks to people like Garry Marsh, a young Michael Bryant and others; and the tour was great fun until it closed after several weeks with seemingly little prospect of the West End. A week or two later, though, John rounded us up, having somehow managed to secure the St Martin's Theatre. The deal was a guaranteed four weeks at £10 per week after which, if the show was a success, increased salaries were to be negotiated.

The first night didn't go very well with the audience but was not a total disaster. The reviews the following day, however, were pretty terrible. One critic said that John should never appear on stage in anything again, or words to that effect.

As I walked into the theatre for the second night all seemed eerily quiet. I asked the stage-door keeper for my dressing-room key.

'You'd better go on to the set, they're all down there,' he said.

There was John Forbes Sempill sitting at a card table in the centre of the stage. He counted me out eight crisp, large, white £5 notes. He had taken that critic at his word and never, as far as I know, acted again. He had taken the play off after one performance.

I am sure this was some kind of record. Even the biggest flops finished after opening week, but *Lion's Corner* ran for one night only. If there are any other one-nighters on record I'm prepared to bet the cast weren't paid four weeks' wages for one performance. I collected my things from the dressing room and walked stunned through the West End taking in the brightly lit scene and clutching my forty pounds.

This early part of the 1950s was pretty tough for me, trying to get a permanent foothold in London. I had to retreat into provincial repertory from time to time. The digs weren't always brilliant and I remember one drunken landlady having to be held up while she cooked me bacon and eggs after the show (and in her case after the pub).

I came in one night and heard her moaning in her bedroom on the ground floor. 'Peter, Peter,' she moaned. Alarmed, I went in to find her in bed. 'Fetch me a glass of water, duck.' Thinking her ill I rushed off to get the water. I returned to her bedside whereupon she smartly took her teeth out and dropped them into the glass of water. 'Put them on the sideboard, duck,' she said amorously. I fled.

H. M. Tennent Ltd and their chief, Binkie Beaumont, almost ran the West End in those days. There were of course other managements, but this was where the real power was and, if you were in favour with them, you were set fair. Daphne Rye, their casting director, combed the good reps and put people under contract to play small parts and understudy. She saw me once or twice but studiously ignored me. She wanted good-looking men and glamorous girls, not moody, quirky devils like me.

Peter Powell, director of the Alexandra in Birmingham at that time, called me into his office once and said to me: 'You worry me. This is a very good company and I can see a future for almost everyone, but I can't place you. You have so much concentration, and in rehearsal you stay in character all the time, even in coffee breaks. I just don't know what is going to happen to you.'

Well, it certainly wasn't going to be with H. M. Tennent, though I did get a job with them on tour in a boxing play called *The Square Ring*. The action was a series of fights in the ring and I played the boxing second. I had thirty-four entrances and exits, very few lines and a sponge. It was pretty hard work as the entrance to the set was high above the stage, down a flight of steps to the boxing ring on stage level. I went up and down those steps like a yo-yo. One of the boxers was played by a young Canadian, just arrived in London. He had, I think, played Hamlet on radio in Canada, and one or two amateur leading roles in Toronto, but that was all he had done. One night just as we were about to go on together he whispered, 'Hey, what's it like to play a small part?' He nearly got a bucket of water over him there and then, but fortunately the cue came up just in time.

That was the sum of my career with the Tennents, but others from the excellent Birmingham company fared better. Ronald Radd was given a contract with them, and Edward Mulhare took over from Rex Harrison as Higgins in *My Fair Lady* in the West End and later played it on Broadway. There was also a wonderful actor in the company named John Le Mesurier, whose Crocker-Harris in *The Browning Version* was one of the finest performances I have ever seen anywhere. John was a joy, with a marvellous dry sense of humour, and a great lover of jazz. I kept up my love of jazz by going to various clubs to catch the great British jazz men like Tubby Hayes, Ronnie Scott, Peter King, Joe Harriott, Allan Ganley and so many more.

Repertory was still going well but some of the smaller companies were beginning to feel the pinch. Derek Salberg's nephew, Keith, was running a small company or two with varied success. Every Saturday after the show Derek gave a drinks party in his office. Keith would ring his father, Stanley, telling him the takings for the week. This particular week they were abysmal.

'What are you going to do?' his father asked.

'I've just made a curtain speech. It went as follows: Ladies and gentlemen of Shoeburyness, as from Monday we are going to try an entirely new policy. We are closing down, and if it's a success we are going to keep it that way,' replied Keith.

Jimmy Viccars was becoming a very successful stage manager in the West End and he put a lot of work my way, understudying and playing small parts. In fact those days could have been pretty thin without him. It was through Jimmy that I came to work with Sam Wanamaker. Sam had settled in London after being outlawed from work in the States by the McCarthy trials. He was a breath of fresh air to me and I fitted into his way of working at once. He directed as well as playing the lead in most of his productions and so, as his understudy, I played his part a great deal while he was directing rehearsals. Obviously I was given direction too, and I learned a hell of a lot from him.

I later went to the Shakespeare Theatre Liverpool and toured with him, by now playing a good part. Sam's American Actors' Studio style of acting and directing appealed to me greatly. I related to it in my own work more than to the traditional British theatrical style: 'Speak your lines clearly and don't bump into the furniture,' as Noel Coward is supposed to have said. If I had any ability at all it was to get right under the skin of the character I was playing. I tried to be truthful without artifice and tricks.

*

In the summer of 1952 I was in a play at a fringe theatre in Notting Hill, and there was a young unknown actress in it by the name of Billie Whitelaw. She was just down from the north where she had done a lot of radio as a child, had been in a few northern reps and had toured with Joan Littlewood and Ewan McColl. She was just twenty and had a warmth and directness on and off stage which was quite exceptional. We moved in together after a week and six weeks later, to the rightful chagrin of Marguerite, we married at Kensington Registry Office. For a honeymoon I took her to Aylesbury where I was playing in *Worm's Eye View*. Not very romantic, but anyway we were both consumed by the business and were going to conquer it together.

Billie was a dazzling young actress with an air of vulnerability about her which the public took to very quickly as she went from part to part in both television and the theatre, and later in films. She didn't hide behind technique, being totally truthful in her work. Always willing to learn, she wanted direction and took it brilliantly. Much later she worked very successfully with Samuel Beckett, absorbing his meticulous direction perfectly.

At this early stage, however, we were pretty poor, moving from furnished flat to furnished flat, finally settling in one near St Pancras. Donald Pleasence's marriage to Miriam being over, he had nowhere to live; and so he became a more or less permanent lodger with us, first in Westbourne Park and then in St Pancras. His career was tailing off as well, both in theatre and films.

I have to admit I can't really remember much about my personal relationship with Billie, but we must have had something going for us as we seemed to be happy enough in those early years. Our careers were paramount, though we had some good times as well.

*

There were some great characters around in those days. Denis Shaw was one. A huge man, best remembered for his prison guard in the film *The Colditz Story*, Denis was well known around the pubs frequented by the actors. He could be frightening and was good at browbeating people into lending him money.

'There's some as can, and some as can't; and you dear boy – lend me five pounds – are the one who...' *Can* or *can't* depended on whether or not the money was forthcoming. It was quite difficult to get a loan back from him. One young actor timidly asked for his fiver back after an eighteen-month wait. 'No, dear boy, you can't have it,' said Denis. 'I haven't finished with it yet.'

Stories about Denis were legion. One night as we were leaving a party rather noisily in the early hours, the local bobby parked his bike against a wall and politely prevailed on us to be quiet. Denis loathed the law. 'You blue-bottled _____,' he cried, mounting the bicycle and heading off down the road before collapsing in a drunken heap.

The copper caught up with him. 'Go home, Mr Shaw; I'm not arresting you tonight, whatever you do.'

*

I was playing a lot of cricket, both in Birmingham and London. I keep mentioning cricket because it has had such an influence on my life and career. Lane Meddick, a former journalist who was in the cast of *Lion's Corner*, ran a team called 'South London Journalists'. Alan Tarrant, then editor of a magazine, was in the team and he applied to become a television director with the newly formed ITV company ATV, run by Lew and Leslie Grade.

Up until 1955 in Britain there was only a single television channel: the BBC. Televised plays were rehearsed in the same way as in the theatre. Camera crews came in and watched a final rehearsal, a camera plot was worked out with the director and the play then transmitted live. Plays were performed on Sunday evenings and were repeated, also live of course, on the following Thursday. We did Priestley's *Time and the Conways* which was something of a challenge as we had to age twenty years for the second act and go back twenty years for the third act, all without intervals or any other break. It was pretty traumatic. I played opposite the superb Margaret Tyzack, and we reminded each other of the experience over forty years later when we worked together again in *Our Mutual Friend*.

The fees were extremely low, based largely on BBC radio money, so the arrival of commercial television was very welcome as it not only created much more work but also caused a bit of competition, thereby forcing the money up a bit.

There was very little filming to TV in those days. As I said, plays and drama series were done live and shot in the studio by television cameras. Eventually they were recorded on Ampex tape with a small amount of external filming inserted. However, this didn't happen until the latter part of the fifties. Live television drama was hectic and terrifying, like a seemingly endless series of first nights in the theatre, only in front of an audience of millions. It was often rough and ready from a technical point of view, but it had energy and was sometimes spectacularly successful.

The advent of commercial television spawned the *Armchair Theatre* series of one-off plays every Sunday. Sydney Newman ran them, having come over from Canada. Sydney was a genius, encouraging new writers and bringing over with him such young directors as Ted Kotcheff, Alvin Rakoff, Silvio Narizzano and Hank Kaplan. Writers such as Harold Pinter and Alun Owen emerged and there began a great age of TV drama. The BBC, not to be outdone, contributed greatly to this.

Rudolph Cartier could transform a TV studio into anything he chose; *Quatermass*, *Nineteen Eighty-Four*, *The Reichstag Five* were all brilliant. I played a German general in his *Battle of Stalingrad*. He had snow, guns, tanks, horses – truly miraculous. Rudi was really a film director at heart, having worked in films in Germany before the war. Whereas most TV directors used the mobile television cameras in a very fluid fashion, Rudi would have about six cameras hardly moving at all. This sometimes meant actors had to get into some strange positions to be in shot, but his results were remarkable.

Granada TV in Manchester under Sidney Bernstein did a tremendous amount of drama at that time, and Anglia in Norwich under John Jacobs did some excellent work as well, as did Rediffusion TV in London. I worked for them all as the decade progressed. From the start of ITV in 1955 I plunged into a seemingly endless amount of work, not only in plays but in comedy sketches and drama serials such as *No Hiding Place* with Raymond Francis, *Boyd QC* with Michael Denison and ATVs *Emergency –Ward 10*.

Then there was my regular 'advertising magazine', *About Homes and Gardens* with Beryl Mason, which went out weekly in the Midlands. The format of an advertising magazine was a series of adverts, each usually a minute long, presented and linked by a serious leading lady – i.e. Beryl – assisted by a young man providing a bit of comedy – i.e. me. In our case the products were associated loosely with homes and gardens, hence the name of the show. We had an autocue for complicated selling points, price lists and so on. Sometimes it broke down leading to a lot of hectic ad-libbing and some strange price lists.

This programme taught me a lot, especially about camera angles and so on and being at ease in front of the camera. I would sometimes be passed a note saying we were under-running so I needed to ad-lib for thirty seconds, or even a minute. I also did a bit of roving interviewing at exhibitions such as the Ideal Homes show in Birmingham. It was an invaluable experience and I did it along with my other work for about a year.

The director was my cricketing friend Alan Tarrant. He was learning as well, and very quickly at that. He was soon directing variety and comedy shows and it was not too long before he was ATV's Head of Light Entertainment. After every show we would repair to the Astor Club, owned then by Bertie Green, one of our advertisers. There, lubricated by Bertie's champagne, Alan, myself and some of the crew would thrash out how the show had gone, how we could improve it and so on. In the cabaret at this club was a young singer/comedian named Des O'Connor. He was terrific and was obviously soon to be a big star, no matter what Morecambe and Wise might say!

I did a lot of comedy sketches, too: with Bob Monkhouse, for instance, in his show *Chelsea at Nine* which went out from the old Chelsea Palace variety theatre on the King's Road. The site is now a furniture store. Bob had a prodigious memory. He would know not only his own lines but everyone else's as well. He was also a good actor. I did a play with him later for BBC Bristol called *The Cat and the Canary*. In the action he had to hit me over the head with a heavy metal gong. The floor manager was supposed to substitute a *papier mâché* version of the gong just before the blow, but failed to do so. Bob hit me with the real thing thinking it was the *papier mâché* one. I was stunned, but they told me my fall was very realistic.

The funniest man I worked with was Tommy Cooper. In one sketch I was a shopkeeper selling him a pair of alligator shoes and, although we had rehearsed it a lot, he actually made me laugh on live television. He was a lovely man and just naturally funny. Years later I met him after a show at Thames TV in the bar at Teddington. 'Have you got a minute? I want to ask you something.' I said yes. 'Right, I'll phone the wife.' He returned in a few minutes, bought me a drink and said: 'Is this funny? There was this house on fire. The fire brigade put it out and there in the bedroom was the owner sound asleep. "How did it start?" a fireman asked. "I don't know. It was going when I came in" '. Not very funny on the page perhaps, but hilarious when told by Tommy. He just wanted my reaction before putting it in his act. I don't think he ever realised just how funny he was.

I have so many memories of this period, but as I kept no records of any kind they are jumbled up and not chronologically accurate. So I'll recount them as they come into my head.

Wilfrid Lawson was the greatest actor I ever knew, and I first worked with him in a play at the BBC directed by a young unknown named Tony Richardson. John Osborne was in the cast as well. We were filming outside Pentonville Prison, and Wilfrid was playing a convict just about to be released. Tony suggested Wilfrid should light a cigarette as soon as he came out of the prison gates. Wilfrid, on 'action', took out the cigarette, caressed it, rolled it round his fingers but didn't ever light it as he surveyed his freedom. Magical. He turned a cliché into a wonderful moment.

Wilfrid was genuinely a great actor. To see him on stage was breathtaking. He was a bit eccentric, and on occasions you could say he liked a drink or two. He was sometimes quite difficult to find before a show. On one occasion at the Royal Court he was found sitting in the audience of a play he was in. 'I wanted to see what I am like in it,' he rasped in that inimitable voice.

Once up at Granada he couldn't be found just before transmission and there was a real panic. He was eventually located at the security gate. He was playing a tramp, had been for some fresh air and security wouldn't let him in, thinking he was a vagrant. We young actors all revered him and would listen to his stories in the pub with reverence, hoping I suppose that a bit of his magic would rub off.

I played Ezekiel Cheever in an *Armchair Theatre* adaptation of *The Crucible*. Sean Connery in one of his first leading roles was John Proctor, and a very young and very beautiful Susannah York was Abigail. I worked with Michael Caine as well, in one of his very early TV appearances at Granada in a series starring John Turner. Michael was a marvellous young actor and great fun too. He was also brilliant in the theatre. I saw him in *Next Time I'll Sing to You* at the Arts and he was superb. Not many people know that.

I did quite a lot of children's TV drama, which of course was all live in the studio. I played a mutinous seaman and Peter Wyngarde was the sea captain. We had a scene together and, being somewhat shorter than me, he stood on a rostrum so that he could dominate the situation. On 'action', keen to get himself a good close-up, he grabbed me by the shoulders to pull me round with my back to the camera. Unfortunately for him I stood my ground and he fell off the rostrum: not quite the effect he was striving for. Peter was such a good actor I wondered why he found it necessary to resort to such tricks. He was more than good enough without any of the starry stuff.

I worked for Ian Fordyce a good deal too. We were great fans of Fulham FC and in one live episode of *No Hiding Place* there was a scene requiring extras in a hotel foyer. Ian asked some of the Fulham players to be in it and they agreed. They were encouraged to ad-lib; on transmission Raymond Francis as Inspector Lockhart came into the foyer and the ad-libbing started. 'Who's that?' said Johnny Haynes to Graham Leggat, who replied in his rich Aberdeen accent: 'It looks like Raymond Francis.'

*

Shakespeare, Somerset Maugham, Balzac, new plays: I did the lot. Then at the end of the decade I got a big break. I was cast as the night news editor in a series called *Deadline Midnight* about a team of investigative reporters. Each of the thirteen weekly episodes was an hour long and was recorded on Ampex tape. We had two hours' recording time to do the whole show which was pretty tight, but the series was a big success; so much so that the producer Arthur Christiansen, formerly a famous newspaper editor, was delighted to sell twenty-six episodes to Australia.

The only snag was that he had not signed me for the further thirteen still to be made, which I did not want to do. Unlike today, becoming associated with a long-running series was often highly dangerous. It was sometimes impossible to get other work at the end of it, as producers were loath to use anyone associated with a particular long-running part. So there they were committed to twenty-six shows with the leading actor signed for only thirteen. A tricky situation for them, and so I was called in to Mr Grade's office for a meeting.

Lew Grade was there, cigar and all. I went on the offensive, offered my hand and said, 'Mr Grade, my name's Peter Vaughan and I used to work for you.'

'I know,' he said. 'And I want you to work for me some more. I've seen some of the stuff you do in odd plays and films, but I want to make you into a big television star.'

'Mr Grade, I don't want to stay but I tell you what I'll do, I'll do one more episode so that...'

Before I could finish, quickly came the reply, '... so that we can write you out.' This was accompanied by a quick handshake, and I was ushered out of the office. Everyone was happy. I did one more show in which Glyn Houston became the next news editor, and I was free. Not rich, but free – and not typecast.

7
STAGE BY STAGE

ESPITE BEING HURLED INTO TELEVISION IN THE FIFTIES I did not desert the theatre. There were small parts in runs at the Duchess Winter Garden and Westminster Theatres.

Jack and Beatie de Leon ran the 'Q' Theatre, unsurprisingly near Kew Bridge. They paid little money but put on adventurous plays and it was a good shop window for other work. In 1954 I got the part of Captain La Hire in Shaw's *Saint Joan*, directed at the Q by Esmé Percy. Rachel Kempson was Joan, and her tall, beautiful teenage daughter Vanessa often watched her mother from the wings.

Esmé Percy was a highly respected Shavian. He had only one eye; his other one had been terminally damaged by his four-footed canine friend. He would sit in the stalls, dog on knee (whether the same animal I doubt) and give precise directions in his beautiful voice. He had just had a successful, if unlikely, professional liaison with a very young Joan Collins in a play in the West End. When asked about this he would say: 'I adored her. Her favourite food was a Mars Bar and her favourite drink, a Coca-Cola.'

Robert Shaw was in the cast. As well as being very engaging, he was just about the most competitive person I ever met. It didn't matter what the contest was: he had to win. I played cricket against him once. He bowled very fast but not too accurately and I was able to smack him around for a few overs. This enraged him greatly and he often referred to me as 'that unattractive left-handed bat'. He took his revenge on me, beating me on the slot machines in the pub during the run of *Saint Joan*. We were all thrilled when, not long afterwards, he landed the lead in a filmed series *The*

Buccaneers, the precursor to his becoming a big film star. Bob had all the charm and cheek in the world. He was supposed to join the Old Vic but, as the film job precluded this, he recommended two brilliant young character actors to take his place, Gareth Jones and Peter Vaughan. Neither of us went, but it was a nice piece of largesse from Bob.

Gareth was a lovely actor who was determined to live life to the full and gave some excellent performances despite having a heart problem. Sadly, he died in the second commercial break whilst acting in a live *Armchair Theatre*. I saw the play, which was set in the Underground after an atomic explosion; I remember being unable to follow the last part of the piece and wondering where dear Gareth had got to. At age 34, Gareth really did die with his boots on.

In 1955 I was cast in a production of Fritz Hochwälder's *The Strong Are Lonely*. This was a play about Jesuit priests in Paraguay in the 18th century who incurred the displeasure of the Pope by becoming too involved in secular matters. They were worker priests and their head, the Father Provincial, was played by Donald Wolfit. This was apt because Donald was putting on the play.

A lot has been written about Wolfit and his eccentricity, but it should be remembered that he was a superb actor. He had great presence and immense strength; and, although perhaps the last of the actor-managers of the old school, his work was totally true, as he proved when acting in front of the camera on film and television. Outside the theatre he could be charming and gentle, but once inside that stage door he became autocratic and suspicious of all around him. Once when a piece of scenery nearly fell on him he was heard to say, 'It's Binkie Beaumont, he's out to kill me.' He seemed to feel the world was against him, but it didn't stop him giving some great performances. His Lear in particular was memorable and he was also wonderful in comedy.

The other leading part in the play was the Papal Legate, sent by the Pope to remonstrate with the Father Provincial not to stray from the edicts of Rome. This part was played by Ernest Milton, an actor of equal presence but totally different in style. Wonderfully eccentric, he stalked the stage like a huge bird. Margaret 'Peggy' Webster came over from New York to direct the play – if anyone *could* direct those two giants, that is. Donald, used to directing himself, always wanted to be in the most advantageous position and perfectly lit. Once Peggy stopped Ernest in full flow to suggest he paused on a certain line. Ernest drew himself up to his full height, looked her piercingly in the eye and said, 'Peggy, I never pause, I only make a silence.' I thought that profound and never forgot it. A silence can mean everything in the theatre, while a pause may mean nothing.

Rehearsals complete, we embarked on a pre-London tour of ten weeks or so before coming to the Haymarket Theatre, London. I was playing Father Clark, one of the worker priests, not a huge part but substantial enough. After a week or two of leaving the theatre at the same time as Donald he said to me, 'Vaughan, I'd like you to understudy me. No extra money but a good opportunity for you. Let me know.' I worked hard on the part and, after a week or two of understudy rehearsals in the theatre in the morning, the great man turned up to watch me play his role. This was an unusual thing for a leading actor to do, but he must have heard something. At the end of my performance he said nothing but came up on stage and went through all the props he used, giving me tips about scrolls, feather quills, seals and so on. This was a generous thing for him to do, and I felt a warm glow that he had accepted me.

Donald, in performance, certainly always gave his all, and often seemed exhausted by the end of the evening. His voice would need lubricating as well and at every performance a young actor in the play, Ronald Harwood, would be in the wings with a bunch of grapes. Donald would sweep off stage in a scene drop, grab a handful of grapes, blast the pips into the wings and return refreshed, almost in one movement, ready for the next scene.

One night just as the curtain was about to rise he said, 'Vaughan, my voice has gone, you'll have to take over, do you know it?' I found this a little unnerving as I had the first line of the scene as Father Clark! Needless to say he was never off. His curtain calls were legendary, hanging on to the curtain in a state of apparent exhaustion bowing humbly and deeply.

His local theatre was the Theatre Royal in Nottingham. This was where he had cycled from his home in Newark as a boy to see all the old actor-managers. When we played there he made a curtain speech which began as follows: 'Citizens of Nottingham, we of the living theatre are in grave danger of extinction due to the incursions of the mechanical media.' I noted that he was starring at the local Odeon in *Svengali*, could be seen on Sunday in one of the first recorded *Armchair Theatres* and could also be heard in a radio drama serial. So much for *his* extinction.

Ronnie Harwood, now the famous playwright, spent a lot of time working with Wolfit both as actor and general factotum when he first came over from his native South Africa, and his brilliant play *The Dresser* must have been inspired by his experiences with the great man.

The tour over, we dress rehearsed for our London opening. 'This is the Theatre Royal Haymarket,' said Donald. 'None of your fancy West End acting here.' This was delivered as several of us stood in the urinal under the stage during a rehearsal break. The play ran for some months, but was perhaps most memorable for one of Kenneth Tynan's greatest reviews. 'The play must be seen,' he wrote, 'to observe Donald Wolfit and Ernest Milton upstaging each other for the greater glory of God.' Donald was outraged, but Ernest purred with delight. 'Spectacular,' he said.

Another memorable play for me was *Paddle Your Own Canoe*, a translation of a frothy French comedy with Moira Lister and Nigel Stock. We did the usual pre-London tour and opened at the Criterion in 1958. I played a French lawyer, a hilarious part dealing with a family will; it was more or less a monologue for the first twenty minutes of the play, but he did not come on again. The first night audience in the West End loved it and I went off to a big round of applause. All I had to do then was put my feet up in the dressing room, have a couple of beers and wait for the curtain call. The reception was pretty good but not outstanding. Harold Hobson, the eminent critic of the *Sunday Times*, had a habit of picking on not-too-well-known actors or actresses and eulogising them in his reviews, particularly if he didn't like the play too much. That is what happened to me with a vengeance. He wrote a column about my performance and said the play never really recovered after my exit.

Moira and Nigel were very charming to me about it. After all, they had to carry the whole of the rest of the play and it can't have been too much joy for them to read Mr Hobson's review. Donald Albery, who put the play on, was less than pleased however, and called me on to the stage a couple of hours before the next performance in order to cut and 'tone down' my part, as he put it. I point-blank refused to alter a thing; he backed down, and we continued at the Criterion for some months. Actually, the public enjoyed the play immensely. Moira and Nigel were brilliant as were Violet Fairbrother, Roy Purcell and the rest of the cast, and it was a very happy run.

I also managed to do a film or two in the fifties, though nothing of any great size or quality. There was the famous *Village of the Damned*. I was the village policeman best remembered for falling off his bicycle. Billie and I were in *The Devil's Agent* shot in Bray, County Wicklow, at the famous Ardmore Studios. There was one memorable day where several of us who weren't working indulged in some marvellous Irish conversation in the bars of Dublin. The locals showed us where to drink in the 'holy hour'; that is, when all bars were supposed to be closed. A local chemist closed his shop at lunchtime and was still with us at Ma Broome's at two in the morning. 'The conversation was too good to miss,' he said. 'Never mind the shop.' A truly memorable day.

I was in *Sapphire* directed by Basil Dearden and a Disney film called *The Horse Without a Head*, and did my first foreign location work in *Two Living, One Dead* directed by Anthony Asquith in a cold Stockholm where I had some good times with Patrick McGoohan and a very young Michael Crawford. Back in London, Patrick and I were out on the town one night when he decided his ambition was to drive around Parliament Square the wrong way which – at two in the morning – he proceeded to do, only to be stopped by the long arm of the law.

'Ah, Danger Man,' the sergeant said, referring to Pat's famous TV series. 'I don't think you're fit to drive, Danger Man.'

'No, but he is,' said Pat, referring to me. I got in the driver's seat and we lurched unsteadily off, watched by the law, with Pat cursing me as I tried to find the right gears. Happy days.

I infiltrated my way into BBC radio drama as well, and by the end of the decade was doing quite a few broadcasts. I had loved radio since my Malaya days, but economically it was a disaster. The fees were low and after a round or two in the George after rehearsals and transmission they became almost non-existent. There were some rich characters about in BBC radio though, and great times were had by all.

Domestically things had changed as well. As our flat in St Pancras was about to be demolished to make way for an office block, in 1957 we bought a flat in Datchet on the Thames near Windsor. It was a good flat and had a garden down to the river. To explain why we moved there I'm afraid I have to mention cricket again. I was already playing for the local cricket club. The captain was O. G. Batcock, also captain of Buckinghamshire and an MCC player. His theatre name was Oliver Gordon; he had directed me in repertory in Birmingham, Wolverhampton and Hull for the Salbergs, and invited me to join Datchet when I was settled in London.

In the side and often opening the batting with me was Bill Harboard, brother of Gordon Harboard, a well-known agent. Bill worked with his brother and took me onto his books and worked tirelessly on my behalf, as well as being a great friend. Cricket had done the trick again. Sadly his only son Tony, a very good modern jazz drummer (as my son was to be some years later), went out to the States to play there only to be later called into the US army and killed in Vietnam.

Billie was by now extremely successful and was away a great deal, as indeed was I. Donald Pleasence had left us and married again, this time to a fine singer-actress, Josephine Crombie. They soon moved down to Datchet in a neighbouring road, then moved to an even grander house almost next door to us with their own river garden and mooring. Donald bought a boat and we managed not to drown as we clattered into moorings and biffed our way through locks. Bob Wilson, who had been working in the Midlands, was moved to Ruislip and he and Toni quickly moved to Datchet as well, and stayed there permanently.

Politically the brutal suppression in 1956 of the Hungarian revolution by the Soviet Union affected most of us pretty deeply. Although still left-wing in outlook, our reverence for the Soviet Union was severely dented. I was still socialist but began to believe that it could best be achieved democratically. As I look back in memory over this decade I am surprised at how much was achieved, or at least changed in such a short time.

From being an unknown Billie had moved virtually to the top of her tree, and I was by now inundated with work. Had we achieved what we set out to do when we married? Perhaps we had. At home I was taken back into the fold after a couple of years of ostracism. Father was the peacemaker, saying the whole situation was absurd. I decided the best way forward was to agree with Mother whatever I really felt. This worked well enough and made peace between us.

I must also mention the thrill of going to the Royal Court Theatre in 1956 to see *Look Back in Anger* with my friend Ken Haigh playing Jimmy Porter. That play signalled a complete change in our business. Plays with French windows and 'who's for tennis' were out, and a whole seam of truthful talent was unleashed. A new kind of writing, acting and directing in films, TV and theatre had arrived and I felt I was part of it.

Oh, and nobody had dropped The Bomb either.

8
HEROES AND VILLAINS

U NFORTUNATELY I CAN'T REMEMBER all of the work I did during this golden era of television one-off plays and serials because I never kept a record. I have to be content with a few random memories of the early-sixties television performances.

TV violence was becoming a concern, and when I played Bill Sikes in the BBC serialisation of *Oliver Twist* questions were asked in the House of Commons about the appalling way Sikes killed Nancy. MPs spoke of her being bludgeoned to death with blood everywhere. Actually, what happened was very interesting and shows the power of suggestion in TV drama. The death was shot as follows: I stood in silhouette, a menacing figure with my back to camera. I advanced on the brightly lit Nancy with my stick raised. As I neared her she went out of shot. The stick went across camera in close-up over and over again with a sickening thud until Nancy's out-of-shot cries stopped. I was in fact hitting a wet sandbag set below the camera. The next shot was of Sikes' dog whimpering on the floor below with drops of blood trickling through the ceiling to the floor in front of him. There was no shot of Nancy being beaten, or even shown dead at all: that was all in the viewers' imagination. It was a brilliant piece of filming and far more effective than if the death had been shown for all to see.

Around this time for some reason or another I was starting to play a lot of menacing, sometimes violent characters, often on the wrong side of the law. They could easily be categorised as villains, but I never thought of them in that light. The human condition is too complex to allow one to just lump together 'heroes' and 'villains'. Whenever I played a hard nut or someone outside the law I always tried to show a vulnerable side to the character and to find a reason for the criminal behaviour. For instance, Commissar Nikitin in *When the Kissing Had to Stop* must have been totally out of his element in London after the Soviet Union had conquered Britain. I played Hitler once on TV but I'm afraid I couldn't find any excuses for him.

One rather sinister character was a police officer called Mr Michael in a 1963 TV play, *The Strain*, written by Alun Owen and directed by Ted Kotcheff. This led to me playing the lead in a play of Alun's at that year's Dublin Theatre Festival. We were a huge success and I had a really good time there. The play was directed by a larger-than-life character named Godfrey Quigley who was also a fine actor. He was tremendous company and we became great friends.

That year the festival club for the artists was in the Intercontinental Hotel and it was a very convivial after-show gathering place. One night our cast was gathered at a table there while Godfrey was up at the bar being interviewed by the American press. One of our actors from England had a very attractive wife who was showing rather a lot of *décolletage*, and this was causing much excitement amongst the Irish amateur boxing team at a nearby table. There was a bit of nudging and winking and guffawing and the odd remark could be overheard. One of our cast, the fine Irish actor T. P. McKenna, was outraged and told them they were insulting his English friends. Plenty of drink had flowed and one thing led to another, and pretty soon fisticuffs broke out which wasn't such good news for the actors.

Quigley, at the bar, heard and saw this fracas, rushed quickly to the scene and declaimed to the boxers: 'Stop, stop! Don't hit my actors' faces – they have to perform tomorrow night!'

Everything stilled for a second; then the boxers obeyed his plea and got stuck into the actors' solar plexuses instead.

The play transferred to the UK for a tour but wasn't very successful there. I had moved on by then and Ray McAnally played the part. I can't for the life of me remember the name of the play. Obviously another eruption of megalomania because someone else played the part.

Although work was abundant I was still just as driven, just as unsure where the next job was going to come from, and was still striving to improve. I don't think you could call it ambition; it was more a question of trying not to fall off the bandwagon. Any slacking off and that would have been all too easy to do.

Around this time I was in another play whose title I can't remember, written by Robert Barr and directed by Gilchrist Calder. It was in essence a stage version of a television series later to become the famous *Z Cars*. It starred Ronald Shiner and Thora Hird and was set in a town in the North. Put on by Peter Saunders of *Mousetrap* fame we went out on the usual pre-London tour. Frankly the play was not much cop (no pun intended), although there were some great scenes and performances in it.

I had a pretty good part as a police sergeant, with a particularly fine scene at the beginning briefing the police (and incidentally the audience) in the style of *Hill Street Blues*. The scene went superbly well for a night or two: too well in fact for the star, Ronnie Shiner, who had to come on after it. He didn't like this at all and had the whole scene bar a line or two cut out. More eruptions of megalomania.

However, we had a lot of fun on that tour with people such as Alan Browning, who had just started acting after working as a journalist, Mark Eden, and of course Thora who was brilliant in it as always. Thora would regale us with wonderfully rich anecdotes of her late beloved husband Scotty, 'our Jeannie' (her daughter Janette Scott) and many tales of early life in Morecambe.

Then there was a huge Dickensian type of character by the name of John Sharp. Besides being a fine character actor, John was a Greek scholar, raconteur and wit. He was also a true *bon viveur* and loved a drink or two, which gave him a florid complexion and caused him to be a little overweight. We used to meet every Monday before the show to discuss our weekends. I would have a couple of discreet halves of bitter while John tore into the large vodkas.

One week we met as usual: 'Large vodka, John?' I enquired.

John, looking particularly florid, replied: 'What! Do you think I don't know how to look after myself? A large Soave, please.'

John was also a well-known radio actor, appearing for a while in *The Archers*, a series which it seemed to me he didn't have the greatest regard for. He put his own words to the famous signature tune, beginning: *Old John Archer's got the clap, picked it up in Ambridge…* etc.

After some weeks on tour Peter Saunders came to see the play and told us on stage after the performance that we were to open in the West End. This news was greeted with muted enthusiasm, to say the least, as we all felt the play hadn't really got what it takes for the West End. The following day we were called in to the theatre for notes on the performance. The director went on and on all morning and, after a short break, into the afternoon. It was a beautiful summer's day outside and we were all getting a bit restless. John was especially bored as he had received no notes at all, not one. Suddenly the director said, 'Oh and John, Mr Saunders doesn't think the alderman of a small northern town should wear red socks. Will you change them to black ones.'

John exploded: 'Socks? *Socks?* I've been sitting here since half past ten this morning and all you've got to tell me is *socks?* Well, I'll tell you what I'm going to do: I'm going to catch the 4.20 train to Paddington. I'll write you out a cheque for two weeks' wages – and don't think I haven't got it, because I have.'

This he proceeded to do and shot off to the station in high dudgeon followed by a pleading management who eventually mollified him and brought him back. The play did open in the West End (I can't remember where) and folded after a couple of weeks.

Commercial repertory as we knew it was by now in serious decline. People could sit at home and watch all the drama they needed, and of a high standard as well. The old ABC cinema in Didsbury had become a television studio and I did an *Armchair Theatre* from there. I explored the place and found the organ still there, sitting in the basement gathering dust. No more 'I Want to be Happy' coming up into the auditorium; those days were long gone, though I think it would have enlivened that particular *Armchair Theatre*.

I was fortunate to be in some wonderful one-off plays on television. I think *The Fire Raisers* by Max Frisch was my favourite, although playing opposite the exquisite Celia Johnson in *The Cellar and the Almond Tree* ran a close second. The author, David Mercer, was a tremendous play-wright and was concerned with the effect of Communist Eastern Europe on us in the West. In this play Celia played a dotty old Czech aristocrat banished to the top floor of her castle; the rest was taken over by the Party as their headquarters. I was the tired Communist official sent up to get the keys of the basement from her. They were needed so that the Party could get their hands on her store of vintage champagne which they wanted for a banquet. However, the old lady thought my character was her butler and told me her whole life story whilst I fetched and carried for her. It was a poignant and beautiful play, and when Celia died years later the BBC showed it again as a tribute to her.

Celia was a delight to work with, and she had a mischievous sense of humour. There was a strike at the BBC when we were recording the play and so we couldn't finish it, and it was some months before we could all be together again to complete it. Things were a bit tense as there wasn't much time at our disposal, and just before one scene I was given several instructions by the floor manager at high tempo.

'Understood,' I replied.

'Shouldn't you say roger and out?' whispered Celia just on 'action'.

Despite her gossamer figure she loved good food and had a healthy appetite. When the company lunched together she would always order last. 'I must know what you're all having or I shall be jealous,' she said.

Then there was *All Things Bright and Beautiful* by Keith Waterhouse and Willis Hall, a brilliant piece about a Leeds working-class family being moved from their slum dwelling to the paradise of a new high-rise flat in the suburbs. Thora Hird and I were the parents. I thought, and still think, Thora was a truly great actress. Her comedy timing was out of this world, but it's the total truth which was so stunning. She could make an audience laugh and cry and then laugh again in seconds. I just loved working with her.

One day in rehearsal we were watching John Hurt and Lois Daine playing the young lovers in the opening scene. They were playing it quite nicely but Thora thought they should have got on with it a bit more. 'If those two young people don't get a move on in that scene there'll not be a set switched on when they get to us.'

She was in great form in the pub at lunchtimes, regaling the cast with her anecdotes. Of course I had heard most of them before whilst on tour. I have a facility for tuning out, resting and almost sleeping with my eyes wide open. During one lunch break I was jolted from my reverie.

'Mr Vaughan, my co-star, would you mind getting sat forward in that chair so that I can see the expression on your face while I tell this story?'

Thora was a wonderful actress and Alan Bennett obviously thought so too; her *Talking Heads* along with those of Patricia Routledge are peerless.

I worked on another David Mercer play for television called *You and Me and Him*. This was a three-hander with a writer wrestling with his Ego (all moral and hard-working) and his Alter Ego (to hell with work and morals, let's go out and have a good time). I played all three parts. It was shot three times with stand-in actors playing the other parts and was then edited together. It was quite early days for such a technical piece of work, and of course I had to get all my positions and eyelines very precise so that it all cut together properly. I found it pretty difficult to learn until I hit on the idea of memorising the parts of the writer and his alter ego together and then I found it easy to learn ego afterwards. The conscious brain could take in the two parts while the subconscious was busy taking in the third.

It was around this time that the film studios were getting on the television bandwagon, and Pinewood, Borehamwood and Shepperton were all busy making such series as *Danger Man*, *The Prisoner*, *The Saint*, *Man in a Suitcase*, *Randall & Hopkirk* (I did one directed by Leslie Norman, Barry's father), *The Avengers*, *The Protectors* and not least *The Persuaders* which starred Roger Moore and Tony Curtis.

They were all hour-long episodes and had a ten-day schedule so there wasn't a lot of time to hang around, and sometimes things became a bit hectic; to go over schedule was disaster. I remember on the last day's shooting of an episode of *The Persuaders*, at three in the afternoon, Tony Curtis and I still had a long dialogue scene to shoot – normally a good half day's work. He was of course the hero and I, of course, a nasty piece of work, and for this Tony had a brilliant idea: we circled around each other menacingly in close shot, and worked it so that for his salient lines and reactions he was in front of camera with my back to it, and vice versa. We shot the whole scene in one, it looked terrific and the day was saved. He hadn't been in Hollywood for all those years for nothing.

Tony was fantastic to work with, a huge personality with tremendous humour. On the first morning of shooting we were standing on location in a field at dawn. 'Here we are,' he said, 'Tony Curtis, Peter Vaughan, still in the business despite all those bastards in the front office.' He was a survivor all right.

He was unhappy because Roger Moore had a better dressing room at Pinewood than he had. Roger's was well furnished with fitted wardrobes, while Tony's facilities were comparatively poor. I arrived one morning and there was a hell of a noise going on with Tony pitching his furniture into the corridor, over the staircase and onto the floor below. He was soon placated and he quickly got a very nicely furnished and smartened-up dressing room.

Tony had been brought up in New York, in the Hungarian sector. 'Until I was five years old and my mother sent me to the street corner to buy a daily paper I thought all Americans spoke Hungarian.' Asked about his short-lived marriage to Christine Kaufmann, an actress who briefly was a star, he said: 'Who the hell wants to sit opposite a broad at breakfast every morning complaining she's only made one movie?' He was a funny, brilliant man with a huge zest for life.

Aged 16, in 1939. A studio portrait at the behest of my mother!

Promoted to Acting Captain at only 23

My first West End play: *Doctor's Delight* at the Garrick Theatre in 1950, with the legend A. E. Matthews

The Importance of Being Earnest, Birmingham Rep, 1950. The nearest I got to being a juvenile lead!

Lion's Corner, taken off after only a single performance at St Martin's Theatre, London, 1952. It doesn't happen often – trust me to be in it!

Deadline Midnight, 1960. My first leading part in a TV serial.

Bill Sikes in the BBC's *Oliver Twist*, 1962. One of my favourite villains!

Playing a guest role in *Hancock*, 1963
(Photo © ITV/REX/Shutterstock)

Early days at Goffs Manor with the dogs

Sunday cricket with Vic Lewis' team, 1966

The most wonderful day of my life: the birth
of my son David in January 1967

A glamorous photo of Lillias

One of my favourite pictures of
Lillias and David

A huge relief to get back to *terra firma* on location for the 1968 film *Hammerhead*

In uniform again for the 1968 British drama film *The Bofors Gun* with David Warner

As Horace Dorrington in the 1971 TV series *The Rivals of Sherlock Holmes*

On location for *Straw Dogs*, above with Sam Peckinpah (an awesome director – how lucky I was to work with him) and below with Dustin Hoffman before I lost my foot!

11 Harrowhouse – an enormous privilege to work with James Mason and Sir John Gielgud

Valentino with Rudolph Nureyev – not his usual sort of partner!

As Quartermaster Sergeant Bloomfield in the 1979 film *Zulu Dawn*

The 1979 film version of the classic sitcom *Porridge*. I loved playing Grouty alongside the hugely talented Ronnie Barker as Fletch. (Photo © Moviestore/REX/Shutterstock)

'King' Billy with his family in the 1980 TV series *Fox* – didn't they do well!

Front cover shot with Richard Weinbaum who played 'King' Billy's grandson, Andy Fox

Winston the Ogre in Terry Gilliam's film *Time Bandits* – a romp with the glorious Katherine Helmond

With Ian McKellen and John Woodvine as Hermann Göring and friends in *Countdown to War*

Mr Tulkinghorn in *Bleak House* – my most eerie portrayal!

Happy memories of working with Clive Owen in the long-running series *Chancer*
(Photo © ITV/REX/Shutterstock)

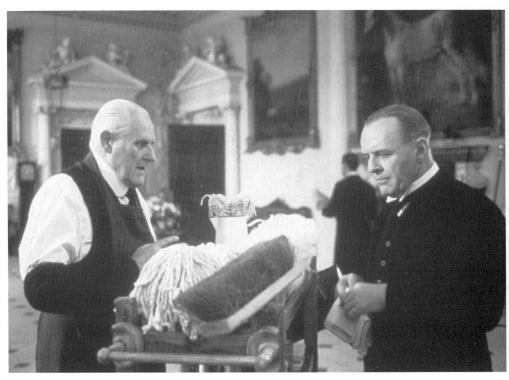

Father and son (Anthony Hopkins) in *The Remains of the Day*, a film which I consider to be one of the greatest of all time (Photo © SNAP/REX/Shutterstock)

On my rounds to see my patients as Dr Hinks in the 1994 miniseries *Dandelion Dead*

With Daniel Day-Lewis in the 1996 film of Arthur Miller's *The Crucible*. A great film to be in, with the added privilege of meeting Arthur Miller himself.

BAFTA nominations night 1996 – damn it, I didn't win!

Fooling around at home

Mr Boffin in the 1998 TV adaptation
of *Our Mutual Friend* – another
lovely Dickens character

As Sir Ensor Doone in the 2000 TV movie of *Lorna Doone*. I have vivid memories of my 'death scene'.

to Peter with thanks, admiration, respect and awe!
best wishes Geoffrey

With Geoffrey Rush in *The Life and Death of Peter Sellers*

Death at a Funeral, with director Frank Oz – the start of a great friendship. What fun we all had making this movie.

9
SLOANE RANGER

ESPITE ALL THIS CONTINUOUS WORK none of it was really very well paid like it is today and so it was necessary to keep the bandwagon rolling along. Politically there was a very real threat of nuclear war which hung over the world, and I of course supported the growing anti-nuclear campaign. Pilloried by the Tory press as left-wing loonies and eccentrics, the movement nevertheless gained in momentum and there were marches from Aldermaston and Wethersfield to rallies in Trafalgar Square attended by thousands.

On the Wethersfield march we were accompanied for some miles by Randolph Churchill (Winston's son) pushing a pram with a gramophone on it playing 'There'll Always Be an England': a somewhat eccentric criticism, I thought, because there certainly wouldn't have been much of an England in the event of a nuclear attack. Bryan Pringle and I carried a huge banner designed by Sean Kenny which was pretty heavy going; when we got to within a mile of Trafalgar Square we had to hand it over to Arnold Wesker and John Neville, bigger names than us who carried it for the last mile in front of press and cameras. However, it was all for the cause and by way of consolation there were lots of lovely lady supporters who dispensed food and hot drinks and gently tended over blistered feet, and any other aches and pains.

I can't honestly remember when it actually happened, but I think it gradually seeped into my naïve brain that all was not well in my marriage. With our two busy careers, we were frequently apart; and, although we were still friendly enough, it was clear that Billie had many admirers, and that she seriously loved someone else – the real love of her life. He was famous, married and a strict Roman Catholic, so it had to remain a secret liaison. I don't remember how I came to know about 'he who shall not be named' but I was pretty upset. He was a good friend of mine and I felt betrayed, much more by him than by her as frankly I felt our relationship was by now not much more than a friendly convenience.

I didn't feel like rocking the boat and bringing things to a head – I was too busy for that – but I did feel that I had the right to take advantage of the situation myself. After all, it was the Swinging Sixties. So I went on the town and had a wonderful time, joining in with the scene and getting far too fond of whisky chasers. There were wonderful times on location; and Manchester, home of Granada TV for whom I worked a great deal, was a tremendously sybaritic city in those days.

I was brought up sharp on one occasion, however, when I was in an episode of *Adam Adamant* and we were shooting at night in the streets of Shepherd's Bush. It was pouring with rain and the prospect of working that night was slim. I was put to wait in the BBC TV Club where I had a convivial evening with friends and acquaintances. Around ten o'clock (still pouring with rain) I was taken to a pub nearer to where we were supposed to shoot. The locals gave me a great welcome and more drinks followed. I was by now in great form, or thought I was. Suddenly the rain stopped and I was rushed to the location where I had to drive a very low-slung sports car up to a precise mark, jump out, assemble a telescopic rifle and aim at a window opposite. Well, I managed the driving onto the mark, but I had great difficulty in getting out of the car; and as for assembling the rifle, that was a joke. The director shot my efforts, printed it and showed me later, and of course we had to go back and do the scene properly. I vowed then never to take a drink before or during work again. I have stuck to this ever since, no matter how long the wait or how little the work to be done.

After work, though, it was a different matter and I was getting to like the taste a bit too much. After a certain point with whisky I would cease to be the life and soul of the party and would become argumentative, unpleasant and sometimes violent. One extra drink would do it, but I never knew which one was the 'extra' one.

This was how my life was looking when I went up to the Glasgow Citizens Theatre in 1963 to play Bottom in *A Midsummer Night's Dream*, directed by Piers Haggard. I had heard a good deal about Lillias Walker's return to acting after her divorce and that she was being brilliant on the Scottish circuit, and I was really hoping that she would be in the production so I could meet her again. Sadly she was working elsewhere, at the Pitlochry Theatre I think it was, so the best I could do was to leave a message for her with her friend Ann Kristen.

I enjoyed playing Bottom, but there was a good deal of unemployment amongst the local Scottish actors at that time and not everyone welcomed me there. One night I was surrounded in a bar with my back to the wall and was asked in no uncertain manner how I could justify coming up to Scotland to play a leading role that could easily have been given to a Scottish actor. This was not a promising situation and I had to think quickly.

'I tell you what I'll do,' I said. 'I promise never to come to Scotland to work again if you all promise me never to come to London.'

There was a moment's silence, followed by guffaws and much back-slapping. I was in, and when you are 'in' in Scotland you are really 'in'. We became great mates and I had a grand time there, but I was sad not to have seen Lillias. The fact that she had divorced some years before and was back in the business interested me greatly. Then it was back to London, working hard – and playing hard as well, so long as there weren't too many lines to learn that night.

The Queen's Elm in Chelsea was a favourite watering-hole. Frequented by a wonderful loose-knit crowd of painters, writers and actors, it was run by a beguiling Irishman, Sean Treacy. Sean wrote a book about this amazing pub and the people who used it, called *A Smell of Broken Glass*: a wonderful title given to him by a regular named Laurie Lee.

After that it would be up to the West End to the Salisbury and to clubs such as the Buckstone, always packed with actors late at night, situated in a basement opposite the stage door of the Haymarket Theatre. Then there was Gerry's Club, at that time in Shaftesbury Avenue, where the genuinely funny John Junkin was often being hilarious at the bar. Keith Waterhouse was often there as well, and when I told him I was going to Brighton to make a rather good little film called *Smokescreen* he took out the keys to his lovely seafront flat saying, 'Here you are. I shan't be using it for a few weeks.' Such was the camaraderie and generosity to be found in the loosely knit social scene.

Peter Cook's Establishment Club had opened up in Soho and was hugely popular with its spacious bar and cabaret room on the ground floor and

Dudley Moore and his trio playing jazz in the basement. I remember Michael Caine lamenting to me there one night that he couldn't get into pictures. His pal Terence Stamp was getting the parts. Shortly after this came *Zulu*, and everyone knows what came after that.

Unfortunately this was the time of the Krays, and one night the happy scene in the basement was broken up by thugs; panic and screaming ensued. I ended up under the piano until things died down.

A well-known Australian actor, Kenneth J. Warren, ran a club in Sloane Square called 'The Kangaroo'. It was a delightful club, popular among actors as well as the local Australian community. Ken had a visit from some of the Krays' mob asking for protection money and Ken told them to go to hell. They left with threats that they would be returning to wreck the place. Ken promptly organised all available Aussies, including some visiting Qantas air crew, and armed them with a variety of weapons. When the Kray mob arrived to carry out their threat they were met by some very tough guys indeed and were quickly put to flight. Ken was never troubled again.

*

One afternoon, having just finished a television show, I was sitting in a basement drinking-club opposite the Arts Theatre near Leicester Square, desultorily studying form in the *Sporting Life*, occasionally going upstairs to put a bet on in the betting shop opposite, going back and watching my horse lose on the club TV, when Dudley Sutton came in. I was sitting gloomily at the bar. Dudley, a brilliant young actor with a huge personality and a face like a battered cherub, stopped in his tracks.

'What are you doing?' he asked. I muttered something about having just finished something. 'Stay where you are. Don't move. I'll be back in a minute,' he said, rushing out of the club.

I shrugged and returned to the paper. He quickly returned with a fresh-faced young man wearing highly polished army boots, neatly creased blue denims, a blue T-shirt and an ex-army gas-mask case over his shoulder. 'That's our Ed,' said Dudley, excitedly pointing me out to this young man.

'Is he heterosexual?' the young man asked.

'Yes, very.'

The young man looked me up and down for a minute, opened his satchel and brought out the script of a play. 'Would you like to read this?'

They returned to the Arts Theatre across the road, and I went to our *pied à terre* in Neal Street, Covent Garden. It was easy to get a flat there in those days and there wasn't much sleep to be had with the fruit and veg market in full swing. I think the rent was £5 per week, and it was close to theatre land and so very useful.

I sat down to read the play and was absolutely bowled over. I rang Bill Harboard and told him to drop everything. I had to do this play at all costs. 'It's called *Entertaining Mr Sloane*, by a new writer called Joe Orton,' I told him. I knew this was the part for me, and this chance encounter with Dudley turned out to be one of the most important moments of my career.

Although the style of the play is common now, it was the first of its kind to us. Joe had had a short play or two broadcast on Midlands radio, but this was the first professional stage production of his work. Patrick Dromgoole, later to become head of drama at Harlech TV, was the director; and apart from Dudley and myself, the cast comprised Madge Ryan as my sister Kath and Charles Lamb as our dad, Kemp.

Rehearsals were very exciting but a bit daunting as we explored how to do the play. We opened at the Arts Theatre Club and it was a sensation. Reviews were ecstatic and audiences entranced. It was a difficult play to control as it was so funny and there was a danger of the audience being 'laughed out' too soon. The play had a great rhythm and we went for group laughs: that is to say, going for two or three laugh lines together, thereby getting one big audience laugh rather than two or three smaller ones. However, different audiences found different things hilarious so it was a bit of a roller-coaster evening on occasion, and a great lesson in audience control.

We transferred to Wyndham's Theatre and later to the Queen's Theatre. Terence Rattigan invested in it and everyone who was anyone came to see it. Laurence Olivier, at the height of his powers and head of the National Theatre, came with one of his directors, William Gaskill. Gaskill didn't like it – he thought it too cruel – but Olivier thought it was marvellous. As we discussed the performance outside the theatre, he purposely stood in the road with me higher up on the pavement. It was a deliberate gesture to indicate that, despite being a great actor himself, this was my evening. He was equally generous with everything he said. (Later, in his dressing room as I watched him make up for *Othello* he said to me, 'Given you can do it, the most important thing for an actor is physical fitness.' I have tried to follow this advice. Muscle control and breath control are vital in acting and

Olivier with his prodigious talent and strength was an example to us all.)

Judy Garland was in London and she adored the play, coming several times to see it. She and Madge Ryan became friends and I went with them to the Blue Angel nightclub a couple of times after the show. Danny La Rue assisted by Ronnie Corbett and his wife Anne Hart fronted a brilliantly wicked cabaret. Judy Garland was delightful, but I felt slightly uneasy in her company. She was just too enormous a star perhaps for me to handle socially.

As I said, the play was a sensation and the writing was superb. One of my favourite lines is when Kath is tending a wound in Sloane's backside: she says, 'Don't be alarmed, Mr Sloane; until I was fifteen I was more familiar with Africa than my own body.' Ed had a wonderful line when Kath, now pregnant by Sloane, asks if he can attend the birth. 'No,' says Ed, 'it's all any reasonable child can expect if the dad is present at the conception.' It is a great play and it was a joy to play it.

However, Joe Orton was not entirely at ease with his success, despite the wonderful reviews and *Entertaining Mr Sloane* being voted best new play of the year. Perhaps this accolade from the theatrical establishment was at odds with his desire to be outrageous and to shock; or perhaps he just didn't like our production very much. He told me how good a Berlin production had been and that his work should be played by comedians, not actors. Tony Hancock should play my part, he told me.

Joe's next play *Loot* had a wonderful part, Truscott, which I fancied playing very much. I discussed the situation with Patrick Dromgoole who shrewdly advised that we get out after our success and leave it at that, so I didn't pursue the matter further. True to his word Joe cast his friend, the great comic actor Kenneth Williams, in the part and the production went out on a pre-London tour. I saw it at Golders Green and it was truly awful. No shape, no control and vastly overplayed with Williams milking every line. That version didn't come into London, but the play was later recast with the fine character actor Michael Bates absolutely brilliant as Truscott and it became another big hit in the West End. So much for Joe's experiment with comedians.

Joe was as complex a person as he was brilliant as a writer. In the bar one lunchtime during rehearsals as we discussed the play he told Dudley Sutton and me that he knew what it was like to be a heterosexual, just as much as we did. 'I was married once,' he said. Whether this was the truth or fantasy I don't know. I wonder whether his diaries were a little extravagant with the truth?

During the run of *Sloane* I got a part in a film called *Fanatic* with Tallulah Bankhead and Stefanie Powers. This was a Gothic piece set in an old house near Eel Pie Island on the Thames; Yootha Joyce and I were the sinister servants. It meant doing the play and then snatching a few hours' sleep before being called at six in the morning to film. Although this became very tiring, there was a rhythm to it and I enjoyed it.

Tallulah Bankhead was extraordinary, very politically aware. Her father was a senator and she was very radical for her time. There was a well-publicised friendship with Joe Louis, the black world heavyweight boxing champion, which broke a contemporary taboo. Very glamorous and the toast of Broadway and London in the thirties, the stories about her outrageous behaviour and wit were legendary. For example, one night when friends came round to her dressing room unexpectedly after the show she poured them champagne and handed her apartment keys over to her lover of the day saying, 'Go ahead, darling, and start without me.'

By now, however, it was the sixties and she was getting on a bit and not quite so dazzlingly beautiful. In the house which we used as our location base there were two dressing rooms, one for men and one for women. Donald Sutherland, playing the simple gardener in one of his first films, strayed in error early one morning into the women's dressing room. He was greeted by the sight of a naked Tallulah who purred, 'Come on in, now you've seen that I'm the only natural blonde in this movie!' He ran.

On the set she was very difficult and her treatment of the director, Silvio Narizzano, was disgraceful. He must have had the patience of Job. Annoyingly she had no idea of film technique and couldn't do the simplest of things such as firing a gun and saying a line in the right position at the right time. We had to do twenty-seven takes of this and I had to bounce onto a hard floor twenty-seven times until she finally got it right.

One early morning we did a scene with me dead, fully clothed in a bath with water dripping from a tap onto my face, while Tallulah threatened Stefanie with a gun. Unfortunately there was no hot water available so I agreed to do the scene in cold water. Tallulah rehearsed a couple of times until I was thoroughly soaked and freezing and then said, 'My feet are killing me; I have to go to my room,' and left me there shivering for an hour or so. What a cow!

Stefanie was delightful and a very good actress but already well versed in Hollywood ways. We had a rape scene to do, and as we rehearsed she told me exactly where she wanted her head to be in relation to the camera as we struggled. I thought this was a bit too technical and stilted.

'Put your head where you like, darling,' I said, 'I'm just going to rape you.'

She was terrific in the scene.

*

One day in the middle of all this furious activity I went into the Salisbury pub opposite the theatre stage door to grab a sandwich and my life changed forever. Lillias Walker, whom I hadn't seen since she had introduced me to her fiancé in Birmingham some twelve years earlier, was sitting there. I felt elated but strangely calm. There was my destiny, and I knew it. It wasn't love at first sight, for I'd known her before; but perhaps subconsciously I had loved her from the beginning, and although we had to go our separate ways it seemed inevitable and natural that we had come together again – this time for good and all.

Roses were sent to the Westminster Theatre where she was playing the lead in *Mr Brown Comes Down The Hill*. Philip Pearman, a leading agent at MCA, had seen her work in Scotland, got her the play in London and was all set to promote her when he died; and, although she had a good career and did a lot of good work, I don't think the potential of this brilliant actress and ravishing beauty was ever fulfilled.

From that moment we were together, and no more than a week later I had packed a suitcase, left my old life behind and moved into the flat in Gloucester Road which she shared with Hilary Crosland, the divorced wife of the Labour Minister Richard Crosland. We were ecstatically in love, and I felt at peace and contented and passionately excited all at the same time. We would rush back to the flat from our respective plays with a cooked chicken and chips from the Italian shop across the road and a bottle of brandy ('There he goes with his leg-opener,' Madge Ryan used to say) and we were blissfully happy.

To my surprise and astonishment Billie behaved in a totally hysterical way. After all, ours had become a marriage of convenience: we were more friends by now than anything else. Her true love was 'he who shall not be named'. And Michael Craig, as he described to me later, was also seriously in love with her and ready to leave home for her; and there were other admirers of varying seriousness. Surely we had outgrown each other and I was entitled to my happiness as well?

I hoped we could remain friends, but this was not to be. I really thought she might harm herself and I did my best to placate her but it was to no avail. Although quickly consoled by Robert Muller she has always branded me as the guilty party, vilified Lillias and done her best to harm me whenever she could. I never answered back or commented on the situation. The relationship was ended and I felt there was nothing to be gained by vituperative discussion about it.

Some fifteen years later when we were on location together but not staying in the same hotel she took me on one side and told me that she did not blame me for leaving her, only in the way that I did it. I was dumbfounded; I didn't answer, merely nodded in apparent agreement. What was I supposed to do? I had bent over backwards in the divorce settlement to let her have everything we had and even paid her notional alimony of £10 per week to be increased if ever she needed it, though she did have the grace to drop this after a while. It was a little ridiculous since she was one of the most successful actresses in the country at that time.

I had no feelings working with her; and ironically 'he who shall not be named' had come over from Hollywood and was in it as well, and as far as I could see he didn't have any feelings for her either, though maybe I was wrong about this.

But all that was much later. Lillias and I rented a place of our own in Chelsea, only to find after a week or two that we had been conned by the people who rented it to us. It wasn't theirs to rent and we had to get out, losing money on the deal (a propensity we have managed to sustain quite consistently over the years). However, we found a nice maisonette in Barnes over a laundry and we were very happy there.

Lillias' twin daughters Alex and Vicki, who were at boarding school in Scotland, spent the summer holidays with us; it was always their mum's intention for them to come and live in London as quickly as possible, and I wanted us to be together as well. Lill's mother had died during childbirth and so she had been brought up by her grandmother and her mother's sister Elspeth. In childhood she spent part of the time on her father's farm which gave her her early tomboy quality, and the rest of the time with her grandmother and aunt in rather more wealthy surroundings which gave her elegance and style. An irresistible combination, and on top of that she was a brilliant actress.

Sloane was by now playing at the Queen's Theatre and was coming to the end of its natural run. Michael Codron came to my dressing room and told me the theatre wanted to put on a new play and asked if I thought we could take another transfer. I said no, and so the run came to a close: the end of a brilliant time in the theatre.

One evening when I arrived home having had far too many whisky chasers and in a somewhat aggressive and unpleasant mood, Lillias told me she couldn't take this: there had been too many alcoholics in her family and she didn't want another one. I gave up spirits there and then, and have since only ever drunk beer or the grape. Fortunately that includes the odd brandy. Times were changing, and some sanity was creeping into my life.

10
FAMILY MAN

O NE EVENING NEAR THE END OF THE *SLOANE* RUN the film director Sidney J. Furie came to see the play. He had previously directed Dudley Sutton in a film and they had become friends. Shortly after, a film script came through the post from Artanis Productions. It was called *The Naked Runner*; it was to be directed by Sidney and star Frank Sinatra. I was offered the leading part of Slattery, the MI5 official luring an ex-agent (Sinatra) back on to an almost suicidal mission.

On the way to work on the first morning I suddenly realised that Artanis was Sinatra spelt backwards, and that the actor I was supposed to manipulate and dominate in the film was actually my boss, and earning something like seven million dollars a year by all accounts. Not bad for 1965.

This was far and away my biggest film break to date. I had played Charlotte Rampling's father in her very first film, *Rotten to the Core* (and brilliant she was too), but apart from this I hadn't done much feature film work; so it was all very daunting as I made my way that morning by worker's lift to the 32nd floor of the not-yet-finished Centrepoint building in Charing Cross Road. This was to serve as our MI5 office location.

I went in and Sidney introduced me to Frank who was surrounded by aides and acolytes. I hadn't met him before as he'd only just flown into London with his new bride, Mia Farrow. Sidney went off to attend to technical matters and I was left with Frank and his buddies. They were preoccupied with the New York stock-market prices; one would occasionally sing out a share price, up or down a couple of points as the case may be, and Frank would reply laconically 'buy' or 'sell' as he thought fit. This was the strangest atmosphere in which to work on a film that I have ever known before or since.

'Let's go though the scene,' said Frank, and so we would. It was a big scene and I had most of the dialogue. His idea of going through the scene was telling me what he was going to say, what he was going to change and what he was going to cut, punctuated of course by the odd 'buy or 'sell'. I took all this for a few pages; and then he said he was cutting something which would have made nonsense of the scene.

'You can't,' I said.

'What?' he said. Our eyes met and I explained why.

There was a silence that seemed to go on forever as we stared each other out. I was pretty certain there was another actor standing by if he didn't like me; but so what, I had to make my point.

Eventually he spoke. 'Okay, see what you mean, I'll say it.'

Phew!

From there on we relaxed and, I think, worked pretty well together. He wasn't really an actor in the true sense, but with his superb sense of rhythm and catlike movement he was mesmeric on screen. He was also in a terrific hurry, for what reason I was never sure. We did a big dialogue shot one day and Sidney said *cut* and *print* after one take. 'We'll do another for safety,' he said. This is normal practice so that there is an alternative take should anything prove to be wrong with the first one when examined later at rushes.

'To hell with safety,' said Frank, 'let's live dangerously and move on.' And this was pretty well the way we shot all the scenes that included Frank.

He had a fearsome temper which, allied to his powerful position, made him pretty formidable. One day, on location in the New Forest, the unit duly set off at crack of dawn or earlier to be ready to shoot at eight. Frank decided to leave London later and go down by helicopter from his place at Grosvenor Square. Unfortunately he got caught in the rush-hour traffic on his way to the heliport in Wandsworth which made him very late.

He stormed out of the helicopter in a rage. 'What the hell do we have to come down here for? You could have shot all this in my garage in Grosvenor Square!'

He and Sidney had a real shouting match which led to fisticuffs where Sidney gave as good as he got. The film was off, with Frank refusing to act and Sidney refusing to direct: impasse. Brad Dexter, remembered for his performance in *The Magnificent Seven*, had saved Frank from drowning at some point and had become his principal assistant and friend. He parleyed from one to the other for two hours and slowly got them back to work.

The following morning I was sitting with Frank at Centrepoint waiting to start work while Sidney was supervising the lighting. Frank watched him at work. 'Look at that guy: Sidney J. Furie, thirty-two years old and the best director to come out of Hollywood.' It certainly paid to stand up to Frank.

He had the common touch as well. One day early on at Centrepoint, thirty-two floors up, Frank was looking out of the window when two faces appeared on the other side of the glass; the window cleaners nearly fell out of their bosun's chair with shock at seeing Frank. He went down and met them and gave them his autograph.

He loathed photographers who interfered with his privacy, and toward the end of the film there was an incident outside a nightclub. I don't know exactly what happened but it must have been quite serious because he took off in high dudgeon back to the States, vowing never to set foot on these shores again. This created quite a problem as he was needed crucially to appear in scenes in the denouement of the film. Even though he was the boss of the film, he refused to come back. What to do?

Sidney set up a night shoot in a disused hangar at Dunsford airfield, put in a radio transmitter or two, fished me out from whatever else I was doing and gave me pieces of paper with dialogue written on them saying, 'This is in American, change it to your character.' I would transmit this stuff to Frank's character, and hopefully some sense was made of the end of the film. *The Naked Runner* wasn't a bad film, but had rather a strange ending and that's the reason why!

Frank Sinatra was just about the most powerful man I have ever come across. Lillias was a huge fan of his and has never really forgiven me for not introducing her to him, but sadly I never had the necessary social rapport with him for this to happen.

Almost at once I did a film called *The Man Outside* with Van Heflin, who was a beautiful actor to work with, totally concentrated and true. I played a nasty Russian villain who, among other things, tortured the leading lady by burning her breasts with a lighted cigarette. One of many charming characters I have played over the years.

Van was for many years under contract to MGM, led by Louis B. Mayer. Everyone lived in fear and trembling of the legendary mogul. Van told me a great story of when he was doing the film *Johnny Eager* in which he played the title role of a policeman with marvellous subtlety and reality. One day he was summoned to Mayer's office. This meant one of two things: either you were being given a really good part or you were being fired.

MGM would have as many as twenty films on the go in those days and the great man would keep in touch by seeing bits of all the rushes. Van was kept waiting, standing in front of his desk while he conducted a long phone call. Eventually he looked up and said: 'I seen your rushes of *Johnny Eager*. Very good but watch your drinking.'

This put Van in a real dilemma. He didn't dare say the character was supposed to be drunk, and he didn't dare make a joke of it. In the end he inclined his head, smiled deprecatingly and left.

He also told me a lovely story about Joan Crawford who wasn't happy having him as her leading man in a film: she'd wanted Clark Gable. In one scene she had to slap Van's face during a row. As happens so often in films, they didn't get around to shooting the scene that day. Van always rang home at lunchtime to check mail and so on, having left very early in the morning for work. This day his wife told him a lovely bouquet of flowers had arrived. Nonplussed, he asked his wife to open the message. It read: *Sorry I had to hit you so hard – love Joan.* Well, at least he knew what was coming.

*

Around about this time my decree nisi came through and so arrangements were made for Lillias and me to get married at once. This was easier said than done. Lillias wanted a church wedding but the C. of E. wouldn't countenance it. However, the more liberal Church of Scotland agreed to marry us in her local village church at Longforgan, near Dundee, and the date arranged was 4th January, 1966.

In December I was finishing a run at the Vaudeville Theatre playing Gladstone to Dorothy Tutin's wonderful performance as the ageing Queen Victoria in *Portrait of a Queen*. Lillias was ending a tour of Shaw's *Getting Married* – an apt title. Her tour should have ended in Sunderland but the famous Prospect Theatre company put in an extra date down in Brighton. Lillias refused to go. She was *really* getting married, and had arrangements to make. This astonished me as, of course, I would dutifully have done whatever the management wanted. I admired her, though: a highly talented actress but never allowing the business to dictate her life.

Lillias' father, Colin, was a handsome giant of a Scottish farmer. The night before the wedding he took me out to the local hostelry and we got down to some serious drinking. On returning to the farm I was completely out of it and he hadn't turned a hair. I remember stroking his head, telling him how wonderful it would be in close-up and that he was a star! He seemed quite pleased by this news but must have thought his daughter had found a right one this time.

Colin was of great stature, mentally as well as physically. He lost the woman he dearly loved giving birth to Lillias, and his second son was killed at twenty-one in a building-site accident in Canada; yet I only ever saw him behave with dignity and delightful humour, especially with children.

The wedding went off well; two lovely near-twelve-year-olds, Alex and Vicki, attended their mother, and there was a good lunch for family and friends and of course the minister. My mother and father didn't come; 'We didn't come to the first and we are not coming to this one,' Mother said. However, Lillias always got on very well with them both, especially Mother, with whom she had a special bond. We went on to St Fillans Hotel by the lovely loch there and found a bottle of champagne in our room from Donald Pleasence who would have come up but he was working.

That evening in the bar a local laird and old friend of Lillias' came in and rather monopolised her in a proprietorial way and looked me up and down with that look which only aristocrats can manage. *My God, surely she could have done better than that*, the look said. Freed of him, we had an idyllic day or two there before returning to Barnes. We were in love and very happy. We still are.

*

The leading Irish writer Hugh Leonard lived across the road from us in Barnes. His output was astonishing: screenplays, television plays and adaptations as well as plays for the theatre. Immensely entertaining and a great raconteur, we became great friends with him and his wife Paula. He wrote several rich and wonderful parts for me in television at that time. I think my close proximity contributed to this and I loved doing his work.

Both Lillias and I were very busy, but I was uneasy that I was not developing the feature film side of my work. I decided it was time to move on from my agents, Gordon Harboard and my old friend Bill Harboard, and signed up with a brilliant and charismatic lady named Joy Jameson. She was dynamite. Casting directors were close friends; visiting American producers and directors were met on arrival at the airport; she was a ball of fire. Originally she was with the Heyman International Agency, but soon set up on her own. Donald was her number one client and, while I never knew for certain, I think he helped set her up. Although I was definitely her number two, she certainly improved things for me. Good work flowed and she was excellent over billing and money.

Lillias was busy, too, both on TV and in the theatre. She was brilliant in Dürrenmatt's *The Marriage of Mr Mississippi* at Hampstead Theatre Club, for instance.

1966 was a really busy and fruitful year for us both, especially when we realised Lillias was pregnant. The twins spent the summer holidays with us and we were all the more determined to live together as a proper family unit. This meant we had to move, and move quickly. It wasn't going to be easy to find a suitable place in London to fit our purse; and then we had an amazing stroke of luck.

Great friends of Lillias, Thea and Kenneth Hunt, were looking to move out of London from their house near Edgware Road to a place nearer his work for the Esso Petroleum plant near Southampton. They saw a place advertised and went to look at it; but the ceilings were too low for their furniture so they passed the details on to us, we who had hardly any furniture at all. We went to see the house and fell in love with it and decided this was where we were going to live. We would make everything fit around it. It was a fifteenth-century Sussex farmhouse with Horsham stone roof, sturdy ship's beams from the Armada and a priest's hole (a hiding place in the Civil War) up the main chimney. This was Goffs Manor, Crawley, complete with an old bakehouse, pond and swimming pool, and it became our home for the next twenty years. We paid £2,000 for a peppercorn rent of £7 a week and rates of £4 from the Commission for New Towns. What a stroke of luck. Lillias, with her genius for home-building and her gardening skills, gradually turned it into a most beautiful house and garden.

At the end of January 1967, a week after his birth in the London Clinic, David Max Vaughan Ohm arrived home at Goffs Manor amid much rejoicing on my part. He was born on a Saturday lunchtime and I missed the actual birth as I was rehearsing the aptly titled *Great Expectations*, a

Dickens adaptation for television by Hugh Leonard, in which I played the lawyer Jaggers.

This was my first and only go at parenthood, and I can't describe the feelings of joy and elation. I felt ten feet tall as I told Peter Bowles as we celebrated that night in the Queen's Elm. It was a truly wonderful moment when I first went into the room and saw them both. Lillias looked so beautiful and serene as I held him for the first time: our love child, we called him, which he surely was. What a strange coincidence that Lillias should have been playing *Getting Married* when we got married and David should be born when I was doing *Great Expectations* a year later.

Alex and Vicki left their Scottish school and were soon waiting for the bus opposite our new home to take them to their school in Horsham, and we were all together at last. I don't know what I was like as a stepfather; not too brilliant, I suspect. Lillias says I was never home anyway as the work escalated. The M23 hadn't been built yet and the journey to London took longer than now, and there was no Gatwick Express train either. Lines had to be learned at night and I must have been a fairly remote figure, either not there at all or demanding total hush as I worked on my script. Lillias was very busy as well, both in television and films, and how she ran the household so brilliantly and had her career as well was beyond me. Perhaps being a lightning study helped; I have to chew over my roles seemingly forever.

So that was family living as I had never known before. When those three pairs of eyes gazed at me in reproof or persuasion, and with David gurgling in the background, I was lost and never happier and more contented in my life.

11
LOCATION, LOCATION, LOCATION

O NE OF THE OCCASIONAL PERKS OF FEATURE FILM WORK is the opportunity to spend time shooting in exotic locations and, as my film career progressed, a share of this came my way.

A Twist of Sand is a Wilbur Smith thriller about lost treasure hidden in a wreck in the desert of German South West Africa (now Namibia). I was cast as a mentally retarded ex U-boat sailor: a pretty menacing, shambling figure. A straightforward part for me! Our locations were to be Malta for the close sea work and Libya for the desert work. Malta went well – there is an excellent sea tank there where storms and rough seas can be simulated. We had completed that, and some work at sea, when the Arab-Israeli Six Day War broke out. That scuppered our plans for Libya as there were several Jews in our unit.

Our film was not alone in having to cancel projects in Arab areas of the Middle East and most, like us, went hot-foot to Spain and the desert area of Almería in Andalucia. The city of Almería became a veritable film town, and locations in the desert itself were at a premium; it was a bit of a scramble to get a good spot. It was not uncommon to turn a corner and bump into a Western getting made, or a modern car chase. We did very well with our permit to work. In a bar one evening I met a location manager looking glum over his drink.

'I've got a permit,' he said, 'but your film's got a better one.' He was referring to the same piece of desert!

Accommodation was at a premium as well. James Mason's film was ensconced in the Agua Dolce, the only decent hotel in the area. At that time tourism had not started, there was no airstrip and the coast road from Malaga was a perilous affair – a dusty narrow road with huge drops down to the sea, the edge marked only with white stones. We flew into Malaga airport, at that time only a wooden terminal and passport building, and embarked on a Greek merchant navy boat loaded with all our gear and on which we were to live in Almería harbour for the duration of our shoot. The bunks were comfortable enough and we usually slept well after a long hard day in the desert.

It took a good hour's drive through the mountains, passing an abandoned gold mine with its ghost town, to get to work. The sand was particularly sharp, like fine glass: not much fun with wind machines blowing it in our faces simulating sandstorms. However, it was my first taste of Spain and I loved the place. We would call in at a little bar on the coast where they would show us their catch of the day and cook whatever we wanted on a wood fire in the middle of the bar. We'd wash this down with local wine and then head back to the boat.

Sometimes on Sundays there would be a bullfight; the excitement would build up during the week, and by Sunday the tension would be enormous. To watch this elegant and dangerous ritual was fascinating and the reaction to the death of a brave bull was almost like a collective orgasm. Outside the *corrida* the poor would queue for cheap meat. This was Spain in all its starkness. What a country – I was in love with it. But not General Franco and his Guardia.

One night there was a birthday party on the small boat we used in the film and which was moored next to our boat. Many of us were there, and if you weren't careful you were tossed into the mucky harbour water on arrival. At the time we were using African extras in various scenes, and their boss arrived in his open-topped American coupé, immaculately dressed and accompanied by his stunning girlfriend, to give instructions for the following day's work. He was directed to the birthday party boat to find the first assistant director and was promptly dumped into the water by some unruly matelot.

As this had been witnessed by his girlfriend, he was enraged and wanted compensation for his suit and wallet, which he claimed was lost in the water. He refused to be mollified, especially as no money was forthcoming, and so he sped off in an ugly mood. As the evening wore on he returned team-handed, all of them armed with knives and sticks.

This presented us with a tricky situation: how to get back to our own boat moored a couple of hundred yards away. Almería harbour, by the way, was not a pretty place but it did have some palm trees dotted about and we weren't too sure how many of this man's mates were lying in wait.

At this stage the Guardia took an interest in the situation. Our leading man, Richard Johnson, put down his glass and strolled over to the Guardia in true British style saying, 'It was harmless fun. My name is Richard Johnson; I am the star of the film and even I was thrown in the water,' upon which he was quickly handcuffed and put in a damp dingy cell in Almería jail. It took the producer and his assistants till the following morning, and only after much persuasion and many pesetas, to get him out. They knew the value of a film star all right!

As the film neared its end the money was coming to an end as well so the last scene, a shoot-out on the beach near Roquetas de Mar, was a bit of a rush job. Our grip, a giant of a man, went up and down the beach with the small camera-operator on his shoulders shooting the film with a hand-held. My friend Jeremy Kemp and I, fellow villains, had to die in the water whilst attempting escape. It is quite tricky to lie dead in the water and keep still, as the tide washes you out of shot at the wrong moment. The only way was to hook a foot under a rock, thereby reducing the effect of the tide and hopefully saving one's close-up!

Jeremy and I found ourselves on location together several times after that. A tremendous actor with a great appearance, he has given many brilliant performances in films and theatre and of course his breakthrough television role in *Z Cars*. Years can go by without our seeing each other, but we always pick up again where we left off, usually with a few tales to tell each other over a glass of claret or two.

I was in a great hurry to get back to England on that last day's filming and as soon as I had finished I had to dash to catch a plane at Malaga. This meant a nightmare drive along the coast road. In those days it was a dusty track with barely room for two cars, a prodigious drop and hairpin bends. How different that road is today, with beautiful tarmac, nice and wide, and barriers in the more dangerous places. In those days there were only stones painted white and often conspicuously missing at crucial bends. In order to make the plane the Spanish driver drove like a demon. I was terrified, cowering in the back with a bottle of Fundador!

The reason I was in such a hurry was that I had to go straight to Lisbon to shoot a film called *Hammerhead*. Hammerhead was the richest man in the world, dressed totally in white and a very nasty character indeed, and I was to play him. I had already flown from Spain during a couple of days off from shooting *A Twist of Sand* and had met the producer Irving Allen and the distinguished American director David Miller, and had a costume fitting. I have to say it was not the greatest script in the world, but I had a good leading part and the locations in Lisbon, on the beach in Cascais and on the water in the Tagus Estuary, were very pleasant spots to be in. Lillias came out for a holiday and all was well until one day on Hammerhead's luxury yacht in the estuary outside Lisbon Harbour.

The idea of this particular shot was to lower Hammerhead (i.e. me) onto the deck in a sedan chair attached to a helicopter; flunkies would open the door, I would step out, and the helicopter with chair attached would then fly away. As we rehearsed I stepped into the chair and was lifted some thirty feet or so into the air, expecting to be lowered back down onto the deck ready for me to step out and play the scene. However, it slowly dawned on me that things had gone wrong and I was being whisked away out to sea hundreds of feet up and was being bounced about in a balsa-wood box attached only by one metal hawser.

Bill Mervyn, one of the actors, was the first to become aware of the situation and panic ensued. The pilot was radioed. His problem was that the box was supposed to be empty but with my weight he was concerned the helicopter was unstable and may crash, in which case he had his engineer standing by with a large pair of shears to cut me loose into the water. And since there wasn't a door handle inside my box I had a very good chance of drowning. It was a strange sensation being bounced about in a balsa-wood box constructed by the art department and I remember wondering if it would break up and should I hang on to one side of it, although it wouldn't have done much good at that height.

Obviously it all ended well and there was a wonderful photo taken by Bill Mervyn of me about to attack the assistant director who had messed up the cue for the pilot. Lillias was blissfully unaware of all this, sunning herself by the hotel pool!

A couple of years later I was in a play in London and the pilot of the helicopter came round to see me after the show. He explained the incident to his girlfriend and started to shake and tremble. Apparently it was a very near miss indeed. Not a good enough film to die on I'm afraid.

Portugal was a lovely country to be in and Lisbon a fascinating city. It was thrilling to hear *Fado*, the Lisbon street songs, sung by brilliant if sometimes temperamental women accompanied by men with beautiful hand-painted guitars. I didn't understand a word, but such was the power and emotion that I was on my feet applauding. I also went to the Stadium of Light and saw Benfica in the European Cup; I was taken round to the dressing room afterwards where I met one of the great soccer legends, Eusébio, who graciously embraced me, being an actor from England.

The dictator Salazar was ruling Portugal at that time and it seemed an even more repressive regime than Franco's Spain. We were told that secret police were in our unit, and this was borne out when an actor got drunk in a nightclub and shouted, 'Down Salazar!' We were told in no uncertain manner that if there was any more of that, filming would be cancelled.

There were lighter moments, however. One day we were shooting in a town square and the local police were keeping it clear of traffic. Despite this, a tourist bus slipped the cordon and a party of American sightseers began getting out of the bus, thereby making it impossible for us to continue. Our producer Irving Allen was outraged and rushed to the scene waving angrily. The police arrived quickly and escorted the tourists back onto the bus. But as it sped away it became evident that a protesting Irving (who was also American) had been bundled up with all the tourists and it took quite a bit of time to retrieve him.

Of course, not every film I made during this period offered the luxury of a sun-kissed location shoot. The action of *The Bofors Gun*, a film adaptation of the play *Events While Guarding the Bofors Gun*, took place over one night's guard duty in peacetime Germany, and we shot it at night in winter in the distinctly mundane surroundings of an RAF barracks near Stevenage. With a cast including Nicol Williamson in brilliant form, David Warner, Ian Holm, John Thaw, and myself as the duty sergeant, and with Jack Gold directing his first feature film, it was a brilliant piece of work and became a great art-movie success. We all worked for minimum expenses and a percentage when the film went into profit. Universal Pictures taught us a sharp lesson here, for despite its success not a penny profit ever came our way. I think they call it creative accounting, or something like that.

I very nearly didn't get the part of the solid, upright Sergeant Walker, for I'd been playing a succession of thoroughly unpleasant characters both on television and film, and Jack Gold wasn't at all convinced I could play him.

'My wife thinks you can but I'm not so sure,' he told me as we met in the snug of a St John's Wood pub.

I'd just about convinced him when an old crone going up to the bar to replace her stout suddenly saw me and shrieked, 'Oh my gawd, he's the one who plays all the 'orrible parts!'

Strangely enough, in an odd sort of a way, I think that clinched it!

A couple of weeks before the film began I went to see Father who was in bed and looking very tired and weary. I've already mentioned the shell that landed on him in the First World War, killing three of his mates and filling Father's back and legs with shrapnel, and the crippling arthritis he developed in later life. Years of continuous pain had taken its toll, and I think he had just run out of steam. He shaved himself, I trimmed his hair, and he went off to hospital quite calmly, taking spare pyjamas, brush and comb and his shaving kit. I went back to start the film. It was February 1968 and the temperature in the barracks where we were shooting was freezing cold.

I was inconsolable the day Lillias broke the news to me that Father had died. I drove to work that night in my black VW completely shattered and numb with grief. I just lay on my bunk staring at the wall. Eventually there was a scene to shoot but I couldn't move. Ian Holm gently coaxed me down. I believe this was the first time I realised how much I loved my father; if only I had told him, although he would have deflected it in some way. What a role model he had been to me without my realising it. *Be ambitious but always skim the top off it. You can be an actor but you must support yourself, always. Always see the ludicrous side of things* – advice I've always tried to follow.

So Max's tempestuous relationship with Eva was over. She said, 'I did my duty by him and looked after him until the end.' And by Jove she did.

*

Joy Jameson had certainly galvanised my career and there was film and television work aplenty, although it must be said that not all the work was of the highest quality; which brings me to a film called *Taste of Excitement*, shot in Èze-sur-Mer below the beautiful village of Èze, situated between Nice and Monte Carlo. A truly sensational location, but not I'm afraid a sensational script.

After we'd been shooting for a week or two, a well-known theatre thriller writer turned up and became very excited and wrote all kinds of complex twists of plot into the script. This was wonderful until he left after a disagreement, leaving many convoluted plots unresolved. The result was chaotic with everyone trying to have a go to make the end of the film work.

I was playing the French detective who supposedly solves the case. As many as three script changes would come to my room, sometimes as late as midnight, and then it would be changed again when we got onto the set. What a shambles; but the sun was still shining and the sea sparkling blue and Nice and Monte Carlo as attractive as ever. Lillias came out and we stayed at the famous Welcome Hotel in Villefranche, where Cocteau created the tiny, beautiful fishermen's chapel and where Graham Sutherland stayed and left a painting or two hanging on the walls.

Donald Pleasence was doing *The Madwoman of Chaillot* further up the coast and introduced us to the Colombe d'Or at Saint-Paul-de-Vence up in the hills on the way to Grasse. Much has been written extolling this amazing hotel with its priceless paintings by Picasso, Chagall and other famous impressionists who donated them to the *patron* when they were unknown and poor in exchange for board and lodgings. They hang there quite without security, open to the world. Someone stole them once but they were too famous to dispose of and they were returned shortly after.

We were having dinner there one evening and at a nearby table sat Simone Signoret and Yves Montand. We needed some salt and called to our waiter who didn't appear to hear us. Simone picked up her table's salt cellar, strolled over to our table and deposited the salt without even breaking her conversation.

Lillias knew Dirk Bogarde, who lived nearby; and there we all were in the bar with the delectable Anouk Aimée whom I admired so much from her recently released *Un Homme et une Femme* with Jean-Louis Trintignant and that haunting music.

The Cannes Film Festival was on at this time: what a carnival. Lillias had returned home to young David and his two extra mums, Alex and Vicki, which meant I saw quite a bit of Donald; and one Sunday we found ourselves on the yacht of legendary film mogul Sam Spiegel in Antibes harbour. And what a yacht it was! I had never seen such opulence on water before. And it was star-studded as well. Danny Kaye was explaining how to rest very tired eyes: keep them open, cover them completely with your hands for one minute and don't blink, take your hands away and you have clearer eyes. It works, more or less. My best moment, though, was turning a corner on deck and coming face to face with Katharine Hepburn. We had a great chat; what a wonderful person, absolutely without affectation.

Loel Guinness had another superb yacht moored alongside and we went on board that one as well. It was even more opulent with priceless original art in the ward room and, in the centre of it all, every type of booze that you could imagine. At the very top of this pile was perched a highly polished bottle of Guinness; just to remind him, I suppose, of where all the wealth came from.

Then it was off to Bryan Forbes' villa for lunch, actually better described as luncheon. I am hopeless at parties even to this day, feeling awkward and very nervous. Sometimes this manifests itself in getting pie-eyed and then behaving very badly. However, on this occasion I was placed at table next to Yul Brynner's sophisticated and elegant French wife. My attempts at conversation weren't too brilliant: I just couldn't think of what to say. Suddenly someone mentioned Scotland and I seized my chance.

'Do you know Scotland?' I asked.

'Fife,' she replied.

'Oh, I know Fife,' I said. 'Who do you know there?'

'Fife,' she replied without the flicker of a smile. Of course I meant the county, but she was referring to the Earl!

Bryan's wife Nanette Newman had produced a wonderful meal, and her young daughter Emma was delightful and about the same age as Alex and Vicki. Nevertheless, I was relieved to be on our way back to Nice in Donald's huge Lincoln convertible, which he had brought over to Europe from California and was his pride and joy. Unfortunately it was now raining and we couldn't get the roof back on, and then the bloody thing broke down on the *autoroute*. Donald went off to use the phone about a kilometre away to get help and I was left in charge in the cold and wet in a lay-by for quite a long time. That'll teach me, I thought, trying to be *au-dessus de ma gare*. Ah well: it had been an amazing day, but now it was down to earth with a bump. Back to Èze-sur-Mer to learn the latest script changes for Monday.

Back in London after *Taste of Excitement* came to its thrilling end I met up with a producer named John Hawkesworth about a project for tele-vision called *The Gold Robbers*. The idea was that a huge haul of gold ingots was stolen from a London bank, driven to a waiting freight aircraft and flown to Switzerland. I was to play the Chief Superintendent hunting down the suspects one by one until we finally got to Mr Big. It became a highly successful programme, and by the time I caught him in episode 13 we had reached the very top of the audience ratings.

John, an ex-regular army officer, was a highly experienced and excellent producer. His private car was emblazoned with stickers saying *Don't Flood Rutland* which we all thought was hilarious, and indeed was unless you happened to live in Rutland, which he did.

We had some fine actors among our gold robbers: George Cole, Roy Dotrice and the wonderful Bernard Hepton among others. Lovely Artro Morris was my loyal sergeant, and the principal director was a guy called Don Leaver. Don and I hit it off at once; I loved his energy and enthusiasm and particularly his ability to excite cast and crew into believing that what they were doing was special and exceptional. There weren't many bored actors doing crosswords on *The Gold Robbers*; there was genuine delight in the work.

It was successful all right, but there was one big snag: it wasn't in colour. It was on tape with filmed excerpts and all in black and white. John moved on to produce *Upstairs, Downstairs* in colour. The days of monochrome were virtually over and so our lovely *Gold Robbers* was never repeated or sold abroad. The age of colour had arrived and I expect our pride and joy ended up in the bin... ah well, it's a transitory game! Actually, Don and I were put under contract for a few weeks to try and make a sequel; but somehow it didn't seem right in colour and so I moved on.

*

I was asked to meet the great Sam Peckinpah who had come to the UK to make a film of his adaptation of *The Siege of Trencher's Farm*. His arrival caused great excitement and the competition to be in the film was keen.

At the interview, after a few questions, Sam suddenly said, 'Not for a thousand years, boy, not for a thousand years.' I was amazed: he had quoted my dialogue to Private Evans on his arrest in the guard room of *The Bofors Gun*. Arrested for murder, Evans asked me, 'Can I go home now, sarge?'

'Not for a thousand years, boy...'

David Warner was Private Evans and he had recently played the priest superbly in Sam's wonderfully lyrical film *The Ballad of Cable Hogue*. Sam had obviously seen *The Bofors Gun*, and that little scene got me the part against much opposition! I was thrilled to bits, and a truly amazing four months or so was under way.

The film's story begins with the arrival in a remote Cornish village of a brilliant American mathematician, played by Dustin Hoffman, and his wife on holiday. However his wife, Susan George, is a village girl who has gone to America and married there. The arrival is greeted with hostility by the men of the village and leads to a violent confrontation.

Rehearsals began at once. Sam called us his 'British Wild Bunch' and we certainly were. I played the head man of the village and my lads were a tough lot. Even so, some of the scenes were quite comical; but Sam said to the crew, 'Never laugh at the actors – they'll start to think they're funny.' (Alan Ayckbourn said the same thing when I did a play of his, but that comes later.) Another edict of Sam's was that actors were not allowed to go to rushes; that is to say, to watch all the takes at the end of the day's shooting. However, he was preaching to the converted: this was a cast more likely to be in the hotel bar at the end of a hard day.

One morning Sam suddenly announced he had changed the film title from *The Siege of Trencher's Farm* to *Straw Dogs*. I was polite about it, but I really had no idea what it meant and still don't really. I believe there is some literary allusion, but I am not sure.

Just before going down to Cornwall on location a party was thrown for the cast: men only, and served by very attractive waitresses. Champagne and wine flowed, music played and, as the meal ended, things got a bit rowdy. I am terrible at parties, and by now I had retreated to the kitchen where I had a quiet beer with the owner and his wife and dog: a nice peaceful scene by comparison. I went back in to see T. P. McKenna dancing on the table. I am not sure whether the table gave way or he just fell, but he crashed to the floor. The next morning T. P. – who was playing the Major, the village squire – was in great pain and, arm in sling, went to see Sam, deeply upset that he would have to drop out. But Sam merely said: 'So the Major's got a broken arm. There's no reference to it in the script, but the Major has his arm in a sling.' I can't think offhand of a director who would not have recast, but that was Sam for you.

Rehearsals over, T. P. McKenna, arm in sling, and the rest of us set off to shoot *Straw Dogs* in Cornwall. Our hotel was in St Ives, the lovely seaside fishing village famous for its community of artists: Ben Nicholson,

Barbara Hepworth and all. We started filming at once. Locations were all in the more remote parts of Cornwall.

With Sam it was as well to know your role inside out. One day there was a scene of us walking down a country lane when Dustin in his E-Type Jaguar sped past, forcing us to jump for safety. My character had a long angry outburst at this but the speech was not scheduled for that day. We rehearsed and, as Dustin sped off, instead of 'cut' Sam said 'Vaughan – speak!' I'd learned the speech, just in case, so all was well. The lesson was to be prepared for all eventualities when filming!

We worked hard and we played hard. Socially we had a really good time, and drinks, jokes and good company flowed freely. Thirsts were quenched regularly in the hotel bar in the evenings and, as predicted, no one worried about seeing rushes. One convivial evening at the bar around ten o'clock, Sam poked his head round the door. 'Wanna see some picture?' He had set up an impromptu screening of our first month's work and despite the 'no rushes' edict couldn't resist showing it to us. So, drinks in hand, we trooped in and watched it with gales of laughter as we sent each other up. Actually I thought everyone was pretty good, except for one fat slob who didn't seem to be doing anything much. I hate watching myself until the job is done and dusted.

Sam hated interferences from above and was not best pleased when moguls from Hollywood complained that our Cornish accents were not all the same and ordered a dialect coach. He duly arrived one morning when I was preparing to do a very emotional scene. My daughter had gone missing and my character was distraught. He got on my nerves telling me my O's were not round enough! Sam saw I was a bit disturbed, came over and the coach explained what was wrong with my O's. Sam listened carefully and then said, 'In every great work of art there is always a flaw,' and walked off. End of dialect coach!

June Brown came on the film as my wife. There was a scene when Susan George brought some laundry to be done by June. I was brooding in the back of the room cleaning my gun. Sam cut out the scene as it didn't take the plot forward. I told June I had asked for it to be cut as she was too good in it. What a lovely lady, and a superb actress. A few years ago she took time out from Dot Cotton in *EastEnders* to do a TV film in which I played her husband once more, and we had a good laugh about our time together on *Straw Dogs*.

If any problem cropped up during the filming, there was an incredible character who dealt with it. He had been a prisoner of the Japanese at the end of the war, working in a factory in Nagasaki, and had survived the dropping of the hydrogen bomb. Small and nimble (and probably riddled with radiation) he was officially the unit driver but would run errands at lightning speed for one and all. We called him Mr Fixit.

One of the cast who had better be nameless wanted a car: he had no licence or insurance, but nonetheless hired a car. Late that evening after much celebration he and a friend went for a drink but got no further than smashing against the car-park wall. Mr Fixit came to the rescue.

'Don't worry, I'll dump it down an old tin-mine shaft and it will be lost for good and all.'

Sadly the following morning the car was still there. In the dead of night Mr Fixit mistakenly put the wrong car, a similar model, down the tin mine. I am afraid it was some poor holidaying hotel resident whose car was lost for good and all.

Sam approached me one morning saying, 'I woke up with a half hard-on this morning. Guess we'd better get some broads up from Plymouth.' Mr Fixit went to work and next day they duly arrived. I don't think many people indulged but it seemed to typify Sam's Wild West approach to life.

With the constant succession of social evenings coupled with carrying the film on his shoulders, Sam fell ill and went into hospital in London. *Force majeure* was called: that is, the film was suspended, Sam's illness being considered an 'Act of God'. I couldn't help thinking, though, that the constant black coffee laced with (probably) brandy dispensed by his lovely assistant Katy Haber might have helped God act a bit. *Force majeure* is a bit nervous-making. Sitting at home with no pay, not knowing how long it will last or even if the film will start up again, is a worry. Sam soon recovered though and it was back to Cornwall to finish the film.

The climax of the film was the attack on Trencher's Farm and was filmed over several nights. The house was totally remote, by the sea at St Just, and we wrecked the place. Whatever Sam told us to do, we did it. It was wild. I went through a window with the curtains on fire only to have my feet blown off by the special-effects department.

These scenes over, all that remained was for us to head back to London to Twickenham Studios to shoot a few interiors. Our time on location was coming to an end. Winding down and returning to some sort of normality was not easy – especially for Sam. On our last night in Cornwall he went back to his rented cottage nearby, threw his new wife out into the road and proceeded to smash up the contents of the cottage. The owner eventually persuaded him to stop by pleading, 'That is a Ming vase, please don't break it!' His wife had to walk back to St Ives and arrived in our hotel cold and distraught. The following day Sam reluctantly got on a train to London crying out, 'I don't want to leave my film!' That's commitment for you.

I left St Ives with many happy memories of the place. One of the best was John Belaris and Bodil, his beautiful Norweigan partner, who ran a great restaurant superbly. We were all frequent visitors and were made to feel part of the place. Startled customers were astonished to be waited on by Dustin, giving one of his best method performances as a very attentive waiter! We had a lovely family holiday towards the end of the film and John took us around in his E-Type Jaguar. The twins were by now teen-agers and both stunning lookers. After Lill, David and I left, they stayed on with John and Bodil and worked in the restaurant – their first job, I think.

When the film was released it caused much outrage and was banned from television for thirty years. Personally I think it is a classic, and its message is even stronger today. How times have changed. Nowadays I believe Susan George's performance would have won her an Oscar. It is simply a great film.

A couple of us were cast almost at once in the film *The Pied Piper* on location in Germany. My colleague from *Straw Dogs* got very drunk on arrival and ended up in the fountain in the main square of Rothenburg ob der Tauber giving the Nazi salute and shouting '*Heil Hitler!*' This did not go down well with the local police, and the following day he was back in England. No *Straw Dogs* behaviour here!

Actually things were pretty tense when John Hurt arrived as his replace-ment. On his first morning there was a big crowd scene. The extras were all lined up ready and John walked through them and up to the director and camera with a bottle of Pils and a glass, poured out the beer and knocked it back in one. There was a huge cheer and the tension was over. It was a brilliant entrance and the point brilliantly made.

The director was French and had not directed in English before. The trouble was, his English was poor, yet he wouldn't allow us to speak to him in French. His reply to any question was always the same: 'What's the matter, you 'ave a problem?'

In the end if we had a problem we sorted it out amongst ourselves. John Hurt, Diana Dors and Roy Kinnear became good mates and we all got on well. I was devastated when Roy was later killed in a riding accident on *The Three Musketeers*. What a loss. A lovely man and a brilliant actor.

Rothenburg, a historic town on the banks of the river Tauber with lovely old buildings and picturesque narrow streets, was badly bombed in the Second World War. After the war it was rebuilt exactly as it was before. History has it that in the sixteenth century, Rothenburg was captured and sacked by warring neighbours but the local beer was so good that the enemy called the whole thing off and got stuck into the beer instead! This event is re-enacted every year, and took place while we were there. Men on horseback in period costume and carrying pikes trotted round the narrow streets and were given a stein of beer at any house they stopped at. As this went on for three days, and the weather was extremely hot, many steins were consumed and the riding got faster and faster!

All this was accompanied by a gathering of the country's Neo-Fascist Party which seemed to be doing extremely well. I found it all both oppressive and depressing. Was my friend from *Straw Dogs* so wide of the mark as he shouted in the fountain?

*

Härte 10 was a miniseries for Bavaria Atelier in Munich, where the interiors were shot. However, the film was mostly shot in South Africa and we were based in Johannesburg. I was signed up not to appear in live theatre in South Africa, but took the view that filming was international and you should go wherever it took you. I was never really happy with myself about that decision. Should I have gone? Ah well. In hindsight I was glad to experience it at first hand as it proved a real eye-opener for me. To witness the reality of living under the system of apartheid was devastating. I saw a woman beaten up by the police at the bus depot. Her crime? She was trying to get home to her township after work, but had forgotten her pass.

Once Jeremy Kemp and I were shooting in a township which had a small shed which turned out to be a cinema. We were both recognised and were made very welcome. At the end of the day our police escort said it was too dangerous to stay and left us. We stayed on and had a great evening sharing root beer and stories with these wonderful people.

The German crew and unit were not the most efficient, being a bit excitable and not very organised. Once, when we were filming in Kruger National Park, we worked a bit late and arrived at the exit to find that we were locked in for the night with a few wild animals for company. Panic ensued until Kemp, with the aid of a couple of ladders, climbed over a high fence, found a warden's house, got keys and let us out. No wonder we won the war.

I had scenes to do in Namibia, which was not then independent, being a South African protectorate known as South West Africa. The journey was amazingly beautiful, across the Kalahari desert to Walvis Bay, all in small aircraft. One eight-seater was run by a husband-and-wife team – he the pilot, she the air hostess. All very friendly and informal. Then a car journey along the Atlantic coast to the town of Swakopmund. There were huge sand dunes that creaked and moved in the winds from the ocean. They had snowploughs which were used to clear the roads of sand. The sand is so rich in minerals that you could scuff your feet and find semi-precious stones. No wonder De Beers had mines there. I met a doctor in a bar who showed me thirty-nine uncut diamonds given him by a grateful patient for saving his life.

Of course the country was under South African apartheid laws. This was heartily disliked by the German hotel manager who was happy to hand over whenever independence came to Namibia and go back to Germany. One day he had a real problem. A planeload of tourists from the Philippines were coming to stay. 'What colour are they to be classified?' he asked the authorities. The answer was that a separate room had to be allocated for meals to be served and also drinks served there; but they were not allowed in any of the hotel bars or the main restaurant. I wonder if they had a happy and relaxed holiday!

*

This is a story about the perils of film-making. *The Blockhouse* was based on an amazing true happening in Poland in the Second World War. The setting was Gdansk, 1942. There were many Todt workers there: that is, forced labour conscripted by the Germans from all the occupied countries of Europe. They were harshly treated, held in camps and made to work without rest.

Early one morning while they were being marched to work there was a severe air-raid. Everyone fled for cover as low-flying planes strafed them. Seven disparate Todt workers took refuge in the entrance to a large concrete bunker. As the bombs fell they found themselves trapped inside; they were bombed in and there was no way out. However, these hungry, overworked men soon found that they were in a huge provision bunker. There was food, wine, candles, blankets – everything they needed. What a celebration.

Seven years later, in 1949, the street above was being cleared ready for redevelopment when faint tappings were heard from below. Two men were brought to the surface. One died at once in the sunlight, the second in hospital a day or two later having told the story.

Those seven years were the basis of our film. The cast featured Peter Sellers, Jeremy Kemp, Charles Aznavour and others. The producer, Antony Rufus Isaacs, was a lovely chap who was hugely enthusiastic about his film. So certain of success was he that he had started shooting before he had all the money needed. He obviously thought investors would flock in on seeing early rushes and rough cuts.

Sadly this did not happen and the money ran out with two or three more weeks' filming to do. The cast and crew had a meeting and agreed to finish the film without pay. Desperate efforts were made to get the money. Our young seventeen-year-old co-producer Edgar Bronfman Junior's father flew in, took a look and flew out again.

In the end Hemdale Films came to the rescue and we all got paid. There was then a problem with who owned it: Hemdale or the original company? This was never resolved and so the film was not released. We saw a video of it not long ago and frankly it was pretty awful. There were some good scenes but it was painfully slow and one-paced, very darkly lit and with poor sound. So maybe it doesn't matter much who owned it after all!

I have to say though that, until disaster struck, it was a very enjoyable film to make. Antony Rufus Isaacs made us very comfortable in a hotel in St Peter Port, Guernsey. Our blockhouse was the former military hospital built by the Germans during their occupation of the island. It was the perfect location and this was our Gdansk bunker: deep underground, with a labyrinth of corridors and rooms on different levels.

We worked French hours: that is to say, from 12 noon to 8 P.M. without a break. We would meet about 10.30 A.M. to plan out the day's work and rehearse a bit, then descend into the darkness at 12 and stay down there as I said until 8 P.M. It took a little time on coming out of the damp gloom to get one's eyes and balance adjusted, but then it was back to the hotel for a drink or two as soon as possible.

On the first evening we turned up at the hotel bar tired, dirty and casually dressed. The head waiter immediately barred us. Jackets and ties only, he said. Our mad assistant director said, 'Right lads, jackets and ties *only*.' So off we went to our rooms and reappeared in the correct attire. It worked. From then on we were allowed in the bar no matter how scruffy.

I really liked my part. I was a Frenchman who had collaborated with the Germans; loathed and ostracised by the others, I was isolated and had to live on my own. Eventually I couldn't take it any more, went mad and killed myself. That was a really good scene to do.

There's always a bit of waiting around when filming. Sometimes we found ourselves outside with nothing to do, and my friend Jeremy Kemp and I would organise a bit of impromptu cricket. We made a ball with gaffer tape, our bats were pieces of wood, and stumps were chalked on a wall. But it was good fun and keenly fought.

Peter Sellers, who normally did not mix or join in socially with cast and crew, asked to have a bat. He was very funny when preparing to bat, taking an elaborate stance and looking to see where exactly the fielders were placed.

'I'm a relation of Brian Sellars,' he told us.

Kemp and I pretended to be impressed even though the great Yorkshire captain's name was spelt -ars not -ers like Peter's.

Many years later, I played Sellers' father in *The Life and Death of Peter Sellers*. I researched his biography and found to my amazement that when Peter was a boy on a variety tour with his family, they arrived in a town to find their name wrongly spelt on the posters: they were billed as Sellers. They preferred it to their real name Sellars and kept it that way thereafter. So was he really related to the great Brian Sellars? Who knows.

12
BEING GROUTY

ON LOOKING THROUGH MY CV I am surprised to see how much work I did. Why weren't we rich? Lillias and I lived well and had a lovely home, but there were family commitments and the money earned from TV work was less than you probably think. The BBC's fees were not high, and everyone else's seemed to be based on those. My first TV work (a walk-on in 1952) paid eight guineas! Things got a lot better than that, but were still nothing like today's possible earnings.

Lillias and I went to Cornwall and played the farmer and his wife in the film *Malachi's Cove*. It was good to be working together on equal terms. The only other film we were both in was *Intimate Reflections*, in which Lillias starred with Anton Rodgers while I had a very minor role as The Salesman. This latter film was directed and produced by the soon-to-be hugely success-ful Don Boyd, who never employed either of us again! Ah well…

Talking of disappointments, I was thrilled to be cast in *The Mackintosh Man*, working with Paul Newman and directed by the legendary John Huston, but what an anticlimax to my hopes and expectations that turned out to be. In the film Newman was supposed to be Australian, but he was really struggling with the accent which made him nervous and unsure. I was interrogating him as the police inspector and had to dominate him. He wouldn't meet my eye so I banged on the table, the blue eyes met mine and we played the scene.

He was a huge star, though. One day on location in London a large department store emptied as staff and customers alike rushed out to catch a glimpse of him passing by. But he still couldn't do an Australian accent!

He and John Huston were obviously great buddies, and one day after a prolonged and apparently liquid lunch they returned to the huge room in which the rest of us were waiting to do the next scene. Huston smiled and said in an authoritarian voice, 'Action.' The only problem was, nobody knew what the scene was to be so nothing happened.

I was on the film for over two weeks and he always called me Brunskill, the name of my character: never, ever Peter Vaughan, on or off the set. His way of directing was to do the scene himself, setting me a series of exact positions for particular lines. The problem was, he was several inches taller than me; so, for example, if I hit my mark, I couldn't reach the door to open it. There was much 'Brunskill!' being called out. I'm afraid I wasn't very happy at all. What a disappointment.

At the weekend I went up to Wem to see my mother, Eva. She had terminal lung cancer but she did not know; she just thought she had some-thing wrong with her chest and would soon be better. She was now living at home being looked after by Meg, her sister, who lived nearby. On a previous visit, before her discharge from hospital, I had been called to the consultant's office and told that she was terminally ill: nothing could be done for her and she should go home. He said it was for me as her next of kin to decide whether to tell her the situation or not. I wrestled with myself over what to do. She seemed happy that she had lost weight; she ordered a jacket by mail order and showed it off like a model.

'Look at my ankles,' she said to me. 'I've always had good ankles.'

I talked to Aunt Meg about it, but in the end it was left to me to decide. I didn't tell her. I didn't want to frighten her; but was I failing this courage-ous person? Would she rather have known? Were there things she would want to do or people to see? I still don't know to this day whether I was right to keep it from her or not.

That weekend I took her for a drive to the Wrekin, a local mountain, and she loved the view and the air. On Sunday afternoon I had to drive back as I had an early film call on the Monday. She was very keen on cross-words, and just before I left she gave me a clue from the *Sunday Telegraph* which I couldn't do.

'Surely you know that,' she said. 'You're supposed to be the intellectual in the family.'

Time to go, we said goodbye and I walked up the street to where my car was parked and drove slowly past the little house. She was standing at the window. I waved, tooted the horn and drove away. The following morning about eleven I got the news via Aunt Meg and Lillias that she had died in the night.

I felt little emotion, unlike when Father died while we were shooting *The Bofors Gun* when I lay on my bunk numb with grief. I calmly got on with filming.

Life had not treated my mother well. An unhappy marriage, a son who fundamentally disagreed with all she stood for, and so much unfulfilled potential. She would have been a wonderful actress had she been allowed. That memory of her standing in the window remains vividly in my mind; and, despite all our differences, deep down I loved her and I believe she loved me.

At the end of the week, my filming complete, I went to John Huston and said, 'Thank you, Mr Huston. I have learned a lot. By the way, my name is Peter Vaughan.'

'I know,' he said. 'And I'm sorry to hear you lost your mother.'

On that note I left for the funeral.

*

In 1974, after quite a long stint away from home on location, the chance to do a play in the West End could not have come at a better time. It was a pretty average thriller called *The Pay-Off* and my part was pretty average too, but the prospect of spending some time living at home with Lill and the family was too good to miss. Nigel Patrick directed and played the lead. We opened to fairly mediocre reviews, but the play was quite commercial and in for a solid run. We had a good cast including Peter Sallis and Dulcie Gray, and I was the villain once again.

Nigel was a quite brilliant actor on stage or screen, but I'm afraid he did get bored playing the same role week after week. He would start to fool around and loved to corpse his fellow actors: that is, make them giggle and laugh. Wonderful Peter Sallis was especially susceptible to corpsing, and on one occasion it got so bad Nigel gave him a dressing down at the interval. A bit unfair, I thought, since he was the one who made him laugh in the first place. I am a bit po-faced about private jokes among the actors. I believe people have paid to see the play and so it's pretty hard to get me to break up, but he did get me good and proper once. Nigel would have made a great ventriloquist. He would assume a fixed smile, in which the lips did not move, and make remarks during other people's speeches. In one scene I had a long angry tirade at him, and one night during a pause he smiled and, lips not moving, said, 'Have you seen the front row? They're all Yappanese!' (It's hard to say 'J' without moving your lips.)

I carried on with my speech, taking in the audience, and sure enough the whole front row was taken up with inscrutable Japanese. I finished my speech. There was a pause; then Nigel clicked his heels, bowed and said, 'Ah so.' That finished me, and I had to turn my back on the audience to recover.

Another night we were standing together by the piano listening to Dulcie holding forth centre stage. Again the lips did not move: 'Look at Dulcie. Her false eyelashes are falling off. She's fucking mad, you know.'

One good thing about a West End run is that you are able to do other work during the day, except on matinee days of course. During *The Pay-Off* I did a very funny biscuit commercial with the hilarious Harry Fowler, and also some radio drama. I've mentioned before that I loved radio acting, and one of my biggest regrets is that my poor sight no longer allows me to do it. I had three wonderful radio directors with whom I was lucky enough to work pretty regularly: Kay Patrick, Jane Morgan at Broadcasting House and Gordon House at the BBC World Service at Bush House. All three were brilliant directors. My favourite actor to work with was Nigel Anthony. We both love modern jazz (he is an accomplished drummer) and we seemed to know instinctively what we were up to. He got rhythm!

I was nominated a couple of times in the seventies for an award for best radio actor. The first time it just so happened that Keith Waterhouse was nominated for best play, so we had a drink and went along together to the Savoy Hotel for the awards. We explained who we were to a somewhat officious lady who coldly told us to go and sit at the back. She warmly welcomed another actor and put him at the front, so I knew there was no way I had won before it even started. A long evening followed, and Keith didn't win either. I must say I thought it a pretty shabby way to treat someone of his stature, but Keith as always shrugged and laughed. I was nominated again the following year but I didn't attend: I couldn't go through all that again. Still, I was very proud to be nominated.

You obviously are not restricted in radio by your physical appearance. I had a very good example of this when Jane Morgan cast me as Old Man

Dorrit in a Dickens serial with Angela Pleasence as Little Dorrit. The old man was small and with a weak chest. There was absolutely no way I could have played him in any other medium than radio.

Whilst in *The Pay-Off* we finished one serial with Jane in mid afternoon and all went to the club opposite Broadcasting House. After a glass of wine or two it was time to go to the theatre, and I thought a nice walk down Regent Street and across Piccadilly to the Comedy Theatre would set me up for the evening. Sadly the cold evening air had the opposite effect, and I staggered into the theatre quite frankly absolutely smashed. Peter Sallis dipped my head in cold water and I sort of pulled myself together for the performance. I thought I was really good that night, but I wasn't! I was so slow I put twenty minutes on to the running time of the play. I expected a most fearful dressing down from Nigel, if not the sack. I think he must have known how upset I was because he just helped me through the evening. I really thought that very special of him. Motto, thespians: don't drink and drive and don't drink and act – ever. I never have since that day.

*

Another job cropped up during the run, this time a TV situation comedy. Had I not been in the play I wouldn't have done it as there were not enough episodes to make it financially attractive and it would probably have clashed with other more lucrative work. However, the scripts were brilliant and I loved the part. The format was to do an episode a week, rehearsing every day and doing the show on Sunday in front of a live studio audience. I didn't realise at the time *Porridge* would become a genuine comedy classic, still hugely popular. I had, more or less accidentally, turned up in something pretty special.

The scripts by Dick Clement and Ian La Frenais were superb, and director Sydney Lotterby guided the proceedings perfectly. No fooling around with Sydney at the helm. As for the cast, one can only admire the principal actors Ronnie Barker (Fletcher), Richard Beckinsale (Godber), Fulton Mackay (Mr Mackay) and Brian Wilde (Mr Barraclough) – all totally believable and giving equally stunning performances week after week. Their standard never wavered.

I played 'genial' Harry Grout, Slade Prison's tobacco baron. He and his minders were in fact far from genial and the rest of the inmates went in fear of him. He lived very comfortably in a neatly furnished cell with his own radio and pet budgerigar, Seymour – that is, until he ate him! He was very funny but also a bit menacing: a real villain in fact. It wasn't a big part, only appearing in a few episodes. He was referred to a good deal, though, and so the part seemed bigger than it really was.

I loved playing him, and to work with Ronnie Barker as Fletcher was very special, a real privilege. Character actor, stand-up comedian, song and dance man and even writer: he had it all. And such a lovely, modest man too. Quite irreplaceable.

I was astonished at the impact my character had made, and for the first time I had to experience recognition wherever I went. 'Let you out, have they Grouty?' was a favourite one, and still is even today. Recognition in general is a natural consequence of appearing regularly on TV and film, but this Harry Grout thing is something different.

A few years ago Lillias and I went to see the stage adaptation of *The Producers*, our favourite film of all time, at Drury Lane Theatre. There were crowds outside, and as we arrived by taxi we were approached by ticket touts looking for trade. 'It's Grouty!' We were immediately escorted by them through the queue and up the steps to the theatre entrance where we were solemnly introduced to the theatre staff as 'Mr and Mrs Grout'.

Recognition is not always such great fun as that. Being hugged and asked for a kiss by elderly ladies, for instance, is not my idea of heaven. But as Lillias rightly says, the time to worry is when you aren't recognised at all.

Supermarkets are tricky places for recognition. There is no escape until the bill is paid; no matter what aisle you go down, the persistent pursuer will be waiting for you at the end. A couple of examples come to mind.

One very hot afternoon in Spain I was shopping alone. At the time I was getting ready to play a very scruffy part: my hair was unwashed and unkempt, I had a two-week growth of prickly stubble for a beard and, despite only being dressed in a thin T-shirt, shorts and a pair of espadrilles, I was sweating profusely. I must have been quite a sight as I was also in a hurry.

As I sped round I noticed I was being watched and pursued wherever I went by a rather sinister figure. He was beautifully attired in shirt, tie and a smart white suit and with not a bead of perspiration. As I queued at the cash desk he slowly came up to me.

'I'm very disappointed in you,' he declared. 'On television you look immaculate. It's very sad to see how you have let yourself go.'

'I'm sorry,' I said, paid my bill and fled!

Another time, in Stratford-on-Avon buying a few things for the journey home to Scotland, I was spotted by a family with a baby in a pram. The man pursued me into a shop and kept asking what he had seen me in. Not having been in his sitting room that was a difficult one to answer!

'But what would it have been?' he repeated.

Fed up with him I said, 'Oh, many.'

'Thought so,' he said and went back to his wife with the news. 'It's *Many*!'

I escaped while he was being given some stick by his wife, but he was right – I have been in 'Many'!

*

I wasn't sorry to see the end of *The Pay-Off*. Not a good play; but it had served its purpose, enabling me to be at home. And what a home it was. I have already mentioned how lucky we had been to get it from the council at a peppercorn rent, and after a year or two we were able to buy it cheaply. It was an ideal family house, and with the birth of David Max in January 1967, and Alex and Vicki leaving their Scottish school to come down to live with us, the family was complete.

The twins were really lovely girls and very close. I was a pretty poor step-parent for them. I should have been more easy-going and relaxed, but I was working hard most of the time and suffered the actor's fear of (a) not knowing my lines and (b) not being good enough in the part anyway.

It must have been quite an austere scene and in great contrast to the times they had with their No. 1 Dad, Peter Burton. No longer doing much acting, he had become a very successful photographic model living in Chelsea where he had a rich social life. Smooth, sophisticated and very good-looking, he would come down and whisk them away for weekends in London. How they must have longed for those visits. Still, although we are a volatile lot and had a few tricky moments, times were good.

Lill, of course, was extremely busy too, but had the gift of working while running a home and family with no difficulty. She always had animals too. She adores them and they adored her. Ben Poodle, for instance, was always in her dressing room and even gave one or two performances – and always knew his cues for entrances and exits! David Max came off best, though, as in effect he had three mothers, always getting what he wanted from one or another of them.

By now, though, it was 1975; the girls had finished school and technical college courses and were now both out in the world. Alex was working in Brussels, where she did voice-overs in English for Dutch and Belgian TV commercials as well as her office work. Vicki was working successfully as an actress in repertory theatres. Straight in with no training, just like me.

Meanwhile young David Max, aged nine years, gave an excellent performance as an ill-treated child in a Thames TV film called *The Shuttlecock*. He was very real and had stillness and concentration rarely seen in one so young. Further work was offered but he turned it down as it would have meant losing his place in the school football and cricket teams. Wise boy: acting is a precarious business. Around this time he was given a snare drum and that settled his future. The jazz scene's gain is perhaps the theatre's loss, but his mum and I are both thrilled listening and watching him at work.

Whilst at home I had done a TV or two and had a smallish part in the film 11 *Harrowhouse* with John Gielgud and James Mason. I was able to tell Gielgud how much his Hamlet had inspired me in Singapore at the end of the war. To me it was the perfect Hamlet, and made me all the more determined to get back into the theatre. He was very courteous and tried hard to reciprocate in some way but I was never in the same league. Modest and charming, he also had a waspish tongue. His voice was louder than perhaps he realised; and once at lunch he said, 'I don't know why James Mason is doing this part. Ralph (Richardson) would have been so much better. But I suppose he has to take everything because of that terrible wife.' James was lunching at a table only a few feet away!

They worked brilliantly together, though. I remember one very long scene in which they both had great chunks of dialogue and I had about ten lines of questions as a detective. It was the end of a long day and, after shooting both their close-ups in turn, it was decided to do my close-up. Although no longer on camera, they both stayed and gave full performances all through rehearsals and takes of my close-up. On some films, cues would be read out by an assistant director or a continuity girl, the so-called stars having gone home. But those two were totally professional and therefore helped me enormously. Two truly great actors and it was a privilege to work with them.

*

There are lots of old jokes about agents: about them taking a percentage of what the performer earns while sitting in the office doing little or nothing. However, this is just not true. A good agent beavering away on your behalf, advising you on the pros and cons of taking or getting a job, is absolutely essential if you are going to stick around in the business; and, on the whole, I have been very fortunate in this regard.

After the huge success of *Entertaining Mr Sloane,* Gordon Harboard took me to meet Cubby Broccoli and Harry Saltzman to see about my being a James Bond villain. Harry said I looked far too pleasant and there was no way I could play a villain. As I was playing almost exclusively vicious, sinister and dangerous men at that time, I felt Gordon might have fought a bit harder for me; but he didn't, so I thought it was time for a change of agent. (Incidentally I have felt sulky about the Bond films ever since, especially when stopped and asked, 'You were in the Bond films, weren't you?' I must look like someone else; I don't know who – I haven't seen them. There's paranoia for you!)

So I moved to Heyman International, which is how I came to be taken on by Joy Jameson. She was full of energy and with a huge personality. Shortly, with the help of Donald Pleasence, she set up on her own and there I stayed for several happy years.

For financial reasons, American films were often set up and made in London, and many American producers and directors were ensconced in West End hotels. Joy was very hot at meeting them at Heathrow on their arrival and therefore was quickly 'in' for potential parts for her clients. However, despite all this work I had an uneasy feeling that she only really saw me as an understudy for Donald and that I was sometimes playing work he had turned down.

Later, with the Americans no longer coming to the UK in such numbers, I felt I needed an agent in Los Angeles to work with her. Donald had one; why not me? This seemed to annoy Joy. She said I didn't need an international agent – she could handle everything. I talked about this to Donald when we were both in *Malachi's Cove.* When I got back to London, Joy told me I was difficult and terminated our association. That's polite for giving me the sack. She dressed it up by saying she would work with me for three months while I found someone else, but I left at once.

I went to see a couple of high-class agents without success, but then Dennis Selinger, head of the London branch of MCA, to my delight and surprise took me on. He had a vacancy, having just parted company with the wonderful Trevor Howard. And so I had, in my view, the best agency and indeed the best agent in London. This was in 1972 and I'm happy to say I have been with the organisation ever since – so perhaps I'm not so difficult after all, Joy.

In 1976 another agency, London Management, merged with us and one or two people moved on, but Dennis Selinger said that I must stay and introduced me to a London Management jewel named Michael Anderson. Michael came to see me in the West End playing Sergeant Rough in the famous thriller *Gaslight*, and thus began an association which lasted until his retirement seventeen years later – far too soon in my view. We worked together brilliantly and I don't remember ever having a difference of view about my work. He kept me in almost continuous employment and gave me great encouragement and confidence.

If things were a bit slack Michael would 'cobble together', as he put it, until something better came along. He always said that, as a character actor, it made no difference to my career whether I played the lead or a minor role. Our occasional lunches when we would plan, plot and sometimes cobble, indulging in theatrical gossip, were always a great joy and I was very sad when he decided he had had enough. I was by then seventy years old and he encouraged me to keep going as there would be plenty for me to do; and here I am, more than twenty years later and still at it!

Before he left he introduced me to a very special agent at ICM (yes, we were now known as International Creative Management, with branches in LA and New York). Michael Foster is dynamite, a ball of fire, and he took me on despite saying I was almost past my sell-by date. An American casting director described him to me as the best agent Hollywood hasn't got. Well, they've got him now; but for two and a half years he got me a lot of very good (and well paid) work until he left for higher things.

And so, from 1996 onwards, I have been with the wonderful Sally Long-Innes. She has a great list of clients, most of whom are much more prestigious than myself: people like Ben Kingsley (sorry, *Sir* Ben I should say), Daniel Craig etc. However, she always has time for me, pursues any suitable job tenaciously and makes sure that in my old age I am properly treated. She is really caring and I love her dearly.

So you can see that I have been extremely fortunate with my agents; but unfortunately this was not so in Lillias' case. I described in an earlier chapter how Philip Pearman, one of MCA's leading agents, spotted her working at the Glasgow Citizen's Theatre, brought her to London and put her in *Mr Brown Comes Down the Hill,* an ideal platform for Philip to show her off to theatre, TV and film companies. Tragically he died suddenly, soon after the play opened.

Despite glowing notices from critics like Kenneth Tynan (see his book *Tynan Right and Left*), no one really took her up; and those that did couldn't see the talent they were dealing with or, if they could, did not have the ability to exploit it. And so this glamorous leading lady and clever character actress all rolled into one became disillusioned and left the business. What a loss. It might have been so different with a really good agent.

*

As well as running house and family Lillias was travelling to (or staying in) Borehamwood where she was playing Rosie Cartland in the long-running TV series, *The Cedar Tree.* She was excellent as always and played the part for about two years. Don't ask me how she fitted everything in, but she did. She was the breadwinner, so when I was asked to go to the Edinburgh Festival followed by a long tour for very little money I was able to do it.

The plays were Shakespeare's *Measure for Measure* and Jonson's *The Devil is an Ass.* The plays would be done in repertoire and I was offered the choice of playing either the Duke in *Measure* or Fitzdottrel, the lead in *The Devil.* Shakespeare addicts will be horrified to know that I chose the latter: I love Jonson's plays, and this one had apparently offended King James I and been taken off after one or two performances. Jonson was a rebel and so am I! Playwright Peter Barnes dusted it down and put it together again so our production was effectively a new play over three hundred and fifty years old.

We had a terrific cast, including a young Alan Rickman and David Suchet to name but two. Alan was obviously destined for a great future both as an actor and director. He taught me a lot about positions and distances that nobody had ever told me before! Alan and I both had small parts in *Measure for Measure*; I was Escalus, and I have to confess I can't remember much about him except that I had to stand around a lot with the odd speech to say while a lot of emoting was going on around me. Act V alone runs for an hour and concentration could wander. However, both plays got very good reviews as the principal dramas of the Festival.

After the show we would go to the Festival Club for a drink or two and something to eat. On the last night we all turned up there for our farewell only to be told the club was closed, despite tables being laid out for meals.

'What's all this then?' I asked the dour Scots manager, pointing to the tables.

'Staff party,' he said.

I saw red and told him that without us there wouldn't be any staff to have a party. Things got worse between us and the delightful Anna Calder-Marshall had to calm us down.

He won the day though. 'I know you,' he said. 'I've seen you on the telly. And if you ever come on in my house again, I'll switch you off!'

After a month's season at the Birmingham Repertory Theatre we became the first visiting company for a season at the National Theatre in London. The public loved the plays and again we got good reviews, but the theatre management were frosty to say the least. I didn't like the atmosphere there and was relieved not to have gone there after *Entertaining Mr Sloane*. It was not for me and I was glad when we moved on for our tour of Europe.

After playing the principal theatres in Holland we were in Germany; and, one Saturday night in Cologne, Alex and her then partner, Richard, drove from Belgium to see *The Devil is an Ass*. I was really touched that they should have come so far to see me and the show, and afterwards I wanted to give them a good meal and a glass of wine or two. However, a very formally attired waiter refused to serve us, saying everything closed at midnight on Saturdays as Cologne was a strictly Catholic city.

As we were rather forlornly saying our goodbyes in the now empty restaurant, the starchy waiter came over and said, 'Wait here, please.' He disappeared and returned some minutes later totally transformed: loose hair, T-shirt, smart jeans and sneakers.

'There is one place open; follow me.'

We ended up behind the locked doors of, I think, the local press club while our friend showed us photos of his five children and told us how much he loved England, especially Halifax where he had spent two wonderful years working in a hotel – did we know it?

Motto: there's always somewhere after hours if you're lucky enough.

It was after a performance of *Measure for Measure* in Zurich that a fragile old lady in a wheelchair was brought round to meet the company, and I went over to remind her that I had worked with her twenty-six years before in the West End. Yes, this is the incident I alluded to in Chapter 5, and the little old lady was none other than Elisabeth Bergner. I was really pleased to see her, even though she had been a difficult person to work with back in 1950. She didn't speak, however: just looked at me with a dazzling smile but through dead eyes. I felt sad that she obviously had no idea what I was talking about. Perhaps I was wrong, though; maybe it was simply that she wouldn't talk to an actor playing a minor role like Escalus.

13
SEEING OUT THE SEVENTIES

TOUR OVER, THE WORDS OF THE OLD BLUES SONG came to mind: *Get out of here and get me some money too; why don't you do right like some other men do?* After my long stint on arty-crafty theatre salary, the sentiment seemed pretty appropriate; so a part in Ken Russell's film *Valentino* staring the legendary Russian ballet dancer, Rudolf Nureyev, came at a good moment.

It was quite an experience working with Rudolf. He had enormous energy and stamina. I played Rory, a sports columnist who looked down on Valentino and thought him a bit of a phoney. So there was a boxing match and drinking contest, both of which had to be thoroughly rehearsed and choreographed.

Rudolf thought actors were an inferior breed, probably quite rightly. When we rehearsed the fight it was pretty physical. He said: 'I am a Tartar; I really fight, and will really hit you.' This he proceeded to do until I remembered my old army days and hit him back. We went through the routine about twenty times, and each time he would say 'Again' hoping to tire me out. Fortunately I was pretty fit so when he said 'Enough' I said, 'Again please'. He loved this and we became good friends. He called me his Fighting Friend and invited me to his many dinner parties after shooting. He was generous and very good company. He was openly homosexual and once asked me, did I like boys? I said it was not my scene and he said, 'Ah, you don't know what you are missing.'

After dinner he could be found at the disco beneath the hotel, where the local girls flocked to dance with him; then from about midnight to 3 A.M. I could hear him in the room above mine working out the steps for a new ballet. I think it was *Romeo and Juliet*. Then up and into make-up at around 6.30 A.M. ready to film the demanding part of Valentino all day. There was an hour's lunch break, but Rudi would do barre work for half an hour and curl up in a blanket on the floor and catnap for twenty minutes or so.

He drove his dialogue coach crazy: despite her efforts he wouldn't, or couldn't, learn his lines which often had to be pinned up around the set, judiciously placed out of sight of the camera.

Ken Russell said *Valentino* was the worst film he ever made. It wasn't; he just got the wrong leading man. But what a man. What talent, and what a pity he never took to acting. I think he thought it beneath him. He ought to have had a good career in films: he had all the attributes but perhaps not the desire to do it.

This great ballet dancer was phenomenally strong and he could lift and fall with ease. For instance, in our drunken fight scene he had to collapse onto the knees of Felicity Kendal who was sitting in a chair. Typically with Ken Russell, we did about thirty takes and she never felt the weight of this six-foot-two man, such was his muscle control. Unforgettable.

*

A BBC backstage assistant volunteered to deliver a rubber plant to the office of the Head of Light Entertainment. Choosing a strategic moment to deliver the plant, he said to the boss, 'Would you have a look at these scripts I've written, please?' He did; in fact he couldn't put them down, and so the sitcom *Citizen Smith* was born. That was the start of the illustrious writing career of John Sullivan, with other successes such as *Only Fools and Horses* to come.

The legendary BBC comedy producer, Dennis Main Wilson, was at the helm and he asked me to be in it.

'Who's playing Wolfie Smith?' I asked. I was told it was a young actor who had just done an army series. His name was Robert Lindsay.

Bob and I got on like a house on fire, but his then wife seemed very suspicious of me. I don't know why that was, unless she thought I might steal a scene or two from her husband. She was wrong on two counts: I never try to steal a scene – to me that is not proper acting – and secondly it would be impossible to do it to Robert Lindsay. He is just too good and I love working with him.

I thoroughly enjoyed doing the series, and I was thrilled to be going on to do the feature film of *Porridge* playing my old part of Harry Grout. Unfortunately it clashed with a third series of *Citizen Smith* which meant I had to drop out of the sitcom. This enraged the new BBC Head of Light Entertainment who accused me of lack of loyalty and said I would never work in BBC comedy again. What loyalty? I certainly had no such clause in my contract.

The film of *Porridge* was great. It was good to do Grouty again. On location I shared a caravan with Richard Beckinsale and sometimes his lovely little five-year-old daughter, Kate. He confided in me that he had not been feeling well, but it was still a terrible shock to hear of his tragic death so soon afterwards. It is fitting that that little five-year-old in the caravan has followed in his footsteps and become the brilliant actress Kate Beckinsale.

*

I write this book in all sorts of odd times and different places, while waiting to go on set or in some dressing room or other; and that is where I wrote about the film *Zulu Dawn* and then left it behind one night when presumably it was consigned to a rubbish dump. I only found this out when revising these chapters about the 1970s and, as it's not a bad story, I had better write it again.

Zulu Dawn is a film about the British invasion of Zululand despite an agreement with the Zulu chief not to do so, and the disastrous consequences of this action. It is a pretty accurate account of what happened and the people involved in it. James Faulkner, the actor-producer, cast me as Quartermaster Sergeant Bloomfield who was in charge of stores and ammunition on the army expedition. I found myself on a plane bound for Johannesburg via Nairobi with Bob Hoskins (a sergeant) and Paul Copley (a private) in economy class. Peter O'Toole, playing the head of the expedition, Lord Chelmsford, was naturally all on his own travelling in first class. The film was after all set in the nineteenth century so perhaps class distinction was appropriate.

The cast list was pretty amazing. As well as Mr O'Toole, Bob, Paul and myself there was Burt Lancaster, John Mills and a host of the best British actors of the day: Ronald Pickup, Freddie Jones, Nigel Davenport, Michael Jayston, Dai Bradley, Simon Ward, Christopher Cazenove, Denholm Elliott and many more.

Bob was in great form on the flight. 'Amazing,' he said to neighbouring passengers. 'Thirty-six thousand feet in the air in a bloody great silver cigar on our way to Africa.' I don't think he'd flown much before. It was near the beginning of his career and he was tremendous fun to be with.

We spent a few days in Durban waiting for everyone to assemble before moving on to Pietermaritzburg in Natal. The cricket ground there was used as the location for the headquarters of the expedition, with tents and horses galloping around. This was hallowed turf to me as Denis Compton once scored three hundred runs on it in a day!

Of course, apartheid was still flourishing, but that didn't stop Freddie Jones who furiously played the bongos and had the locals dancing in the streets. The police looked on impassively but thought it better not to intervene. Nobody interrupts Freddie when he is in full flow! Michael Jayston, a great practical joker, put copious orders for breakfast on everyone's doors one night and forged John Mills' signature on them all. Sir John, not noted for his generosity, took it all in good part.

Our director Douglas Hickox shot a lot of scenes prior to the invasion of Zululand in and around the cricket ground. Douggie was not immensely popular with cast and crew. He had a habit of picking on those he thought were the most vulnerable. One day Phil Daniels, then fifteen years old and playing my bugle boy, became a victim. Phil was an East Ender and a product of the famous Anna Scher school. She produced an array of talent including Pauline Quirke, Linda Robson and many others. Nevertheless, in a scene with about two hundred extras, Douggie had a go at trying to make Phil look small. This didn't work too well. At the end of the scene Phil said, 'Mr Hickox, thank you very much. I have learned so much from you today.' This was greeted with cheers and applause. I have never seen the tables turned so neatly before or since.

Then the day came when we actually crossed Rorke's Drift into Zululand. It was one of the most exciting moments in my whole career: driving three pairs of oxen pulling stores and ammunition across the water, waving a whip and exhorting my oxen with the cry '*Hamba!*' Little things…!

We were told to keep in character the whole time as they were using a 500mm long lens and we would not know when we were in shot. As we approached Zululand there was a huge area of empty veldt before us. Right in character my bugle boy Phil said, 'Quartermaster, ain't the Zulus got big gardens?' That finished me. Fortunately we weren't in shot at the time.

A huge tented village had been built for the film and this was our home from now on. It even had its own telephone exchange – the phone number was Heidelberg 1. Zulu Chief Buthelezi allowed the village to be built on his land but decreed that it should be completely erased at the end of the film which was in fact done. A great leader to whom I was lucky enough to be introduced personally.

So preparations began for the battle of Isandlwana which was to be filmed as close as possible to the location of the real historical event. Hundreds of extras, largely comprising university and college students on vacation, were recruited as Redcoats. Similarly, thousands of young Zulus were recruited. What a wonderful crowd they were: turning up in jeans and baseball caps, they would change into their loincloths, pick up their spears and shields and form up into impis. They still knew how to chant their war cries, how to handle their spears and how to move silently and without being spotted.

Lord Chelmsford encamped his army for the night in what he believed to be an ideal location with a good view all round, not realising an army of Zulus was waiting. Hidden on the horizon, at dawn they swept in and overran the unprepared British, 'washing' their spears as they went. A Zulu was not considered a man until he had washed his spear in blood – he could not own a cow or take a wife – so this made him a formidable enemy.

In real life it was all over in a day, but to film it took some weeks. With only two weeks to go we had still not shot close-ups of the battle and thus the deaths of the principal characters. This became a bit of a rush job as the director refused producer James Faulkner's offer of a two-week extension to the schedule. Fortunately, we had a brilliant second unit director to shoot some excellent hand-to-hand fighting and death scenes. The hand-to-hand scenes with the Zulus, as they swept down on us chanting their war cries, were quite scary even though they were really local workers. I say again, what wonderful people they are.

Each evening when we returned to base, Burt Lancaster would receive us with Shiraz red wine asking, 'Who died today?' Whoever it was then had to do a parody of his death for Burt whilst the rest of us booed and cheered with derision. Burt was a huge star at that time, but he was enormous fun and stayed and mucked in with us all.

I was very happy with my death scene – shot in the back whilst running from my on-fire ammunition carriage – but Bob Hoskins was not at all pleased with his. We were forbidden by the director to see rushes, but Bob managed to hide in the rushes tent and was very unhappy with what he saw. Unknown to Douggie he got hold of a cameraman, rounded up a few Zulus and reshot his death himself! No wonder, with such dedication, that he became such a star and producer. All power to him: he was such a lovely bloke.

Apart from that dreadful word 'apartheid', I think most people had a truly memorable time doing *Zulu Dawn* and James Faulkner is to be congratulated on making it. It was a pity that Peter O'Toole chose to swirl in and out by helicopter each day and (to my knowledge) did not socialise at all with us. It must be remembered, though, that he was giving a superb performance as the unfortunate Lord Chelmsford. After all, we have all used 'method' acting in our time. I say this because I know that on some projects he was tremendous fun to be with. And I was grateful for the lovely silk scarf he gave me at the end of shooting.

Filming over, Lillias and twelve-year-old David came out to join me for a holiday at Umhlanga Rocks, a terrific resort on the coast just outside Durban. It was a joy to have them with me after living away so long. On the very first day I took David on to the beach and suddenly he shot off to chat to an old Crawley schoolmate whose father lived in Durban. Talk about a small world!

We met a South African Air Force crew in a bar and they arranged to take Dave on a reconnaissance flight over Mozambique. Off they went – David must have been in seventh heaven.

Later I drove us in our fine jeep to Umfolozi Game Reserve near Swaziland. The reserve was abundant with wildlife and game. We were so excited at being near to a family of cheetahs, the tamest of the big three cats, resting in the shade and then taking off at lightning speed. We drove on and round a bend met a young rhino standing facing us in the road. I stopped and switched off the engine and we waited for what seemed an eternity. If we had disturbed it, it could have charged us which would have been very bad news indeed; but suddenly it turned and walked away. Phew!

We later went for a drink in a bar where local whites were loudly indulging in racist chat. Lillias was outraged and wanted to intervene so I quickly steered her out – no, rushed her out! What a tragedy that this wonderful country was still blighted by prejudice. To sit alone in the Drakensberg Mountains, as I used to sometimes when not working, gave me a feeling of being at the very centre of creation and one had a sense of total calm.

All too soon our holiday came to an end and it was back to the dear old UK; an unforgettable time for me, and I think it was a bit special for Lillias and young David too. The film isn't bad either.

*

Before the seventies came to an end it was back to the theatre, this time the Royal Exchange in Manchester. Robert Lindsay and I went up to do two plays, Chekhov's *The Cherry Orchard* and Gorky's *The Lower Depths*. We had an excellent director, Braham Murray, and I really got to know Robert and admire his work. I knew from *Citizen Smith* that he was a very special comic actor, but these two classic Russian plays showed up his all-round brilliance. There is really nothing that Bob cannot do or, in my opinion, achieve. He was always questing, looking for new ways to do things.

An extreme example of this came well into the run, at one of the matinees of *The Lower Depths*. As Luka I had to dominate him in a long duologue. Shortly after the scene began he suddenly produced a knife and put it at my throat. Try dominating the scene after that! As I said on his *This Is Your Life* TV programme, I suppose he thought I'd got stuck in a bit of a rut.

This was my first and only experience of theatre in the round. On the first night as Lopakhin in *The Cherry Orchard* I was absolutely terrified. As I walked on, completely surrounded by the audience, I froze and almost carried on walking across the stage and out the other side, never to be seen again! But I soon got used to it, and loved the intimacy of it. The only way to act was 'the truth, the whole truth and nothing but the truth'. Another great experience for me in the theatre. Bob and I have crossed paths only two or three times since then, but there is a bond between us and I am thrilled by the way he has developed into one of our truly great actors.

I have one big regret about my season at the Royal Exchange though. The next production was to be a wonderful play by Ronald Harwood called *The Dresser*, based on Ronnie's experiences as Donald Wolfit's dresser and general assistant in *The Strong Are Lonely* and others. Leo McKern was rehearsing the Wolfit part when he dropped out and the role suddenly became vacant. As you may remember, I had understudied Wolfit and had observed the man pretty closely. I was on the spot, free to rehearse and would have dearly loved to play it; but I was not asked. Instead, up came Freddie Jones, and he had huge success in the part both in Manchester and subsequently in the West End. Freddie is a marvellous actor but I still think I could have had a good stab at it.

However, all was not lost because Graham Benson (who had produced me in a film for TV called *Freedom of the Dig*) and a writer called Trevor Preston came up to Manchester to talk about a new project they wanted me to be in. I was a great fan of Trevor as he was a brilliant jazz critic on the *New Musical Express*. I confess I didn't know too much about him as a screenwriter, but that was about to change.

The series they were planning was the story of a south London family called *Fox*. I was to play Billy Fox, the head of the family. He was a seventy-year-old father of five sons and the boss of his patch: that's why he was known as 'King Billy'. One of my very favourite directors, Jim Goddard, was to direct. Back in 1971 Jim had directed me for ITV as the Victorian detective Horace Dorrington in *The Rivals of Sherlock Holmes*. Horace was a great character, brilliant at getting somewhat dubious clients acquitted. However, he would then blackmail them! We did two glorious episodes before the powers that be decided you could not have a hero who was also a bit of a villain and stopped the series. A bit much, we thought, as after all it was set in Victorian times; and are all detectives whiter than white even today?

Never mind: I was seeing out the seventies with Jim again at the helm, wonderful scripts and a great cast: all my five sons were superb. My favourite character actress Elizabeth Spriggs, whom I have often had the pleasure of working with, was to play my wife. So it was with great excitement and anticipation that I launched into the 1980s.

Before going on, though, I would like to pause a moment to reflect on the sixties and seventies. They were two such eventful decades in every way. Writing about them has made me realise what a journey it was through those years, how richly exciting they were. First, my career blossomed enormously. The catalyst in that respect was undoubtedly the huge success of *Entertaining Mr Sloane* in the theatre, and all the plays, films, television and radio that followed.

143

Second, and much more importantly, there was my personal life. The sixties started on a fairly low-key note for me until Lillias, my soulmate, reappeared in my life. We married in 1966 as soon as my divorce came through; David Max was born exactly a year later and by the end of the seventies was a teenager already hard at work on the drums. The twins came down from Scotland to settle with us in '67, but by the end of the seventies were twenty-five years old and had long flown the nest, with Alex working in TV advertising in Brussels and Vicki a successful actress in theatre and television. Meanwhile Lillias was combining running the whole outfit with her own brilliant acting career.

I know I have written a lot of this before but I really had to let it all sink in to my memory. What a great time it was. And now I go on into the eighties a sober (not always), solid (not always) fifty-six-year-old – how time flies by.

14

A Decade of Change

S O AS I HAVE SAID the eighties started out with a great part for me. *Fox* was a thirteen-part serial for ITV about a south London family. Liz Spriggs and I were the husband and wife, with five sons: Bernard Hill, Derrick O'Connor, Larry Lamb, Eamon Boland and Ray Winstone playing the lads. Not a bad cast eh? Bernard was the builder with a profoundly deaf son (played by a lovely boy who really was deaf). Derrick was inclined to be on the wrong side of the law; Larry was a taxi driver fond of the ladies. Eamon was the serious student and Ray was the young boxer. They were a 'one for all and all for one' family ruled by their father, 'King Billy'. It was the Foxes' patch despite attempts by others to take over.

Jim Goddard directed. He knew exactly what he was doing, and as far as I remember we were always on schedule. I loved working with Jim again and woke up in the morning really looking forward to the day ahead. Then, horror of horrors: in episode 7 King Billy had a heart attack and died. I always felt that he should have recovered slightly from the attack but remained a sick man, watching his power and authority crumble as it became taken over by others. He could then have had a fatal attack an episode or two later. However, he had a huge funeral through the streets of south London in episode 8. I'm afraid I was not in the coffin so did not get a fee!

Sadly, *Fox* was never sold around the world and never repeated. This was because Euston Films who made it were a branch of Thames TV who soon afterwards lost their franchise. So that was that: no repeats or sales. This is a great shame as it was brilliantly made and, I am certain, would have been just as entertaining today as it was then. UK Gold would have had a ball!

*

Terry Gilliam of the *Monty Python* team is not just a brilliant comedian but also scriptwriter, animator and perhaps above all film director. Everyone loves working with him. He has only to ask and people like Sean Connery and Robert De Niro drop in and play cameo roles. I was thrilled when he asked me to play the Ogre in *Time Bandits* and jumped at the chance.

I had to be up early as my make-up took a couple of hours to put on. Katherine Helmond of the cult American comedy series *Soap* came over and played my wife, and I loved being the wicked Ogre – which was just as well, because life was a bit hectic as I was doing a play at the same time. *Travelling North*, with Rosemary Leach and myself in the leading roles, was a very good Australian piece, directed at the Lyric Theatre Hammersmith by renowned National Theatre director Michael Blakemore. The elaborate set was designed by his wife; I may have been wrong but I always felt that the production was designed to show off the set, rather than the set being designed to illuminate the play and accommodate the cast. This seemed to me a pity as it was such a good play, and Rosemary was excellent as always. I can't say that I was totally sorry when it ended, but in fairness Michael did have a nasty bout of 'flu through rehearsals and a lot of people did love the play.

After a telly or two I found myself in the theatre once more, this time in the London premiere of Alan Ayckbourn's *Season's Greetings* for six weeks at the Greenwich Theatre. It was joy unconfined to be in this brilliantly funny play. I had a lovely part and was very happy, but then came a bit of a blow: I was summoned to St Albans Magistrates' Court for three speeding offences. I was determined to defend myself, but luckily for me Nigel Havers, son of the then Attorney General, was in the cast and introduced me to his brother Philip, now a famous barrister but then just starting out on the circuit. I stood to automatically lose my licence as well as being heavily fined so there was a lot at stake.

We arrived at the court one cold morning at 8.30 A.M. I was soberly attired and had been instructed by Philip Havers to look humble and to slightly incline my head when being admonished by the chief magistrate. Philip gave an impassioned defence on my behalf, pointing out that I was having to film in the daytime and play in the theatre at night, and explaining that without my car it would be virtually impossible to carry on my work.

The magistrates then left to discuss my fate in private.

Whilst I awaited their decision, the police sergeant who brought the case said, '*Vis-à-vis* your complicated character make-ups, it would please my son very much if you had played a monster in *Doctor Who*.'

'No, I haven't,' I replied, 'but she has,' and pointed to Lillias who was sitting quietly at the back of the courtroom doing a crossword! She had, too, having been very frightening in the *Doctor Who* story *Terror of the Zygons*.

The clerk of the court then instructed me to remain standing when the magistrates returned. 'And may I say,' he added, 'how much I enjoyed your double-glazing commercial.'

The magistrates duly returned. The chief magistrate (a lady, incidentally) fined me £70 and warned me that should there be any further offence I would lose my licence. We then drove to Folkestone races and backed a winner or two – enough to cover the fine and the case of claret in grateful thanks for Philip Havers' brilliant expertise. And a big thank you too to Nigel Havers for stopping me trying to defend myself!

Season's Greetings duly transferred to the West End and I remember the first night very well. Walking through Piccadilly on my way to the theatre I passed ex-international footballer, Jimmy Logie, who sold papers there. He asked me where I was going.

'To do a first night,' I replied.

'Bloody hell, Peter, when are you going to pack it in?' Not good for the confidence but I knew what he meant!

On arrival at the theatre stage door I was met by my friend Elizabeth Spriggs. 'Just wanted to wish you luck, darling.' She was in very good form. I got her a seat and invited her to the Dress Circle Bar after the performance where the cast and friends were going to have a little do.

The performance was a special one, with gales of laughter and huge applause. In high spirits we assembled in the bar. Liz Spriggs appeared, and as I handed her a glass of wine she said, 'You know how much I love your work, darling, and I know you would not want me to tell you anything but the truth... Darling... it was awful!' And if she thought it was awful it obviously *was* awful as she had impeccable taste and knowledge of theatre. It must have been one of those hysterical first nights. Too many friends, relatives and well-wishers egging us further and further 'over the top'. Thanks Liz, a lesson well and truly learnt.

The play settled in to a very successful run and it was a joy to do. Alan Ayckbourn came to see a performance some weeks in. His comment was priceless: no one to play for laughs, but if you don't get your laughs you're fired! In other words no conscious comedy playing, please. May I say we do see quite a lot of it, and often from people who should know better!

*

My friend Jeremy Kemp, who by the way does not know I am writing this book, once said he thought that actors' memoirs were often very tedious to read, tending to be a litany of their work: 'then I did this and then I did that', that type of thing. I am trying hard not to fall into this trap. A lot of work came and went without incident so I am just going to write about those that stand out in my mind. A full CV of my film and television work is at the end of the book should anyone be interested.

Despite the large amount of TV work, the fees were no higher and I found myself owing the tax inspector quite a bit of money. What to do? No films were in the offing, so touring the provinces seemed to be the answer. First I played Mr Birling in *An Inspector Calls*. This went on for a month or two and proved to be a pretty miserable experience. Besides being a cliquey company, they weren't very good, apart from Alfred Marks who played the inspector. As well as being a great variety comedian he was a fine actor and a lovely man. We became good friends, but in all other respects I was relieved when it was over.

My next tour was playing Hobson in the wonderful *Hobson's Choice*. Rehearsals went well and we opened at the Theatre Royal Bath, one of the loveliest old theatres in the country. The dress rehearsal went extremely well and, apart from the usual first-night nerves, I was raring to go. On I went, said a few lines – and then it happened. My body froze, my mind went completely blank. I just stood there for what seemed like an eternity. I didn't get a prompt, and no one in the cast came to my aid.

It was like the whole place was in shock. The silence was intense; and then from someone in the audience came a long, painful sigh. This seemed to jolt me back into the play and I found myself speaking lines and carrying on with the performance. A truly frightening experience: I shudder now when I think about it.

A lot of actors have gone through something similar, many of them far more eminent than I, but fortunately it has never happened to me before or since. I am sure the person who gave the long sigh was my then agent Michael Anderson, but he never mentioned it. Gareth Davies, the TV director, was in the audience and was heard to say, 'At least it shows he's human after all.'

We went on to tour *Hobson* up and down the country for twenty-two weeks and it was really good to meet provincial audiences in different towns. It was tough on family life, though, as one had to drive home after the show on Saturday nights and leave for the next date first thing Monday morning. Just about time to do the week's mail, mow the lawn and have a row. No, I'm joking! I remember we played Leeds one week and Plymouth the next; I still made it home though. I had a great time playing Hobson and would dearly have loved a West End season. Ian Albery, the theatre owner, came to see us but it sadly didn't happen. I paid my income tax all right though!

Films were a bit thinner on the ground for me in the eighties. Many were being made, just not with me in them. Perhaps, on reaching sixty years old, things were changing a little. So I was delighted to have a part in *The Razor's Edge* starring the wonderful comedian Bill Murray. We were on location in Lille and it was good to be back in an area I knew so well from my World War II days. *The Razor's Edge* is a Somerset Maugham story set in the coalfields of northern France at the end of the nineteenth century. It gave Bill a wonderful opportunity to play a dramatic role as opposed to his comedy.

The role must have made Bill extremely weary as we had to hang around for hours in the mornings waiting for him to emerge in a somewhat 'tired' state. My part was a French miner, and Bill got very suspicious when I ad-libbed a few lines in French as he didn't know what I was saying! I loved my part, though I personally think it could have been a better film.

My next film was a thrill to be cast in: *The French Lieutenant's Woman* starring Meryl Streep and Jeremy Irons. Harold Pinter adapted the screenplay from the novel in a uniquely brilliant way, and Karel Reisz was an inspiring director.

I played the father of Jeremy's fiancée whom he abandoned. We had a very good scene where I confronted Jeremy about this. Karel directed the scene meticulously and did a lot of takes. At one point he gave me the best note I have ever had from a film director. He said: 'Many of the takes where you are acting being the character are good; but once or twice you are just being the character, and they are the ones that are very good.' I have carried that note in my head ever since, and it is the hardest thing to achieve but very satisfying when I manage to do it.

Another lesson learned from Karel concerned the process of editing the final cut of the film. Any scene, however brilliantly done, that held up or was a digression from the main central story of the film had to be cut out. Leo McKern, David Warner et al: we all lost scenes for this reason. Even Jeremy Irons had a beautiful scene with a prostitute whom he felt sorry for when he learned her story: just gave her money and left. It must have held up the main action as it was not in the film. Since then, whenever I suffer this fate, I think of Karel's lesson. Sadly, not all film-makers are as astute in this matter and important moments are lost to the detriment of a film. Ah well, shrug shoulders and on, on, on!

Terry Gilliam's *Brazil* has become a classic cult film much admired by movie enthusiasts. Terry called it the second in a trilogy of films, the first being *Time Bandits* and the third *The Fisher King*. *Brazil* is a dark film set in a pretty frightening future and I found myself playing the Minister of Information Retrieval in a wheelchair. Film buffs sometimes quote my lines at me and I find this a bit awkward as I have long forgotten every word!

I do remember, though, a complicated scene where Jonathan Pryce wheeled me into a loo, got me out of the wheelchair, helped me have a pee, put me back in the chair and wheeled me across to the washbasin where I spread powder on the washstand and, with my finger, wrote a long-forgotten message. It was a perfect take and we got it in one; Terry couldn't believe it and, to begin with, wanted to do it again. This was just an automatic reaction as he had just been working with Robert De Niro who had a guest cameo in the film. De Niro's working method was to rehearse on film; he would often go to thirty takes or so before being happy with the result. A very different way of working, but who's to argue? In my view Robert De Niro is truly one of the screen's greatest actors, and it was thrilling to have him in the film. But then everyone wants to work with Terry.

Shooting the torture-chamber scene at the end of the film remains vividly in my memory too. The location was a disused cooling tower near Putney. It was about a hundred feet high and there was only a narrow walkway, barely wide enough for my wheelchair: no handrails or safety nets, just a sheer drop. Michael Palin had to wheel me to the top of the walkway where we played the last scene. As I mentioned before, I am terrified of heights and have this awful urge to jump, so I just clung on to the wheelchair arms and looked straight ahead. Steady as a rock, Michael never wavered. We reached the top, played the scene with Jonathan Pryce, and Michael pushed me safely back. No alarms, but no safety nets. But that's Terry Gilliam: *que sera sera*.

Later I had a cameo in *The Missionary* in which Michael Palin had a leading role. It was a complicated scene and it went well. I was very touched when Michael took the trouble to write to me explaining that my part had been cut out because it didn't take the film forward. What a caring and thoughtful thing for Michael to have written to me. Actually I wasn't surprised to be cut; Karel Reisz had taught me all about that.

*

The TV ratings war with channels battling against each other has almost completely overwhelmed 'one-off drama'. The individual play stood or fell on its own value; it had no cliffhanger to make the audience want to see a further episode. Nonetheless, it survived the seventies and eighties; and some memorable ones refuse to be forgotten by me. I've already mentioned Max Frisch's *The Fire Raisers*, my number one favourite, and I am going to list a few more – whether I am boring or not!

Under The Hammer directed by Richard Wilson was a really good one. Richard had us playing games, throwing bean bags at each other and so on, each day before starting work. This may sound foolish but in fact it turned a roomful of comparative strangers very quickly into a group of actors working easily together. If I ever direct (heaven forbid!) I think I would do the same. *The Signalman's Apprentice* by my friend Brian Phelan with Dennis Waterman as the apprentice to my signalman was a good one too.

The Strain by Alun Owen, in which I played the sinister Mr Michael, was directed by Ted Kotcheff. We did the play; Ted said it was awful and made us do it again straight away. 'That's better,' he said. I told him I thought it was better the first time, which I know it was. He said he cut my first performance into the second one but I don't suppose he did.

Sadly I am certain some of those plays no longer exist, having been destroyed along with so much other work of that time. I hope *The Fire Raisers* at least has survived, but I doubt it.

Meanwhile BBC producer Shaun Sutton was keeping things going with full-length classics like Galsworthy's *Strife* and Priestley's wonderful comedy *When We are Married*, both of which I was lucky enough to be in. Timothy West and I had great confrontational scenes together in *Strife*, while in the latter I met and worked with Patricia Routledge. She had been in the play on the stage for a year and I thought it wise to do exactly as she suggested I do.

Later I was to play the Abbot to her Hildegard of Bingen, the famous twelfth-century nun. The director was the son of Archbishop Runcie and so I found myself on location in Canterbury Cathedral. The music for the piece was written by Harvey Brough, of the jazz group Harvey and the Wallbangers, evidently also a serious composer. He was there one day with his friend Jacqui Dankworth. I tried to tell them that my son David Ohm was a jazz drummer and that I was a huge fan of her mother, the singer Cleo Laine, but I didn't get very far. They seemed a bit snooty. Hardly surprising really: an old boy dressed as an Abbott trying to talk jazz in Canterbury Cathedral!

Our next location was a very cold one in the North East. Some of the night shooting was the coldest I can ever remember doing in Britain. I made a huge mistake in the hotel one night: I introduced Patricia to someone and pronounced her name Rutledge. She was outraged.

'It is not Rutledge,' she said angrily, 'it is *Routledge.*'

Shades of 'Bouquet' and 'Bucket', I have since thought. She is a marvellous artist in all she does and her performance in Alan Bennett's *Talking Heads* will stay in my memory always. And I still treasure the lovely hip flask she gave me after *When We Are Married*, even though I don't drink shorts.

There is one more very special one-off drama which I must include. *Countdown to War* in 1989 marked the fiftieth anniversary of the start of World War II and chronicled all the events leading up to the war. It was a seriously good programme in which I played Hermann Göring, second in power in Nazi Germany only to Hitler himself. Ian McKellen played Hitler and I had a great time working with him. He also has a great sense of humour and we had a load of laughs when we weren't actually filming. He wasn't knighted then; dare I say less of a Sir, more of a Madam? Sorry Ian, only joking!

*

Huge changes took place in all the family's lives during the 1980s, so perhaps it's best to go through us all one by one in alphabetical order so as not to upset any egos!

First there was Alex. After spending a while in London working for London Weekend TV she went to Moscow for the Olympics Games there. At the end of the Games she took off for India, landing in Goa, and took a couple of years or so working her way up into Nepal, all over India and even spent time at the Everest Base Camp. Quite a journey! I may be wrong but I think she did Goa to Nepal and back more than once.

Her wanderings in the subcontinent over, Alex returned to the UK to be met by her mother who was shocked to find her almost unrecognisable. She had developed Guillain-Barré syndrome, an acute disorder of the nervous system which reduces you to almost nothing. She was rushed straight to the hospital in Crawley where she was put into isolation and carefully brought back to health.

Fully recovered, she was soon on her way again. This time the intrepid traveller was off to Australia where she landed in Sydney. It didn't take her long to find her feet and she was soon working in one of Sydney's best restaurants, run by Lorenzo Pagnan, and they became close friends. In a phone call to her twin sister she told her of being pregnant. 'So am I,' said Vicki; and Alex's Chloe and Vicki's Alexander were born within weeks of each other. And quite without collusion with each other too. That's twins for you.

Lillias went out to see her new granddaughter, the lovely Chloe. A visit to Ayers Rock via the camel train from Adelaide was a highlight for Lillias, though she told me she could never stay long in Oz because the women's accents drove her mad, especially when several were talking together!

Sadly Alex's relationship with Lorenzo was not to last and she returned to Europe with her daughter. By now we were in 1986/87, and this time she returned to Brussels to work once again with her old friend Richard Wells. So it was back to the advertising world, doing voice-overs and commercials on Belgian and Dutch TV and radio. Quite a journey through the decade.

I said I would go through the family in alphabetical order, but Dave will have to wait a bit because the twins are so intertwined I feel Vicki's decade has to come next.

Victoria Burton, actress, was hard at work in the eighties. She took her work seriously and was a very popular member of all the companies she was involved in. She was loved for her sunny disposition, her positive approach to all things and for the quality of her work.

Her partner for some four years at this time was a lovely man named Barry McCarthy, highly talented as both an actor and writer. They lived together in Clapham, and Barry and I became very good friends, probably because of our love of all sports but especially horse racing! Many an hour was spent mulling over form and what to lose our money on, although sometimes we were quite successful – especially Barry. He is still a good friend to us all.

Like her mother, Vicki was in a TV series for a year or two. This one was called *Gems* and was a long-running show about fashion. The director was Stuart Orme whom I worked with many years later; he told me that as well as Vicki's work he still remembered her lovely smile.

In the early eighties she went up to do a repertory season at Dundee. In the company was a young actor called Gregor Fisher. I am not sure which year this was, but it must have been in the early part of the decade because by 1986 their first son, Alexander, was born. He was followed by a second son, Jamie, and by 1989 their daughter Cissie. Three wonderful grandchildren for Lillias.

What can one say of their dad? Well, he is probably the most talented comedy actor of his time. He first caught the public eye in a sketch show called *Naked Video* in which he played a series of characters, all totally different, totally real and all very funny. Among the many characters was a hard-drinking Glaswegian in a string vest called Rab C. Nesbitt. For the next ten years Gregor's Rab C. was one of the truly great characters of television.

Returning to Victoria, don't think that the sunny, lovable, sometimes dizzy person is all there is to her character. Oh no! She is very shrewd, highly intelligent (though often pretending not to be) and with a good business sense. She is also a tough cookie with a rod of iron down her back and woe betide anyone who tries to cross her. What a woman. We don't always agree but she'll do for me.

David Max was thirteen years old at the start of the eighties and nearly twenty-three by the end of them so he did a lot of growing up in that time. He was a boarder at Eastbourne College until he was sixteen, after which he went on to take A-Levels at Horsham Sixth Form College, travelling each day from home. He then went to North London Polytechnic where he got a degree in Modern History. This gave him a very detailed knowledge and insight into modern politics. He and I had many passionate discussions on the state of things and, since I largely agree with his views, we didn't fall out, just ended up in a state of mutual despair for the future.

David also has a huge sense of humour and is incredibly funny. Gallows humour, he calls it; and we rarely meet without rocking with laughter over some ludicrous situation or other. Even difficult teenage differences ended up with a laugh and a hug.

As well as the drums Dave has a great passion for cars and motorbikes. Mention Valentino Rossi and he practically swoons and rattles off detailed current statistics about him. As a young teenager we would take him by car to nearby sandpits, hump his 50cc bike out of the car and off he would go practising motorcycle scrambling. Even an empty field would do for him to roar around. At seventeen he had an old minivan and it soon became clear that he was a natural driver and biker. Very quick but very safe.

As for his drumming, that went on the whole time. Even at mealtimes his fingers would be beating away on the table with a faraway look in his eyes. He was in various bands, practising in a back bedroom at Goffs Manor and playing all through school and polytechnic. By the end of the decade he was already a professional of a couple of years' standing. His mother and I knew that with his good looks, great personality and acute perception and observation he could have been a natural actor. However, having seen his parents doing it he thought it a rather insecure and uncertain way of life, and chose the music business instead! He truly loves his work though; and that is a tremendous bonus in life – to love your work, difficult though it sometimes may be.

By the end of the eighties David had become the man he now always is: passionate in what he believes to be right and absolutely honest (sometimes when it might be better to fib a little bit). He has no truck with deviousness or duplicity and does not suffer fools or injustice, to himself or others. He isn't perfect by any means: he can be stubborn, irritating and fail to see other points of view when it would be advantageous for him to do so. On the other hand he is kind, caring and totally supportive, especially to his mother and to me. I can't think of a better friend or son. I love you, David.

There is no doubt that the most fundamental change concerned Lillias. At the beginning of the decade Lillias Walker was playing Rosie Cartland in the long-running *The Cedar Tree*. When it ended, around 1982, she just missed being in the BBC serial *Tenko*, about women imprisoned by the Japanese in World War II. She would have been superb in the part and it would have been perfect to take her career forward. However, this didn't happen and she found herself out of work for about the first time in her life. If they didn't want her, she didn't want them! So that was the end of Lillias Walker, a superb and brilliant actress. I am sure that with better representation and perhaps a bit more patience and perseverance she could have continued her very special career. What a waste of talent. That agent and others should be ashamed.

Perhaps being a farmer's daughter has something to do with her affinity with animals and, having said farewell to acting, they became her next project. Dogs and cats became her working life. German Shepherds recruited from the famous Norwulf kennels were shown and the bitch, Delilah, had two litters of puppies. These were reared, trained and most of them sold on to carefully selected homes. One or two, however, were kept and grew up to be a big part of our lives.

The next step was to build a boarding kennels for both dogs and cats in the ample grounds of Goffs Manor. So Goffs Kennels came into being and thrived happily for over two years. Even I got involved, being principal dog-walker whenever I wasn't working! The kennels were meticulously run by Lillias, and all the animals were looked after individually with care and affection. Some regular owners were a little crestfallen when their much-loved pooch rushed into Lillias' arms to start their holiday! However, they were reassured when the animal rushed back to them when they came to pick them up. That's dogs for you!

Cats were a different proposition as they would exercise themselves in a run from which they could not escape. Or could they? On one occasion the double doors were not properly closed and one got out and settled high up in a nearby tree. After some hours the cat was coaxed down with the aid of a tree-surgeon friend. Fortunately the owner never found out what had happened!

*

After nearly three years, running the kennels 24/7 without a break took its toll and Lillias closed them down. It was time for a change. And what a change.

Our favourite vet, Terry Fogarty, and Mary his wife had become good friends; and through them we met David and Jenny Cherry who lived nearby. Jenny happened to mention that they had a holiday flat they were selling on the Costa del Sol, in the village of La Cala de Mijas halfway between Malaga and Marbella. We thought this might be a nice idea for holidays for us and the family. So Lillias went out to see it.

She loved the fishing village but didn't think the flat was right for us. However, she went for a walk up the hill to look at the lovely views of the hills above and of the village and sparkling sea. There she fell into conversation with a chap walking his dog. 'This villa is for sale,' he said, producing a key and showing her around. She immediately fell in love with it.

The chap with the dog was Ray Thorpe whose wife Di ran the office which controlled the urbanisation of Los Claveles (The Carnations). Di and Ray were invaluable to us, helping us to do a deal with the owner, finding us a good *abogado* and steering us through the intricacies of buying a house in Spain.

Lill came home to the UK. The wonderful Goffs Manor was sold, and the top storey of Well House, Crawley Down was brilliantly bought by Lillias and became our UK office and *pied-à-terre*. No more holiday flats: Spain was to be our main home.

Just like Upper Well House, the villa was bought by me unseen. I went out on my own to complete the deal and I shall never forget going onto the upstairs balcony, soaking in the view and watching a beautiful sunset going down behind the villa. I fell in love with it too. Everything was signed and sealed the following day and Lill's taste as always had done the trick.

We soon found ourselves in Portsmouth, sitting in an ex-Dutch-army camper van waiting to join the night ferry to Calais before starting the long drive down to our new home. In the back we had a suitcase or two, a few paintings and three German Shepherd dogs: Ben One, Sam and young Hannah. We arrived in France and disembarked at about 7.30. The dogs had to stay in the van during the crossing and we think the ship's crew must have teased them as they had destroyed the netting around the windows. However, they were none the worse for it and we were soon on the open road, full of excitement and anticipation as we set off on the first of our many journeys to come through France and Spain.

We took turns to drive every two or three hours. We managed to get off the dreaded *Périphérique* (the Paris ring road); it can be disastrous if the badly signed turning to the South is missed. Round and round you go! Apart from a stop or two for the dogs to stretch their legs and a *péage* (toll road) or two, the old camper van did us proud and by early evening we found ourselves just outside Bayonne near the Spanish border. By more luck than judgement we found a small hotel with lots of grounds and a field leading into woods which was perfect for the dogs to roam in. The owners were delightful and we had a lovely evening and a good night's sleep.

Next day we were soon over the border into Spain, changing our francs for pesetas, and on our way via Burgos, Segovia, Toledo and then to Madrid. Getting through Madrid for the first time was a bit tricky, to say the least: road numbers change inexplicably and road signs change confusingly. In the end we made it and were soon going through La Mancha and the wine growing region of Valdepeñas.

What a glorious country Spain is. I always think of *la belle France* as a beautiful girl and *España* as a macho man off to a bullfight. Both are wonderful in their different ways; but I do love the drama of Spain a wee bit more!

We pulled in to what looked like a truck-drivers' greasy-spoon cafe. How wrong we were. It turned out to be one of the government-controlled *hostales* of which there are many along the main routes. A large bar serving a delicious selection of tapas, a waiter-service restaurant with food of the highest quality and stairs leading up to (as I found out in future years) scrupulously clean bedrooms and bathrooms. However, on we went as we had set our sights on staying the night at a *parador* in Bailén. As is well known, *paradores* are also government-controlled, many of them in quite superb buildings and locations.

We searched for the one in Bailén but couldn't see it anywhere. We enquired of some locals in our best Spanish, '*Dónde está el parador, por favor?*' They shrugged and we gathered there was no such place. We showed them a written address.

'*Ah,*' they said, '*el para-*DOR.' We had given the wrong inflection. That put us in our place!

As it happened the *para-*DOR was some distance out of our way; it was a lovely moonlit night and we decided that, as we were only three or four hours from our destination, we would keep going. Through the mountains of Andalucia we went, passing Jaen and Granada (more of that later) before the long descent into Malaga. Then on to Fuengirola; and finally around midnight we were in our new home.

We sat by the pool, toasted our new life with champagne and counted thirteen fishing boats in the bay. Sam, who loved water, jumped in the swimming pool and was a bit shocked to realise it was only about a third full! He didn't care though, and neither did we. We opened another bottle and stayed up all night. We were happy. We were home. Our new life had begun!

15
LIFE IN ESPAÑA

W E SETTLED STRAIGHT AWAY into our new way of life. Breakfast outside on the patio, a light lunch of *boquerones* and a beer on the beach, and in the evening discovering our favourite restaurants or staying at home and eating outside in the cool of late evening, and then following up with a midnight swim.

The way of life in Spain was beautifully relaxed and easy-going. In the heat of the afternoon everything closed down for a couple of hours' siesta. Besides the occasional dog bark, the constant swish of the sea and very rare motorbike there was silence. I would walk the dogs high up into the hills where there were spectacular views of the sea and the mountains. Apart from a few villas here and there and a small school it was all uninterrupted country. The Spanish building frenzy was to come several years later.

Meanwhile Lillias was in her element transforming a pretty basic villa into a special one, putting her own individual stamp on it. She is a quite brilliant home-maker. Soon the neglected garden was flourishing, the swimming pool refilled and repainted. The exterior of the villa was also repainted with the aid of Salvador and Luis from the village who worked happily with her. Inside she altered and replaced the kitchen and bought new furniture. This sounds easier than it actually was. You could order things and be promised delivery dates with a smile, and then nothing would happen. Spain was not noted for punctuality and efficiency in this regard and chasing things up could be frustrating to say the least.

We still had the old army camper van but thought it time to get a left-hand-drive car. Off we went to Gibraltar to buy one. We got a second-hand

Citroën, taxed, insured and with a Gibraltar registration number. It was an ideal car for the dirt roads and unexpected streams we encountered, as it had a hydraulic system that could be raised or lowered which we found indispensable.

Gib was also very good for duty-free shopping and cheap petrol. The only snag was getting in and out of the place. If they had a political dispute with Britain the car queue could be long and tedious, and even longer to get out again as the local police examined the car and its contents. However, when relations were good you could be in and out in no time!

I found it a really fascinating place with its busy harbour, barbary apes and narrow streets teeming with traffic and people. British servicemen and women from all branches of the Forces were everywhere. The Rock itself towering above was allegedly loaded with missiles, bombs and weapons, some of which were ready and pointed in the general direction of Libya. The guard outside the Governor General's building was changed at eleven o'clock just like at Buckingham Palace. You can't get more British than that; and, in a referendum, the local population voted almost unanimously against becoming part of Spain.

Incidentally the measures of drinks in the local bars were very British too: rather alarming after generous Spanish servings. There was a tapas bar we would go to on our way home to make up for that and the dreary British food! I am afraid the Spanish way of living wins hands down.

We had a television set at home but the only English-language programme came from Gibraltar TV, and pretty awful it was too. News was nearly all local, read by British ladies who really should have stuck to their day jobs, fluffing and mispronouncing their way through the news bulletins. Even though we love sport, hearing the results of all the Forces' football, cricket and hockey matches did not thrill us greatly. After a year or two of that, cable TV came to our aid. We loved Gibraltar though and were very relieved when the IRA's attempt to infiltrate and blow the place up ended in failure. That would have been quite a bang.

We didn't want a cat, but Di Thorpe persuaded Lill to take one of the many stray kittens and cats that congregated for food round the urbanisation. They were half wild, coming in from the hills to be fed by kind ladies. So a ten-week-or-so-old kitten joined us. We called her Jessica and she became part of the family for the next seventeen years. Not the most beautiful animal but certainly one of the most entertaining. Quite fearless, she immediately took control of our three large German Shepherds. When we took the dogs for a walk she came with us, dashing on ahead, waiting for us and then dashing on ahead again. She was also very protective of her dogs and once leapt on a Yorkshire Terrier innocently passing by. The little dog fell seemingly dead but luckily came round, having had a catatonic fit. Jessica was not half wild for nothing.

Sadly we were not so fortunate with our dogs. Over a period of fifteen months, two died from bloat. Bloat comes suddenly and without warning. Like colic in horses, the intestines become twisted; the animal is in agony and there is no cure. Hannah was the first to get it. I shall never forget driving around one Sunday morning trying to find a vet but all were closed. We had to go all the way to Malaga with lovely young Hannah in terrible pain. Police veterinary surgeons took her in and handled the situation with great sympathy and care but there was no way back for her.

Big black Sam who so loved to swim was the other victim. Woken by his cries in the night, Paul our local vet came out to the villa. Paul seemed to do the trick and Sam's pain eased; but an hour or so later it returned even worse and again there was no way back for him.

The death of these great friends cast a blight over our lives. Ben died too, but at a good age and of natural causes. Even though two more Shepherds, Sally and Joshua, were flown out and were wonderful animals, we never fully got over those deaths which I think had quite a bit to do with our leaving Spain after six years.

All was not doom and gloom, though. As I said, we loved the way of life, the climate was superb and we had quite a good social life. The urbanisation was multi-national and most were pretty friendly. My old friend Donald Pleasence had a villa further up the coast and a townhouse in Fuengirola so we saw quite a bit of him and his wife. Ray and Di Thorpe became very good friends, and Adrian and Clugel Buchel lived nearby. Adrian, an ex-Fulham footballer, would spend a few weeks as a taxi-driver in London and then a few weeks having a good time in Spain. Not a bad way to arrange things.

David and Jenny Cherry who put us on to Spain in the first place had come out to live in the hills beyond Estepona and we had some splendid times with them. David, a clever businessman, would build a villa and Jenny with her unerring taste would do it up beautifully. Meanwhile they had built another villa and so moved into the new one and sold or rented the first one. This they did a time or two. La Coloma is a most beautiful area and we flirted with buying a villa high in the hills there. Fortunately sanity prevailed as no one was really sure what Spanish family actually owned the land!

*

As far as work was concerned it was a busy time for me. I could commute easily to the flat near Gatwick for UK jobs. This was the age of the mini-series so there were a good many trips to various parts of Europe as well.

The miniseries was an American idea and was really a long film for television in several hourly episodes. They took me to Paris, Monte Carlo, Vienna, Zagreb and elsewhere, and so our villa in Spain was an ideal base from which to work. Ray Thorpe would nip up on his moped with scripts delivered to the office (I called him my Spanish agent!); I would learn my lines by the pool, having a dip now and then to cool down; and off I would fly to wherever required. Just about the perfect life for an actor!

Actually, it was pretty hard going sometimes. Deadlines had to be met come what may, and large chunks of scripts would be changed at the last minute; but I still loved it all. A good example of this was the miniseries *Monte Carlo* which we shot along the Riviera from Abbeville to Monaco itself. We lived in Nice for the duration of the shoot and the director, the excellent Anthony Page, frequently asked me to join him at the famous Negresco Hotel, where he was staying, to have supper and work on my scenes for the following day. 'You can't say this rubbish,' he would say, and so an evening's rewriting would begin. An hour or two later I would go back to my hotel up the road and start to learn all the new stuff for the morning. This happened a time or two, but I never got supper!

This was the film in which Joan Collins had a deadline to go back to the States for her part in *Dynasty*. There was a great rush to get her away in time. I played a nasty Nazi who had to interrogate and torture her. She was very heroic and remained silent. This was just as well as we didn't shoot the scene until a week or two later by which time Joan was safely back in *Dynasty*. I actually tortured her look-alike double! Needs must when the devil drives!

Later, in the feature film *Forbidden*, I played another nasty Nazi, this time in Berlin. Anthony Page was again the director. Obviously just a coincidence! At any rate it was a good script which we didn't have to alter. Tony Page, also a wonderful theatre director, worked with Lill for a long time at the Dundee Repertory Theatre and I know she loved working with him too.

As we were living in Spain and there was so much work in Europe, Michael Anderson thought it would be a good idea for me to have an Italian agent working in conjunction with him. A lot of films were still being made in Rome, and Lill and I set off to meet one of the best agents there. Although I had an appointment the lady agent was not the slightest bit interested in me and was apparently too busy even to meet me. I was fobbed off by her assistant and never heard another word! Still, Lill had never been to Rome before so all was not lost. We had time to explore this beautiful city and sample the food and wine.

On the journey home we changed planes in Madrid onto the shuttle to Malaga. It was a Friday evening and the plane was mostly packed with businessmen off to the coast for the weekend. A couple of attempts to take off were aborted before we got to the end of the runway. The perspiring pilot, hat and uniform askew, emerged from his cabin and a lot of rapid Spanish ensued. The gist was that we could get off and wait for another plane, or stay on board and he would have another go. There then followed one of the quickest mass exits from a plane imaginable. All that were left on board were four children and their chaperones, one of the three air-hostesses, Lillias and myself. We reckoned the perspiring pilot wouldn't want to die any more than we did so we stayed in our seats. This time the plane took off smoothly and we had a very pleasant flight to Malaga in a near-empty plane. Lill and I did hold hands until we were high in the air!

Andalucia is a stunningly beautiful region of Spain and we had a memorable holiday motoring round it in our car. We chose midsummer to do it and it was incredibly hot. In one town known as 'the frying pan of Europe' the locals claim you can fry eggs on the pavement, and with storks nesting in the church spire who could doubt them. One advantage of the heat was that not many people were mad enough to holiday in it so it was all quiet and unspoilt by hordes of tourists.

The region is steeped in history. We stayed in Carmona near Seville where there are Roman ruins and where they claim the first known settlers in Europe arrived in 7000 B.C. The cities themselves are all fascinating to visit: Seville for its beauty and for the painter Murillo; Cadiz, from where

Columbus set sail to discover America; and Jerez where sherry comes from. The most awe-inspiring of them all, though, has to be Granada. The Moorish Alhambra and Alcazar is known as one of the seven wonders of the modern world and not without reason.

For us, though, Córdoba became our favourite city of all. Not too far from home, we spent quite a bit of time there. The old Moorish Mezquita with its whole interior lit by sunlight is just stunning. There is a hotel there right in the city centre with a swimming pool on the roof so you can sunbathe and watch the world beneath. It also boasts our favourite Spanish restaurant; perhaps that's really why we loved it so much!

We also set off on a motoring holiday to Morocco. We crossed on the ferry one morning to Ceuta, a small Spanish possession on the North African coast, and after a couple of hours and a bit of negotiation passed through Customs into Morocco. Feeling hungry we stopped at a very nice-looking restaurant for a spot of lunch. We were surprised to find the place empty and nothing much going on, although we were treated with the utmost courtesy by the manager. No one had told us about the two-hour time change and it was only eleven in the morning. We stayed on though and later had a lovely lunch.

It was the month of Ramadan which meant no food or drink, including water, from dawn until after sunset. This was scrupulously observed by the locals although hotels and restaurants remained open for tourists. It was amazing that lovely meals from copious menus were served by waiters and kitchen workers who would not even have a sip of water or a bite of food all day. There was much rejoicing over their meal in the evening, though. Ramadan went on without a break for a whole month. We had nothing but admiration for such dedication.

We drove round quite a bit of the country. After the film, Casablanca was a bit disappointing: it's not beautiful or romantic, being a typical industrial port. However, the Hyatt Hotel is just about the most luxurious we ever stayed in. Rabat, the capital, is a lovely city; and Fez was where I was recognised as a Nazi from films, bringing the kasbah to a halt.

One day driving high up in a very remote spot we got a puncture. We were struggling with the jack when a couple of lads turned up and took over, changing the wheel in no time. Where had they come from? It seemed miles from anywhere and they certainly had no transport. As we drove round the country we noticed bottles of water placed on the side of the road at intervals. This was for truck drivers should they feel faint at the wheel during Ramadan. We learned so much on that holiday. Such a totally different culture and way of life, and yet only a few miles across the water into Europe.

Life in *España* was truly one of the best times of my life. I have so many happy memories of our time there: our villa, the sun, the sea, the food, the wine and all our friends; keeping very fit by running round La Cala with the dogs every morning and playing lots of tennis with Lillias and so many others. Leno, the lovely Spanish owner of the local shop, and I had many battles with the sun at its hottest during his lunch break.

I'm afraid all that pounding on hard courts and hard roads had a price to pay. My left hip gradually packed up and had to be replaced. I had a wonderful surgeon, Juan Oliver, who explained the whole procedure and showed me exactly what he was going to do. The job done, I recovered in a Malaga hospital, which was spotlessly clean and highly efficient with medicines and food arriving dead on time, although there was a couch in the room for the patient's family to do the rest of the nursing. But we managed, and after a day or two I was stretchered into an ambulance and we set off for home. From time to time I had to rise from my stretcher to give the driver directions as he hadn't much idea where I lived!

There then followed several weeks of some pretty tough physiotherapy in Malaga. This was hard for me but even harder for Lill who had to get me in and out of the car and into the building and back. After a few weeks of this I was pretty well back to normal; but sadly there was no more tennis and no more running, both of which I really missed, especially the running. There is nothing like a good run to clear the air and brain!

Robert Lindsay offered me a part in a sitcom he was doing and I thought it would be a nice little number to ease my way back to work. Not a bit of it: I had to dive through a window onto some mats below. No harm was done though; Juan Oliver had done a good job!

*

It was now 1990 and I found myself cast in a TV serial called *Chancer*. Little did I know at the time but it was to involve me in a couple of series over a period of eighteen months or so. It was set in the Midlands, and I played a Middle European tycoon, the owner of a sports-car factory.

Strangely enough I don't remember a lot about the story; but I well remember my first day on it. The series was well under way when I arrived. The young lady producer was obviously not too sure about my being right for the part, or indeed whether I would know my lines, as she sat about a yard or so from me with the script in her hand. Once her fears were allayed we got on very well and I enjoyed working with 'the divine Sarah' as she was affectionately known by one and all.

On that first day, Leslie Phillips asked me to lunch. We hadn't met before and it was over lunch that we agreed that neither of us had ever been out of work in our careers. He won though: I had started at sixteen years of age but he began when he was a child actor aged about eleven. In *Chancer* he played London banker Jimmy Blake and he was tremendous fun to work with.

The biggest bonus of all, though, was working with the young actor playing the title role. Clive Owen and I had immediate rapport; both perfectionists, we really hit it off. Clive is so brilliant, so real, you didn't feel you were with an actor but the character itself. With this quality it is no surprise to me that he has become one of the very top film actors worldwide. Both liking a flutter on the horses, we visited most of the race tracks within fifty miles or so of Birmingham; when we both had a day off we would end up having a great time, win or lose.

Almost a decade later I worked with Clive again in the television series *Second Sight*. I was yet another villain, this time a completely blind one. Our rapport had not diminished over the years, and one of the cast (I won't say his name to spare his blushes) watched all our duologues and described them as a masterclass in how to act on film. Very flattering, but it's hard not to be good when acting with Clive. He was just the same lovely, unspoilt man, and an even better actor with a decade of experience under his belt.

Being in *Chancer* for all that time had its ups and downs but working with Leslie Phillips and especially Clive Owen made it a memorable experience. However, there was a real downside to all this fun and games: I missed being in Spain at home with Lill. I was either in the flat at Well House or in the Holiday Inn in Birmingham. When the weather was bad and the schedule had to be changed it meant it became difficult to get home; and in the end I think all these inconveniences contributed considerably to our decision to sell up in Spain and come back to England. Life in *España* was over.

Well, not quite. There was a bit of an economic depression at that time and we couldn't sell the villa. We still wanted to get back to England though. Lillias was saddened by the loss of her three dogs, and lonely when on her own, so was keen to get away. She was dropped socially when I was absent: single women were not invited out much.

As we couldn't sell the villa we rented it through a very reputable agency for short-term holiday lets for a year. We flew back home to Gatwick with Josh, Sally and Jessica in the hold of the plane; they were then to go into quarantine for six months. Life in Spain was certainly over for them. The quarantine kennels were good though, and not too far away so we managed to visit them every day. Jess had a great time snarling at her neighbours in the cattery, and we managed to give the dogs a run at the back of the kennels on Sundays though this was not really allowed.

Meanwhile, thanks to a generous non-interest loan from Gregor, we bought the lower storeys of Well House; and Lill's next project was joining our flat with the rest of the property and turning it into one big beautiful home.

16
OUR FRIENDS IN THE NINETIES

I T WAS NOW 1991 and Lillias was creating a lovely house and garden in Crawley Down. We had let our Spanish villa and our animals were out of quarantine with a lovely garden to roam in. We also had a fish pond which the cat, Jessica, had to be ducked in to dissuade her from doing a bit of fishing with her paw. Our friends Linda and Graham Ling were our neighbours on one side and Mary Warren sold fruit and vegetables on the other. Directly across the road, Peter Cook and his family had a wonderful farm shop. All in all a splendid place to live.

However, renting out our home in Spain was not a success. At the end of a year it took us a month's hard work to clean the place up, so we decided we had no choice but to put the villa up for sale. Due to the economic downturn of the time, finding a buyer was none too easy; but we did manage it after a month or two and got out more or less unscathed.

So that was the end of our Spanish holdings... well, not quite. Over our years in Spain we had stashed away some money in a Gibraltar bank. I had closed this account some weeks earlier and left the money with my friend David Cherry for safe keeping. I was in Spain on my own tying up the sale of the villa; that done, it was now time to leave and of course take the cash with me. The trouble was it was only legal to take a small amount out of the country. I decided to risk carrying the money in my hand baggage and hope it would not be checked. Airport security was not so strict in those days but, even so, going through the departure gate at Malaga the odd bag was opened and looked through. I just had to hope for the best; but to my horror mine was picked out and all my illicit gains were revealed.

'*Muchos dinero,*' the man said, raising an eyebrow.

Quick as a flash I replied, '*Casino!*' rubbing my thumb and forefinger in a gesture of triumph.

Obviously a gambling man, he seemed very pleased for me, closed up my bag and let me through.

I had a fairly nervous flight wondering whether I would be so lucky getting out of Gatwick. In the event I strolled through the NOTHING TO DECLARE gate unmolested. Yes, I suppose for once I was a real villain as opposed to all my acting ones. I must say the money was very useful when I finally got it to the UK. We didn't have to draw cash from the bank for quite a while! Selling the villa meant Gregor could be repaid his generous interest-free loan, and Lillias could set about using her creative skills to make Well House a really lovely home.

Leaving Spain was a real wrench for me. I love that country and its way of life. That being said, I know we left at the right time. The tourist boom and building binge was just getting out of hand. I still yearn for those late meals followed by a midnight swim, though.

*

As far as work is concerned I suppose I was, by 1990, reasonably well established. Well, I should be, at sixty-seven years of age and having already spent about fifty years in the business. However, the old doubts and fears remained. Would I get another job and, if so, would I be able to do it? Actually, this insecurity is essential to an actor and I really need it to keep on going.

For some strange reason my CV in the nineties has great gaps in it. This is probably just as well as it will stop me boring Jeremy Kemp with a litany of 'then I did this and then I did that'. However, I do have a few random memories that I am going to put down.

In *Dandelion Dead*, a dramatisation of the true story of the Hay-on-Wye murderer, I played the local doctor who went on his rounds on horseback. I hadn't ridden for years but thoroughly enjoyed myself. Each year I send out Christmas cards from the Injured Jockeys' Fund; in my innocence I sent one to Mike Hodges, our lovely director, who thought it was absolutely hilarious to receive it from the horse-riding doctor. I hadn't seen the joke at all and sent it without thinking. A bit slow on the uptake there.

It was a very pleasant shoot with a brilliant cast. Bernard Hepton and I had not met up since *Season's Greetings* in the theatre ten years before. We just picked up our friendship as if it were ten weeks, not years. The bond between actors who have worked closely together never fades. We are a unique tribe! Clive Owen dropped in during the shoot and jokingly sent me up, saying that I was sliding down the slippery slope of success. 'Not yet, Clive,' I said, 'not quite yet.'

Back home my uncharacteristic optimism was fuelled by Michael, my agent, who said there was a part in the next Merchant Ivory film which he thought would be perfect for me. I found myself in James Ivory's office with Anthony Hopkins by his side. I was being interviewed for the part of Mr Stevens Senior in the film adaptation of the superb novel *The Remains of the Day*. I had read the book, and just occasionally you find a character you know you have to play: in this case the aged butler, father of the head butler of the household to be played by Tony Hopkins. The interview went quite well. I hadn't met either of them before and I wasn't really sure what they thought of me. To my absolute delight I got the part. Without a doubt the best film role of all for me, before or since, was mine.

Working under James Ivory's direction was different to anything I had known before. On my very first day of shooting I had to carry a very large tray of silver and crockery across a courtyard, slip and crash to the ground. As we set up the shot James said nothing to me. So I asked him if he had any ideas as to how I should do it.

'Well,' he said, 'I think you have got a bit of arthritis in your hands and aren't too good on your feet.'

That was all I needed to know: not only for that scene, but I integrated it into my whole performance. Absolutely perfect direction, and he probably wouldn't have said it if I hadn't asked him!

Later in the film I had quite a long scene where I tell everyone about my life as a butler in India. We rehearsed and shot it and James said absolutely nothing to me. After several takes I could stand it no longer and asked him if it was all right. He said he was enjoying it so much he didn't want to intervene. That was just inspirational to me. He was equally brilliant with crowd scenes, noting every detail and picking out anything that was not quite right. Quite a director, and I loved working with him. Later Denholm Elliott, who had done a film or two with James, described him to me as being like one of those men sitting at the edge of the Serpentine with a radio-controlled boat on the water, only pressing his button when required to guide it away from the edge and avoid touching other boats: very gentle but in total control.

His partner, Ismail Merchant, was the producer and money man, though he did direct me with the second unit in a couple of kitchen scenes. A very clever man and also renowned for the curries he made for the whole unit at the end of each week's work. This was a weekly ritual which one was expected to attend.

Socially I had an evening or two with Hugh Grant around the pubs and clubs of Bath. Not a great star then, he told me how he went each morning and sat on the steps of our agency until eventually they saw him. Like Bob Hoskins before him, you have to both be brilliant and go the extra mile of effort to get right to the top.

During filming I became good friends with Christopher Reeve, a really stimulating and uplifting person to be with. We would talk politics over dinner. He was very active in the Democratic Party and a great supporter of Al Gore. He was also extremely fit, and full of energy and curiosity about things. No wonder he had played Superman. I thoroughly enjoyed being in his company. The terrible horse-riding accident which paralysed him and, after a long struggle, finally overwhelmed him was a real tragedy. What a loss.

Tony Hopkins is a quite extraordinary actor. Terribly funny and a great mimic when not filming, he would go straight into a serious or emotional scene without a pause. Off the set I noticed he followed me about and spent quite a bit of time with me. I soon realised this was to study how I walked, how I ate and drank, how I gestured and so on. Nothing was said, but it was all to do with playing my son.

One day after a scene together he said to me, 'I knew you'd be all right when I met you. You're loosely tied, aren't you?' I think he meant that I am open to different ideas, different ways of doing scenes. Maybe I'm wrong, though: he could have meant I'm like an old bag, about to fall apart at any minute.

Brilliant though he was, one morning he did a scene which was frankly over the top, doing extraneous business and ad libs. Going to lunch in a car with James Ivory and Emma Thompson, our leading lady, we all agreed something had to be done.

'You tell him, Emma, he'll listen to you,' said James.

And after lunch she did tell him and he did listen. They played so superbly with each other. Some of their work together is breathtaking, and at times heart-stoppingly moving. I think the film is a true classic. But then I would, wouldn't I?

On its release *The Remains of the Day* was universally acclaimed and is now regarded as a film classic. Although I died about a third of the way through the film, I came out of it pretty well. In fact the bosses at Columbia Films tried to get me nominated for a Best Supporting Actor at that year's Oscars, but alas they did not succeed!

Agent Michael thought it a perfect time for me to go out to Los Angeles (at my own expense I might add!) and meet the top casting directors at various studios; all this to be laid on by the LA branch of our agency. So I found myself emerging from the airport to be met by the driver of a huge stretch limo. Who did they think I had brought with me: wife, family, secretary, make-up artist, personal trainer? But no, there was only me and a suitcase, so I sat in front with the driver. There had recently been an earthquake and the journey into town was pretty sobering as I saw some of the devastation it had caused. The San Andreas Fault runs through LA and one couldn't help wondering about the future.

I was duly delivered to the Chateau Marmont Hotel on Sunset Boulevard, a veritable oasis in a sea of concrete with its own cottages and swimming pool. I stayed in the Chateau itself with its pretty basic amenities. The guests were, without exception, employed in films or television. This was *the* place to stay. I knew this as Donald Pleasence always stayed there. The place buzzed with deals being done over breakfast and people meeting up as they passed through. I found myself in the pool swimming with the producer of *My Left Foot* telling me about Daniel Day Lewis whom he had known twelve years earlier in Dublin. It was to be my base for an absolutely fascinating couple of weeks.

Our LA agents had done their stuff and I had a whole itinerary of studios to visit. Most of them were out of town and, as I had no car and there is virtually no public transport system, there was nothing for it but to hire a succession of taxis. This was a slightly tricky business as many of the drivers had only recently arrived from Russia and the former Communist countries of Eastern Europe and had not yet totally mastered the language, or indeed the routes involved. However, we got by and so it was Paramount one day, 20th Century Fox the next and so on.

LA is wholly devoted to the film and TV industry and those connected with it. Everyone seems to be involved in the business or (more likely) trying to become so. In the meantime would-be actresses work as waitresses and would-be actors as hotel receptionists. There was a lovely example of this when I turned up at Disney Studios. The man at the gate greeted me with, 'Peter *"Time Bandits"* Vaughan – welcome to Disney Studios!' He told me he was writing screenplays which he was hoping to get put on. I was greeted with enthusiasm and plaudits wherever I went. Being British and in a successful film, I couldn't go wrong.

Columbia were casting a big film and there was a part they thought I could play. Unfortunately the director was not in town and John Neville, my old friend from Birmingham days, got the part. Why not? He lived there, and anyway was more right for it than I was. Next morning over a coffee and a bagel with the boss of Columbia I was told to go home and not join all those British actors on Malibu Beach moaning about their near misses. I took him at his word, but not before a final meeting with HBO (Home Box Office). I had an excellent meeting with the casting director for a part in *Fatherland*, a TV film to be shot in Prague. The boss was called in. He asked me if I had come to clean the office (he had seen *The Remains of the Day*) and gave me the part. Not a bad joke from my point of view.

I had an amazing time in LA, meeting lots of important people and seeing all those studios which had just been romantic names to me. I had a nice time socially too, being taken by friends Earl and Barbara Barrett to a couple of great restaurants; and I came away with a job or two. However, there was no stretch limo to take me back to the airport: I had to pay for my own taxi. The *Fatherland* deal was done by Michael in London, so there was nothing in it for the LA office. That to me summed up the place in a nutshell: a great place for a quick raid only. It confirmed to me that I am strictly a European through and through.

I did look in the phone book in search of long-lost cousins and got quite excited to find several Ohms there. Further investigation, however, showed that they all came from countries like South Korea and were named after the traditional Buddhist chant, *Ohhhmmm...* Not a Middle European amongst them.

*

Fatherland was an adaptation of the best-selling Robert Harris novel. Set in the 1960s, the premise was that Hitler had won the Second World War and was occupying Czechosolvakia.

Prague had only recently emerged from Communism when we arrived there. This beautiful city was untouched by the war: it was just too far away for Allied bombers to reach. It seemed to me, though, that it was now being overrun by the worst of Western capitalism, from McDonald's to Mickey Mouse architecture. Second-hand cars were being imported from Germany in droves. A quick buck was easily to be made and companies and individuals from the UK and USA were doing just that. I know all this from chatting to various people in the hotel bar.

I played the Chief of Police, and the filming was interesting in that our office location was the old Communist Central Office. It was quite an eerie feeling to be playing scenes sitting at the actual desk in the actual room of the former Government Chief of Police, especially as there was a switch at one's foot which would at one time have been pressed to summon officers to deal with uncooperative or unwanted interviewees.

We left Prague for a few days on location at Stratavice, a lovely old town the centre of which had been ruined by ugly tower blocks. This was the first time the Czech members of the crew had left Prague since the so-called liberation, and they were determined to enjoy themselves. I found myself one morning waiting for my driver outside my hotel in the freezing cold for three quarters of an hour. He turned up with an obvious hangover, grinned and, together with a certain gesture, said: 'Jig-a-jig very good.' Fortunately for him I was not in that day's first scene. Under Communism such words as fired, sacked or redundant didn't seem to be in the vocabulary.

On a day off back in Prague I visited the Jewish Cemetery and Synagogue. There was a museum there with pictures on the walls of children at Treblinka concentration camp. The tourists going round looking at them with remarks like 'Isn't she pretty?' 'Oh, what a shame,' and 'This one survived Dachau' sickened me and I had to leave.

I went back to Prague a year or two later to play the Bishop in *Les Misérables*, an adaptation of the Victor Hugo novel. The city seemed to have moved on from its Wild West excesses of the period immediately following the fall of Communism, at least so far as one could tell from surface appearances. The film was pretty unremarkable, though I had a good scene or two with Liam Neeson, and I met up with Geoffrey Rush, whose father I played some years later in *The Life and Death of Peter Sellers*. In this latter film Geoffrey played eighteen different characters: a stunning piece of work. Miriam Margolyes played his mother and therefore my wife. On her first day she announced herself to everyone in the make-up room as follows: 'My name is Miriam Margolyes; I am a sixty-three-year-old Jewish lesbian.' This brought a rather stunned silence which I broke by saying, 'Oh Miriam, surely you're not 63?' This got a pretty good laugh and broke the ice. I loved working with her. To go with her huge, even outrageous, personality there is a highly sensitive and wonderful actress.

Work was prolific in the UK during the nineties too, and I have to mention *The Moonstone* with Anthony Sher and *The Choir* with David Warner. There was also *Our Mutual Friend* playing Mr Boffin and with a young Anna Friel giving a lesson in how not to treat people in the unit such as hair, make-up and costume. I am sure that by now she will know that is not the way to make friends and influence people!

Then there was *Our Friends in the North*. I knew I had to play the part and almost bullied them into giving it to me. The story brilliantly covered some thirty years on Tyneside seen through the eyes of four young friends. I played Felix, the father of Nicky, one of the four, played by Christopher Eccleston. I can safely say this was my most thrilling TV experience. At the story's opening I was a real hard nut aged forty-seven! As I was now over seventy this was a tough one for the hair and make-up departments, but I think we got away with it.

Luckily as the story unfolds the character gets older and older. Eventually the old shipyard worker who started as a sixteen-year-old in the Jarrow hunger-strike march ended up going through all the stages of Alzheimer's disease. To try to do justice to these scenes I spent some days at the Crawley Centre for dementia. What I saw and learned there about this terrible and underfunded disease made me take it up as my charity work, and I was later able to help raise money and awareness through both the Alzheimer Research Trust and Disease Society.

Working with Chris Eccleston as my son was magical. We even looked like each other, and we became great buddies right from the start. Sadly I have never worked with Chris since. What an actor he is. Daniel Craig was also in it and I have been in a couple of films with him since; he is another fabulous actor and that year he and I found ourselves nominated for Best

Actor by the Royal Television Society. We were each happy for the other one to get the award, but neither of us did: it went to David Jason. Our cry of 'Oh no, not him!' was pretty audible, but fortunately we were not on camera. Never mind. *Our Friends in the North* was my greatest TV experience and I loved every minute of it.

My last scenes on the series were shot at night, after which I had to go straight to Newcastle Airport and catch a plane to Boston, Massachusetts. I had been cast in the film version of Arthur Miller's *The Crucible*, about the famous so-called witches of Salem, and that is where the film was being made. After the drive from the airport I was welcomed by Daniel Day-Lewis who took the trouble to show me around and point out where everything was. I really appreciated Daniel taking such trouble and making me feel so at home.

I played the farmer Giles Corey: a very good part, with the famous 'more weight' scene. If you don't count Daniel, as he is from Dublin, I was the only British actor in the film. As I met the American actors and crew they were all extremely pleasant and friendly to me, none more so than Winona Ryder. She would ring me up and ask me to a movie or to have a meal. She was a quite delightful and caring person. I am so pleased that she is back working again after her personal difficulties in the early noughties.

The director was also from Britain – Nicholas Hytner, the well-established London theatre director – but I am not sure that he had done much filming. I never felt at ease with him, and I got the feeling that he would really have preferred someone else as Giles Corey. Fortunately, quite early on a voice boomed out as a large man bounded towards me saying, 'Peter Vaughan, my Giles Corey! I am thrilled you are able to do it.' He gave me a great bear hug; and that was my introduction to my hero, Arthur Miller.

Meeting and talking with Arthur made the whole trip really special to me. There was still hostility towards him in some quarters. His son Bob, who produced the film, said that he had great difficulty getting the film put on as he insisted that his father should write the screenplay. This seemed unbelievable to me: such was his unpopularity in Hollywood. I discussed this later at the premiere with American writer Earl Barret who said that he had not been forgiven for Marilyn, whatever that means. Don't tell me his politics didn't have something to do with it.

To get back to the making of the film, Daniel Day-Lewis and Joan Allen as John Proctor and his wife were both superb and it was a privilege to be working with them; but there was one more joy to come. Paul Scofield – in my opinion Britain's finest actor of all – arrived to play Judge Danforth, and I had a scene with him. Only a short one, but it was really something special. After the somewhat mixed reviews the film received, he wrote me a letter which I treasure saying *But we know we made a good film.*

It was a pretty lonely life on that film, stuck in a hotel in the countryside, and it was a huge relief when Lill came out to join me. She brightened things up straight away (Joan Allen thought she was wonderful). One day we went out to sea from Gloucester on a whale-watching trip. We were lucky enough to see those wonderful creatures at very close quarters as they came right up to our boat, spouting and diving round us. But for us perhaps the most satisfying experience of all was to be in a bar when the news came on the TV that we had won the Ryder Cup. Our unconfined pleasure was not much appreciated by the locals. Americans must always be winners!

Lillias came out to LA for the film's premiere, too. Daniel was strongly tipped for a Best Actor Oscar; but a couple of days before the premiere he married Arthur Miller's daughter, Rebecca, and suddenly Daniel was no longer mentioned. Was this a coincidence, I wonder?

The whole trip was quite an experience, and one of my fondest memories of it was breakfasting in the Beverly Hills Hilton with Bob Miller and his wife plus Lillias and Arthur. Addresses were exchanged and we were all going to meet up in the future, but of course we never did. I was going to do a film with Rebecca Miller, but sadly the money fell through at the last moment. A pity because we got on really well and I know how talented she is, obviously taking after her dad.

*

Back home I went straight into rehearsals for a theatre production of *Twelve Angry Men*: on the face of it, not the best move after just finishing a big film, but I couldn't resist being summoned by the director – none other than Harold Pinter. I had known Harold socially for many years, but apart from acting with him on radio this was the first time I had worked with him.

I played the unpleasant racist Juror No. 10. I would have loved to play the Lee J. Cobb part, but Tony Haygarth had got it. Why not? His wife was part of the management. Never mind: I had a very good contract, Dressing Room 1 and a hotel room on matinee days.

After a packed-out six-week season at the Bristol Old Vic, we came to the Comedy Theatre in London for sixteen weeks. Although best known as a playwright, Harold was also an excellent actor and director, and I think it was a very good production with a fine cast. My being in Dressing Room 1 was quite amusing. Timothy West was given Dressing Room 4 at the end of a long corridor. Tim and I are good mates, having done plenty of television plays together, and he didn't seem too bothered about the situation. Not so Mrs West, namely Prunella Scales, cutting me dead as she stalked past me in the corridor a couple of times. I wanted to remind her of the fun we had doing Shakespeare excerpts live on children's TV when she was just beginning.

Early on in the run, the phone rang in my room. 'Hullo,' I said.

'Timothy...' a voice replied.

I discreetly suggested she try number 4.

Harold loved to have a jar or two with the actors after the show. We would talk politics; he absolutely loathed American capitalism and the influence it had on the world. He would never go to America, yet his plays were regularly being performed there. Lillias and I saw a production at the Lincoln Centre when we were in New York. This made me feel better about doing *Zulu Dawn* in South Africa during apartheid, which I was never sure I should have done. Our other topic of conversation of course was cricket, both of us being cricket nuts.

Talking of cricket, Lillias and I had done a couple of tours with the England team to South Africa, and later to Zimbabwe. One incident there is worth recalling. We were sitting in the pavilion at Harare Sports Club watching a test match when Robert Mugabe arrived. Lillias brushed past him on her way to the loo, and to this day believes an assassination would have been all too easy! Actually, this lovely country was in very good order at that time with no hint of the terrible events to come later. I think she still regrets the possible missed opportunity though!

Twelve Angry Men had completed its London run and Harold wanted me to do a revival of his play *The Homecoming* which would have meant going straight into rehearsal. I thought long and hard but decided it was time to get back into TV and films. I don't think Harold was best pleased with this decision, but I was feeling pretty tired or perhaps I just chickened out. Probably the latter – I've always been a bit of a coward.

17
SCOTLAND HERE WE COME

BY NOW WE HAD MOVED from our beloved Well House back into Crawley itself, for the somewhat bizarre reason that our family doctor, Ian MacIntosh, could no longer look after us in Crawley Down so we had to move into Crawley. Redwood Lodge was a rather tatty B & B with a gorgeous redwood tree at its gate. A great project for Lillias: she turned it into another lovely family home, and we lived there happily for four years or so. By now it was the end of the century.

Unfortunately during my time in Crawley I developed macular disease of the eyes. Briefly this meant that I could no longer drive or read except very slowly and with a high-powered magnifying glass. My long sight is not bad, but I have to get very close to people to distinguish their features. This can sometimes quite alarm people, especially young girls!

I was incredibly lucky to have an extremely delicate operation which at that time only three eye surgeons in the UK were capable of performing. One of them, John Bell, did the operation on both my eyes quite brilliantly and I was saved from gradually going completely blind except for a tiny bit of peripheral vision. I feel so deeply sorry for the thousands of people going blind because they are unable to pay for this operation. Anyway, I am now registered partially sighted for the rest of my life, although I can see things on TV if I get close enough to it.

Where would I be without Lillias? A superb driver, she takes me everywhere; she reads interesting bits of news and sport to me and generally keeps me going. As far as work is concerned she reads my scripts aloud to me (quite brilliantly, I might add; why did she give up acting? What a loss);

she then helps me learn my lines so that, by the time I go to work, I know them inside out. She also keeps me going when I feel a bit sorry for myself with either a hug or a good talking-to, but usually with a hug. Without her love and devotion I could not have coped at all.

I must say that the people of our profession (our tribe) have been pretty marvellous too. Steering me about, saying who they are and showing me where the loo is. However, once on the set no quarter is asked or given.

Gregor Fisher, that dyed-in-the-wool Scot, first put the idea of moving to Scotland in our heads: cheap living and low property prices were very alluring. Lillias was thrilled at the idea of having three young grandchildren whom she rarely saw living close by. Quite soon, therefore, Redwood Lodge was sold up and I found myself buying a house unseen (shades of Spain) in the small town of Langholm on the Scottish borders.

Once again Lillias had done the trick. Warren Heights, our home for the next four years, was a really good house with a fine garden and views over the town. Of course, it needed extensive alterations in both house and garden to suit our taste, so Lill was in her element with another large project.

From my own point of view, though, there were major difficulties, especially as far as my work was concerned. London was a long way away and I think some people assumed that I must have gone up to Scotland to retire! Going to London for a meeting was an expensive business: the drive to Carlisle, a five-hour train to Euston and sometimes an overnight stop cost money.

I did some good films during this period though: *The Queen of Sheba's Pearls*, *The Mother* and *Malice Aforethought* for example. Most excitingly I met up with the American director Frank Oz, who showed me a script called *Death at a Funeral* which made me laugh out loud when Lill read it to me. The part of Uncle Alfie was made for me and I was determined to get it. Frank was not easily persuaded. In the end, over lunch, he gave me the part.

Working on this film was one of the happiest times ever. Frank Oz is a genuinely funny man and a highly thought-of Hollywood director. He is also the voice of Miss Piggy in *The Muppet Show*. A great cast and we all had a ball making it. The film was very successful around the world until it came to the UK where the critics absolutely slated it. One of them said none of the cast should ever be allowed to work again. Sorry dear, we're all still quite busy! I still think it's a hilarious film, and working with and knowing Frank was one of the peaks of my career.

Back to writing about Scotland, I have to say that I never really felt accepted there. With one or two exceptions I never got beyond a 'hullo' or two. I have lived in many varied places around the world and always got on well with people, but not so in Langholm. A few miles away in Longtown the atmosphere was completely different – relaxed and friendly. Longtown is in England! Could it be because I don't have a drop of Scottish blood in my veins? Langholm has beautiful countryside, with superb views from the hills, and Ben and I had some lovely walks. The local ice-cream is great too, but the winters are cold and wet and the summers accompanied by swarms of midges. All in all I was never happier than when the four years were up and I returned to the ironic humour of sunny Sussex. I suppose if I have any roots at all, Sussex has become them. Living there and with the occasional trip round my old London haunts suits me fine.

Though more selective, I was still doing good work; and I was excited when I was asked to be in a big film named *Is Anybody There?* Set in an old people's home in the 1980s, it was beautifully cast with a set of uniquely different characters played by Sylvia Syms, Leslie Phillips, Rosemary Harris and others. I loved my part, an old World War I veteran suffering from shell shock. Michael Caine played an old magician who comes to the home and he and the twelve-year-old son of the owners become friends.

With this cast, a lovely script and a really fine director, John Crowley, what could go wrong? Surely this was to be a hugely entertaining, successful art movie. How wrong could I be. The end product was nothing like the film we had made. The powers that be, and presumably the editor, had seen to that. All we different characters in the home were reduced to mere background caricatures with little to commend them. Instead the relationship between the old magician and the boy was developed and meandered on and on without much happening. Sir Michael Caine is one of our best film actors: he has a great presence, energy, precision, peerless comedy timing and power. I have to say, though, that in my opinion sweet, loveable old men are not high on the list of his attributes. To be honest I think it is a pretty ordinary film, soon to disappear in the mists of time.

'Is anybody there?' the cinema box-office manager asked of the usherette.

'Not many, not many at all,' came the reply.

18
WHAT'S NEXT?

B Y 2009 WE WERE EXPERIENCING what was euphemistically called an 'economic downturn'. In other words, the country was skint, with little money to invest in our profession. I hadn't worked for almost a year, but strangely I felt pretty sanguine about it. Am I past my sell-by date, I wondered? My agent, Sally, told me definitely not; and I felt sure if an interesting job came along I would leap at it with my usual energy and enthusiasm.

Then, just as it seemed I might finally have to face the prospect of quiet retirement, I was offered the chance to play a recurring guest role in a new big-budget fantasy drama series called *Game of Thrones*. They told me that the character, who was called Maester Aemon Targaryen, was around a hundred years old (cheek! I was a mere eighty-seven at the time), but still sharp-witted and sought out for his wise counsel – and also blind. I said it sounded interesting... But that's another story.

*

Last year, after five enjoyable years, I played Maester Aemon for the last time; and now here we are at the beginning of 2016, with my ninety-third birthday approaching fast.

Asked whether the process of acting is the same as when I began some seventy-five years ago, the answer is a definite yes. The world in which we now live has changed and the circumstances in which we act have changed enormously too; but the actual process remains the same.

In my view there are three distinct types of actors and actresses. There are those who are admired for their looks and personality and give exactly the same performance whatever part they play. Then we have the *look at me* ACTING, *aren't I clever?* school. I call them the 'demonstrators', and they are often hugely popular with the public.

The third school are those who try to transcend 'acting' and really *become* the character they are playing. I try to do this and it is often very difficult to achieve; but when you pull it off it can be a bit special. I call it 'finding the man'. Well, that's just me, and as we are dealing with the human condition I am sure there are infinite variations on the theme.

That's enough of me pontificating about acting. It's best to just do it and see what comes out. Kenneth Haigh summed it up perfectly after watching a class at the Strasberg School of Acting in New York. He said, 'It's simple – some people act better than others!'

*

While I am more or less *compos mentis* and before I go off to join the Big Repertory Company in the Sky, here are a few random thoughts. First of all: here I am! It's a miracle but, despite near misses in both peace and war, I have somehow survived.

As an old unwavering socialist I am in despair of the world I find myself in. Market forces prevail and western capitalism thrives. Wars, genocide, starvation abound. In our own country, governments of differing colours come and go, and yet still the rich get richer and the poor get poorer. I just shrug my shoulders and hope for the best.

Despite these woes I have to say that I am an incredibly lucky person. Early on in my army career a sergeant said, 'Ohm, you were born lucky. If you fell out of an aircraft you'd land in a haystack.' I think he was right. All my working life I have been paid for what I love doing. Here I am, living in a pleasant village in a lovely period cottage made perfect by Lillias in another of her brilliant projects. There are roses round the door and even a friendly pub for a neighbour. I have a wonderful family enriching my life. Vicki and Gregor and Alex and their children Al, Jamie, Cissie and Chloe are all amazing in their different ways. David Max is constantly on hand, always with a word or two of wisdom and to help us with any problem or difficulty. What a mate he is.

I am so grateful, firstly to Alex and then to Georgia, David's delightful partner, for all the devoted work they have done on this book, turning my dodgy longhand into neatly legible type. I'll say I am lucky. Who could ask for anything more? As Lillias' Aunt Elspeth said: 'I have nothing to come back for.' Neither have I, Elspeth, but despite being so ancient I hope to be here a little while longer, touch wood. It might be hard to get a decent part in that rep in the sky. Too much competition.

Meanwhile I'll try not to be too much of a nuisance, but I don't suppose I'll succeed. Once a villain…

FILM AND TV APPEARANCES

Films (including short films)

2011	*Albatross* (Grandpa)
2008	*Is Anybody There?* (Bob)
2007	*Death at a Funeral* (Uncle Alfie)
2006	*Care* (Archie)
2004	*The Queen of Sheba's Pearls* (Edward Pretty)
2004	*The Life and Death of Peter Sellers* (Bill Sellers)
2003	*The Mother* (Toots)
2001	*Kiss Kiss (Bang Bang)* (Daddy Zoo)
2000	*Hotel Splendide* (Morton Blanche)
2000	*Canone Inverso – Making Love* (Old Baron Blau)
1999	*An Ideal Husband* (Phipps)
1998	*The Good Son* (Mick Doyle)
1998	*The Legend of 1900* (Pops)
1998	*Les Misérables* (Bishop)
1997	*Face* (Sonny)
1996	*The Crucible* (Giles Corey)
1996	*The Secret Agent* (The Driver)
1993	*The Remains of the Day* (William Stevens)
1990	*King of the Wind* (Captain)
1990	*Mountains of the Moon* (Lord Houghton)
1986	*Haunted Honeymoon* (Francis Abbot Sr)
1985	*Brazil* (Mr Helpmann)
1984	*Forbidden* (Major Stauffel)

1984	*The Razor's Edge* (Mackenzie)
1981	*The French Lieutenant's Woman* (Mr Freeman)
1981	*Time Bandits* (Winston the Ogre)
1979	*Porridge* (Harry Grout)
1979	*Zulu Dawn* (QSM Bloomfield)
1977	*Valentino* (Rory O'Neil)
1974	*Intimate Reflections* (Saleman)
1974	*11 Harrowhouse* (Coglin)
1974	*Symptoms* (Brady)
1973	*Massacre in Rome* (Gen Albert Kesselring)
1973	*Malachi's Cove* (Mr Gunliffe)
1973	*The Mackintosh Man* (Brunskill)
1973	*The Blockhouse* (Aufret)
1973	*The Return*
1972	*Savage Messiah* (Museum Attendant)
1972	*The Pied Piper* (Bishop)
1971	*Straw Dogs* (Tom Hedden)
1970	*Eyewitness* (Paul Grazzini)
1969	*Taste of Excitement* (Inspector Malling)
1969	*Alfred the Great* (Burrud)
1968	*A Twist of Sand* (Johann)
1968	*Hammerhead* (Hammerhead)
1968	*The Bofors Gun* (Sgt Walker)
1967	*The Man Outside* (Nikolai Volkov)
1967	*The Naked Runner* (Martin Slattery)
1965	*Rotten to the Core* (Sir Henry Capell)
1965	*Fanatic* (Harry)
1964	*Smokescreen* (Roper)
1963	*The Victors* (Policeman)
1963	*The Punch and Judy Man* (Committee Man)
1962	*The Devil's Agent* (Chief of Hungarian Police)
1962	*I Thank a Fool* (Police Inspector)
1961	*The Court Martial of Major Keller* (Purvey)
1961	*Two Living, One Dead* (John Kester)
1960	*Make Mine Mink* (Policeman in Car)
1960	*Village of the Damned* (PC Gobby)

| 1959 | *Sapphire* (Detective Whitehead) |
| 1959 | *The 39 Steps* (2nd Police Constable on Train) |

Television series, plays and TV movies

2011-2015	*Game of Thrones* (series regular, Maester Aemon)
2011	*Doc Martin* (William Newcross, 'Born with a Shotgun')
2011	*Silk* (Michael Dodd)
2009	*The Antiques Rogue Show* (George Greenhalgh)
2008	*Holby Blue* (Clarence)
2008	*Lark Rise to Candleford* (Reverend Ellison)
2007	*Christmas at the Riviera* (Glen)
2007	*Mobile* (Grandad Stoan)
2005	*Heartbeat* (Mr Andrews, 'The End of the Road')
2005	*Malice Aforethought* (Widdicombe)
2004	*Beauty* (Mr Robbins)
2003	*Life Beyond the Box: Norman Stanley Fletcher* (Harry Grout)
2003	*Sweet Medicine* (Laurence Barber)
2003	*Margery and Gladys* (Troy Gladwell)
2003	*Thursday the 12th* (Edgar Bannister)
2003	*Casualty* (Henry Lambert, 'Friend or Foe')
2002	*The Jury* (series regular, Michael Colchester)
2002	*In Deep* (Clayton Waddington)
2002	*Heartbeat* (Arthur Wainwright, 'From Ancient Grudge')
2000	*Second Sight: Kingdom of the Blind* (Harold King)
2000	*Lorna Doone* (Sir Ensor Doone)
2000	*The Thing About Vince* (series regular, Ray)
2000	*The 10th Kingdom* (Wilfred Peep)
2000	*Longitude* (George Graham)
1999	*Hornblower: The Frogs and the Lobsters* (Admiral Lord Hood)
1998	*Our Mutual Friend* (series regular, Mr Boffin)
1997	*The Moonstone* (Gabriel Betteredge)
1996	*Our Friends in the North* (series regular, Felix Hutchinson)
1995	*Oliver's Travels* (Delaney)
1995	*The Choir* (series regular, Frank Ashworth)
1994	*Hildegard of Bingen* (Abbot)
1994	*Birds of a Feather* (Monty, 'Still Waters Run Deep')

1994	*Fatherland* (Nebe)
1994	*Rab C. Nesbitt* (Brother Adam, 'Buckfast')
1994	*Murder Most Horrid* (Doverson, 'Overkill')
1994	*Dandelion Dead* (Dr Hinks)
1993	*Arena* (Harold Listings, 'Radio Night: The Seven Ages of Radio')
1993	*Circle of Deceit* (Liam McAuley)
1993	*Heart of Darkness* (Director)
1993	*Nightingales* (The Inspector, 'All at Sea')
1992	*Lovejoy* (Marek, 'The Prague Sun')
1992	*Mistress of Suspense* (Winston Greeves, 'Under a Dark Angel's Eye')
1991	*Boon* (Ray Beckett, 'The Night Before Christmas')
1991	*Prisoner of Honor* (Gen Mercier)
1990-1991	*Chancer* (series regular, Tom Franklyn)
1991	*The Case-Book of Sherlock Holmes* (John Turner, 'The Boscombe Valley Mystery')
1989	*Countdown to War* (Hermann Göring)
1988	*War and Remembrance* (Col Gen Kurt Zeitzler)
1988	*Game, Set, and Match* (David Kimber-Hutchinson)
1988	*Theatre Night* (John Anthony, 'Strife')
1988	*The Bourne Identity* (Fritz Koenig)
1988	*Codename: Kyril* (series regular, Stanov)
1987	*Harry's Kingdom* (Sid Harris)
1987	*Our Geoff*
1987	*When We Are Married* (Joe Helliwell)
1987	*Screen Two* (The Chiropodist, 'Coast to Coast')
1986	*Season's Greetings* (Harvey)
1986	*Monte Carlo* (Pabst)
1986	*Sins* (Chief Prosecutor)
1985	*C.A.T.S. Eyes* (Woodbridge, 'Cross My Palm with Silver')
1985	*Bleak House* (series regular, Tulkinghorn)
1984	*Hammer House of Mystery and Suspense* (Bullneck, 'Czech Mate')
1984	*Play for Today* (Les Stone, 'Under the Hammer')
1983	*Jamaica Inn* (Squire Bassatt)

1982	*Coming Out of the Ice* (Belov)
1981	*Winston Churchill: The Wilderness Years* (Sir Thomas Inskip)
1981	*BBC2 Playhouse* (Mr Hugh Peter, 'A Last Visitor for Mr Hugh Peter')
1981	*Shelley* (Sergeant Brunton, 'Nor Iron Bars a Cage')
1980	*The Crucible* (Judge Hathorne)
1980	*The Morecambe & Wise Show* (Park Bench Bully, Christmas Show)
1980	*Fox* (series regular, Billy Fox)
1977-1979	*Citizen Smith* (series regular, Dad)
1979	*The Danedyke Mystery* (series regular, Det Insp Burroughs)
1979	*The Famous History of the Life of King Henry VIII* (Gardiner, Bishop of Winchester)
1979	*Crown Court* (Gerald Elliot, 'Beyond the Limits')
1978	*Premiere* (Emerson, 'Freedom of the Dig')
1978	*ITV Playhouse* (Harold Praed, 'Ten Days That Shook the Branch')
1978	*The Doombolt Chase* (series regular, Lieutenant Hatfield)
1977	*Philby, Burgess and Maclean* (Philby's Control)
1975-1977	*Porridge* (Harry Grout)
1976	*Life and Death of Penelope* (Sir George Cartwright)
1975	*The Sweeney* (Tony Kirby, 'Stay Lucky Eh?')
1975	*Against the Crowd* (Don Macintyre, 'We Are All Guilty')
1975	*The Squirrels* (Hawke, 'The Fiddle')
1974-1975	*Härte 10* (Mr Mackintosh)
1974	*The Pallisers* (Mr Chaffanbrass)
1974	*Fall of Eagles* (Izvolsky, 'Dress Rehearsal')
1974	*Zodiac* (Richard Meade, 'Saturn's Rewards')
1973	*The Protectors* (Quin, 'Quin')
1973	*Black and Blue* (Miles Miles, 'Glorious Miles')
1973	*Thriller* (Anderson, 'The Eyes Have It')
1973	*Thirty-Minute Theatre* (Coster, 'You and Me and Him')
1973	*Full House* (Inspector Foot)
1973	*Madigan* (Lyman Bleak, 'The Lisbon Beat')
1973	*The Adventurer* (Roberts, 'Somebody Doesn't Like Me')
1972	*A Man Without Friends* (Det Insp Crouch)

1972	*A Warning to the Curious* (Mr Paxton)
1972	*No Exit* (Calder, 'Man in the House')
1971	*ITV Sunday Night Theatre* (Frank Rogers, 'Some Distant Shadow')
1971	*ITV Sunday Night Theatre* (Albert, 'The Signalman's Apprentice')
1971	*The Rivals of Sherlock Holmes* (Horace Dorrington, 'The Case of the Mirror of Portugal' and 'The Affair of the Avalanche Bicycle & Tyre Co Ltd')
1971	*The Persuaders!* (Lance Schubert, 'Chain of Events')
1970	*Big Brother* (John Cliveden, 'The Eleventh Commandment')
1970	*The Wednesday Play* (Sladeck, 'Emma's Time')
1970	*The Wednesday Play* (Volubin, 'The Cellar and the Almond Tree')
1969	*Strange Report* (Morrison, 'Report 3424: Epidemic – A Most Curious Crime')
1969	*Randall and Hopkirk (Deceased)* (James Howarth, 'Never Trust a Ghost')
1969	*The Gold Robbers* (series regular, DCS Cradock)
1968	*Treasure Island* (series regular, Long John Silver)
1968	*The Avengers* (Dr A. Jaeger, 'My Wildest Dream')
1968	*The Wednesday Play* (Ron, 'The Drummer and the Bloke')
1968	*The Expert* (Richard Toller, 'The Long Hate')
1968	*Omnibus* (Benvenuto Cellini, 'My Name Is Benvenuto Cellini')
1967	*Man in a Suitcase* (Felix De Burgh, 'Essay in Evil')
1967	*Haunted* (Denzil Hogg, 'Living Doll')
1967	*Theatre 625* (Ernst Torgler, 'Firebrand')
1967	*This Way for Murder* (Insp Frant)
1967	*Great Expectations* (series regular, Mr Jaggers)
1966	*The Informer* (David Janner)
1966	*Adam Adamant Lives!* (Dr Mort, 'The Doomsday Plan')
1966	*Public Eye* (Fowler, 'What's the Matter? Can't You Take a Sick Joke?')
1966	*Armchair Theatre* (Sir Robert Byass, 'The Wager')

1966	*Our Man at St Mark's* (Rev John Spencer, 'The Silent Village' and 'The Peppermint Man')
1966	*Quick Before They Catch Us* (Yeoman)
1966	*ITV Play of the Week* (Anthony Sellman, 'The Move After Checkmate')
1966	*Coronation Street* (Arthur Johnson)
1966	*Dixon of Dock Green* (Insp Gordon, 'Routine Check')
1965	*Knock on Any Door* ('The Boot' Winter, 'First Offender')
1964	*The Saint* (Walter Devan, 'The Saint Steps In')
1964	*Armchair Mystery Theatre* (Sgt George Burtonshaw, 'The Blackmailing of Mr S')
1964	*Espionage* (Waring, 'Once a Spy…')
1964	*First Night* (Albert, 'All Things Bright and Beautiful')
1964	*Crane* (Max Goddard, 'The Death of Marie Vetier')
1963	*First Night* (Mr Michael, 'The Strain')
1963	*Armchair Theatre* ('Mr Big')
1963	*Festival* (Schmitz, 'The Fire Raisers')
1963	*Festival* (Gonnern, 'Stalingrad')
1963	*Walt Disney's Wonderful World of Color* (Police Sergeant, 'The Horse Without a Head')
1963	*Maupassant* (Chicot, 'Husbands and Wives')
1963	*BBC Sunday-Night Play* (Passenger, 'Night Express')
1963	*Dimensions of Fear* (Dr Read, 'Deltas of Death')
1963	*Hancock* (Detective Sergeant Hubbard, 'The Eye-Witness')
1962	*ITV Play of the Week* (Mr Tarleton, 'Misalliance')
1962	*ITV Play of the Week* (Nikitin, 'When the Kissing Had to Stop, Act 1: The Hammer')
1962	*No Hiding Place* (Tony Rye, 'Contents Noted')
1962	*Richard the Lionheart* (Caspar, 'The Warrior from Scotland')
1962	*Oliver Twist* (series regular, Bill Sikes)
1962	*The Cheaters* (Stacey, 'The Safe Way')
1961	*A Book with Chapters in It* (Ben)
1961	*No Hiding Place* (Joe Mulvaney, 'Dead Ringer')
1961	*A Chance of Thunder* (Yardley)
1961	*Top Secret* (Leader, 'The Men from Yesterday')
1961	*Three Live Wires*

1960	*Boyd QC* (Sgt Reginald Curtis, 'The Dog with the Bad Name')
1960	*Deadline Midnight* (series regular, Joe Dunn)
1960	*No Hiding Place* (Mitchell, 'The Head Case')
1960	*No Hiding Place* (Alfred Fitch, 'Victim of the Dark')
1960	*Man from Interpol* (Karl, 'A Killer with a Long Arm')
1960	*Knight Errant Limited* (James Eggerton, 'Man on the Pier')
1960	*Inside Story* (Wilfred Barlow, 'A Song for a Sparrow')
1959	*ITV Television Playhouse* (Guard, 'The Advocate')
1959	*ITV Television Playhouse* ('Oggie')
1959	*Probation Officer* (Mr Anson)
1959	*ITV Play of the Week* (Cheever, 'The Crucible')
1959	*Interpol Calling* (Inspector, 'Diamond SOS')
1959	*Saturday Playhouse* (Hendricks, 'The Cat and the Canary')
1959	*Played Upon a Stage* (Malvolio, 'Twelfth Night')
1958	*Boyd QC* (Richard Good, 'The Not So Civil Servant')
1958	*Mary Britten, MD* ('The Wrecker')
1958	*The Adventures of Ben Gunn* (Sergeant Hoxton, 'The Taking of the Walrus' and 'The Parson's Son')
1957	*BBC Sunday-Night Theatre* (Gerald Thornton, 'Time and the Conways')
1957	*Potts and the Phantom Piper* (Stannard, 'The Stranger in the Dungeon' and 'Potts Sets a Trap')
1956	*Armchair Theatre* (3rd Journalist, 'It's an Ill Wind')
1956	*Tales from Soho* (Prison Padre, 'The Message')
1954	*Stage by Stage* (Foretop/Porter to Sir Tunbelly Clumsey, 'The Relapse or, Virtue in Danger')
1954	*Stage by Stage* ('Pageant Wagon to Citizens' Theatre')